THE DEMING
MANAGEMENT
METHOD

THE DEMING MANAGEMENT METHOD

by Mary Walton

FOREWORD BY
W. Edwards Deming

A PERIGEE BOOK

Perigee Books
are published by
The Putnam Publishing Group
200 Madison Avenue
New York, NY 10016

Library of Congress Cataloging-in-Publication Data

Walton, Mary, 1941–
The Deming management method.

Reprint. Originally published: New York : Dodd,
Mead, 1986.
Bibliography: p.
Includes index.
1. Deming, W. Edwards (William Edwards), 1900–
Contributions in management.   2. Management.   I. Title.
HD38.D439W35   1988   658   88-23822

ISBN 0-399-15024-2

Material from *Out of the Crisis* by W. Edwards Deming reprinted by permission of the author. Published by MIT, Center for Advanced Engineering Study, Cambridge, MA 02139.

Material from *Quality, Productivity and Competitive Position* by W. Edwards Deming reprinted by permission of the author. Published by MIT, Center for Advanced Engineering Study, Cambridge, MA 02139. Copyright 1982 by W. Edwards Deming.

Grateful acknowledgment is made to W. Edwards Deming for permission to quote from material used in his seminar which the author attended on February 5–8, 1985.

Grateful acknowledgment is made to the Growth Opportunity Alliance of Greater Lawrence for permission to reproduce charts from *The Memory Jogger,* © 1985 by GOAL.

Copies of Dr. W. Edwards Deming's textbook *Out of the Crisis* are available from the Center for Advanced Engineering Study, Massachusetts Institute of Technology, Cambridge, MA 02139.

Charts and diagrams designed by Carol Estornell.

Printed in the United States of America

2   3   4   5   6   7   8   9   10

To W. Edwards Deming,
with gratitude, respect,
and affection

Contents

————•————

PART THREE
MAKING DEMING WORK

Foreword

by W. Edwards Deming

Why is Western industry on the decline? Why has the balance of trade of the United States of America deteriorated year by year for twenty years? The deficit in export of manufactured goods is worse than the overall figures indicate, as export of agricultural products has been on the increase. We have people; we have natural resources, experience. Why the decline?

The cause of the decline is that management have walked off the job of management, striving instead for dividends and good performance of the price of the company's stock. A better way to serve stockholders would be to stay in business with constant improvement of quality of product and of service, thus to decrease costs, capture markets, provide jobs, and increase dividends.

In the decade after the War [the Second World War], the rest of the world was devastated. North America was the only source of manufactured products that the rest of the world needed. Almost any system of management will do well in a seller's market. Success in business in North America was confused with ability to manage.

Management in America (not all) have moved into what I call retroactive management: focus on the end-product—look at reports on sales, inventory, quality in and quality out, the annual appraisal of people; start the statistical control of quality and QC-Circles for operations, unfortunately, detached from management's responsibility; apply management by the numbers, management by MBO. [Management By Objective], work standards.

The follies of the systems of management that thrived in the expanding market that followed the War are now all too obvious. They must now be blasted out, new construction commenced. Patchwork will not suffice.

Everyone doing his best is not the answer. Everyone *is* doing his best. It is necessary that people understand the reason for the transformation that is necessary for survival. Moreover, there must be consistency of understanding and of effort. There is no substitute for knowledge.

A conjurer may pull a rabbit out of a hat, but he cannot pull quality out of a hat.

The biggest problem that most any company in the Western world faces is not its competitors, nor the Japanese. The biggest problems are self-inflicted, created right at home by management that are off course in the competitive world of today.

Recognition of the distinction between a stable system and an unstable one is vital for management. The responsibility for improvement of a stable system rests totally on the management. A stable system is one whose performance is predictable. It is reached by removal, one by one, of special causes of trouble, best detected by statistical signal.

Understanding of a stable system discloses devastation of people wrought by the annual appraisal of performance, futility of management by the numbers, management by MBO. A numerical goal that lies beyond the bounds of capability of a system will not be reached except at the expense of some other activity in the company, thus, in the end, raising total cost to the defeat of the company.

Teamwork in a company, except for putting out fires, is impossible under the existing annual appraisal of performance. Everybody, once the fire is conquered, goes back to his own life preserver, not to miss a raise in pay.

It is a pleasure to commend this book by Miss Mary Walton to readers that wish to study her point of view on the theory and examples that guide my work and form the content of my seminars and my book *Out of the Crisis* (Center for Advanced Engineering Study, Massachusetts Institute of Technology, 1986). The applications, examples, and comments that she provides will be especially appreciated by her readers.

Washington
March 10, 1986

Preface

I first heard of W. Edwards Deming on a trip to Japan several years ago to research a story on workers at Kawasaki Heavy Industries, Inc., which had won contracts to build trolley and subway cars for the Philadelphia mass transit system. It never occurred to me at the time that the American who had taught the Japanese statistical quality control and principles of management after World War II was still living. Indeed, I supposed that he had died shortly after educating the Japanese. Otherwise, he would surely have been famous in this country as well.

I was therefore surprised to learn in 1984 that Dr. Deming was coming to town. He had been retained by the Greater Philadelphia Chamber of Commerce for a four-day seminar in March of that year. I was assigned by my employer, *The Philadelphia Inquirer*, to write a profile.

Dr. Deming was not only very much alive, but was in rare form when I met him for the first time on January 19, 1984. He was in Philadelphia that morning to give a speech in advance of his March booking, after which his schedule called for an immediate departure for San Diego. I was headed for San Diego as well, to take his seminar there as part of my research. His delightful and protective secretary, Cecelia ("Cele") Kilian, had turned down my request to travel with him, and my flight left later than his.

After the Philadelphia speech, in which he soundly scolded his audience of executives for their poor management practices, Dr. Deming himself invited me to travel with him to San Diego. I quickly changed my plane reservation and off we went. He traveled with only a large briefcase and an inexpensive tan canvas shoulder bag. I remember watching him in the airport as he made a phone call, then pulled a train schedule from his pocket and nearsightedly consulted the pocket-size date book he lived by, jotting down arrangements for an engagement a year hence.

The Deming profile that appeared on March 11 in the newspaper's Sunday magazine, *Inquirer*, drew more response than any piece I'd written in fifteen years of reporting. People wanted to know how to reach Dr. Deming, where to buy his book, how they could attend the seminar. We ran out of copies of the magazine article and then of reprints as well. When later I proposed doing a book on his method, Dr. Deming replied that he would help in any way he could.

Over the next year or so, I visited him on weekends at his Washington home near the Maryland line, treading the flagstone path that led past the big holly tree down to the basement entrance of his office. As he sat at his big blond desk, around the corner from the washer and dryer, he was surrounded by a lifetime of books, journals, curios, and awards. If time permitted after we talked—or rather, after he talked and I listened—there was lunch or dinner with him and sometimes with his wife, Lola, and other guests at his beloved Cosmos Club near Dupont Circle, where popovers and catfish were a specialty. Dr. Deming would order hazelnut ice cream all around, without even asking. Usually he piloted a stately white 1969 Lincoln Continental; its black seats exuded a rich leather smell. Once we took the bus. He was a fan of public transportation. "I ride for twenty-five cents," he said with satisfaction in one of the few references he ever made to his advanced age. (During the course of researching the magazine article, I had inquired obliquely whether he was worried about who would carry on his work. "I'm all right," he answered tersely.) I found him in all respects to be a kind and thoughtful individual, if occasionally impatient at his student's failure to immediately grasp his conclusions.

Dr. Deming was good enough to read and comment on many chapters of this book, particularly on those dealing with the Fourteen Points and the Seven Deadly Diseases, and to make available the unpublished manuscript of his forthcoming book, *Out of the Crisis.* He also provided journals of his early trips to Japan. We traveled as well to several of his clients, and he supplied introductions to others.

The companies that had turned to Dr. Deming's method shared a sense not only of urgency and commitment but also of optimism and excitement. Suddenly, there was a new philosophy that promised answers where none had previously existed. Trained to gather and interpret data, their problem-solving teams were like detectives turned loose with a new sheaf of evidence. At last they had the ammunition to eliminate long-standing glitches in their processes, and they went after them with the enthusiasm of crime-stoppers. Show the slightest interest in their work, and out would come sheets of numbers and stories of misinterpreted clues and, finally, success. Probe a little more into the psyche of the employees, and their stories would bring tears to your eyes: what it meant to be taken seriously rather than to be treated with disdain. To be sought out for one's knowledge and to be asked to contribute to the future of a company. To *want* to go to work. I heard, too, from executives who had discovered how pleasant it is to share responsibility—and to sleep better at night. How good it is to know their employees respect them. And to know that these feelings of satisfaction come at no cost to profits and productivity. Just the opposite—their companies were doing better than ever before and saw no end to the improvement.

These ventures into the American workplace showed clearly that whether the product is hardware or service, whether the company employs two hundred or two hundred thousand, Americans still care about quality. The country is full of intelligent, courageous people who would change if they only knew how

In Part Three, Making Deming Work, I sought to report from the factory floor—or the office cubicle, as the case might be. I wanted to talk directly to the people involved in the change and to find out exactly what had taken place. I wanted to deal with specifics rather than generalities. Wherever I went, I found the same kinds of problems and the same human reactions. An executive who thinks his or her company is different from the ones in this book—who says "We don't have those problems" or "That doesn't happen here"—doesn't really know what's going on, hasn't really talked to the company employees in an atmosphere free of fear.

By the same token, although evidence presented here of the Deming method's success is anecdotal in nature, to borrow a term from medical research, it would be a mistake to interpret it as atypical. The Deming method will work anywhere. It is universal.

The question arises, Is America ready? Must we continue the precipitous decline of our value-added economy, living on borrowed time and borrowed money and throwing up protectionist barriers, until we reach the cataclysmic state that more and more experts believe is inevitable? Must it be that only then our businesses and corporations will be prepared to accept a radically different style of management? Or can we act now?

Acknowledgments

Aside from those people whose contributions are evident in the writing, there were several whose keen understanding of the Deming method added significantly to my own. In this regard, I cannot thank the people of GOAL (Growth Opportunity Alliance of Greater Lawrence) enough for their generous help, particularly Director Bob King, for his suggestions, knowledge, and good humor, and statistician Diane Ritter, for holding my hand through histograms and control charts, and for her hospitality as well.

In Philadelphia, Mary Ann Gould was indispensable. So, too, was Brian Joiner, who gave of his time, insights, and considerable expertise during his trips to the city. At the Greater Philadelphia Chamber of Commerce, I am grateful to Rick Ross for his encouragement and to Rosalie DiStasio for keeping me abreast of developments.

Friends helped beyond measure. I thank Peggy Anderson for guidance, Bob Schwabach and Don Drake for general support and expertise with word processors, and Beth Gillin, Jane Marie Glodek, Ellen Karasik, Ron Cole, Bill Eddins, Patsy McGlaughlin, and Jane Barr. For their interest and companionship during the long and vexing newspaper strike when this book was completed, I am grateful to my union colleagues Bill Barry, Kitty Caparella, Rick Tulsky, Lila Roisman, and others on the Newspaper Guild negotiating committee.

I am also grateful to David Boldt, editor of *The Philadelphia Inquirer* Sunday magazine, both for assigning the story that led to this book and for a happy, long-standing editor/writer relationship. All the people at the magazine, where I work, were a constant source of good cheer. Sally Downey, his assistant and my friend, was wonderful. My gratitude as well to Dr. Deming's devoted secretary, Cecelia Kilian, who put up with my many calls. Artist Carol Estornell gave both elegance and coherence to the illustrations in this book. Harold Tassell, Jim Naughton and Katherine Hatton gave important advice.

Finally, my love and thanks to my darling daughter, Sarah, for her patience and understanding; to my father, Joseph Vogel, to my stepmother, Lucia Yu, and to my mother, Mary Vogel, who did not fail me.

THE DEMING
MANAGEMENT
METHOD

PART ONE

W. EDWARDS DEMING— THE MAN AND HIS MISSION

————•————

Chapter 1

W. Edwards Deming:

A Biographical Note

Born on October 14, 1900, William Edwards Deming is as old as this century. He was sixteen when the United States entered World War I, and forty-one when the Japanese bombed Pearl Harbor. He was in his fiftieth year when Japan, its economy staggering from the effects of war, decided it needed the help of a "foreign expert," and he was in his eightieth when NBC featured him on a broadcast entitled "If Japan Can . . . Why Can't We?" and he was, at rather long last, discovered in his homeland.

He grew up on a Wyoming homestead during the period when irrigation was taming the Wild West and transport was by horse and buggy. His work has taken him to the frontiers of technology. Few have lived through so many important eras in history.

The son of a man who was trained in the law and a woman who studied music, he is named for them both: His father was William Albert Deming and his mother, Pluma Irene Edwards. From his father he derived a penchant for scholarship; from his mother, who had studied at Oberlin College's conservatory of music, a love of composition.

In the early 1900s, William Deming, Sr., moved his family from Sioux City, Iowa, to Cody, Wyoming, where he had a business arrangement with an attorney. He and Pluma had two small sons by that time, William and Robert, who was a year younger. Cody had been named for Buffalo Bill—William Frederick Cody, the colorful nineteenth-century army scout and buffalo hunter and the organizer in 1883 of "Buffalo Bill's Wild West Show." The Demings lived in a small house on the grounds of the Irma Hotel,

3

named for Buffalo Bill's daughter, and Buffalo Bill himself would put in frequent appearances. The two boys were entranced by the long-haired, mustachioed blond showman. Robert Deming remembers visiting an aunt in Los Angeles when Buffalo Bill brought his show to town. The aunt and her two charges elbowed their way to the front of the crowd, and Buffalo Bill recognized the two boys from his hometown.

In 1906, William Deming moved his family to nearby Powell, Wyoming, named for John Wesley Powell, a one-armed geologist who had surveyed the Colorado River, passing by boat through the Grand Canyon, a hazardous feat. The town of Powell had been targeted for a reclamation project and was opened to homesteaders. A three-hundred-foot dam was being built astride the sulfurous Shoshone River—the name is Crow Indian for "stinking waters." At the time, it was the highest dam in the world.

The town of Powell was in on the Shoshone irrigation project, and William Deming filed a claim for a forty-acre homestead on the edge of town. He moved his law library and his wife's Steinway parlor grand piano into a tarpaper shack and proceeded to farm while his wife taught music and voice. They could have claimed an eighty-acre site farther away, but in truth, William Deming was not all that enthusiastic about tilling the soil. As a child, Robert Deming remembers hearing his father explain to a friend the difference between a farmer and an agriculturalist: "A farmer makes his money on the farm and spends it in town. An agriculturalist makes his money in town and spends it on the farm." Said William Deming, "I'm an agriculturalist."

The family kept a cow for milk, chickens for eggs, and a garden for vegetables. As Powell grew, William Deming built up a business selling insurance, real estate, and legal services. He had a reputation for writing contracts that couldn't be broken.

Those early years were difficult, particularly for Mrs. Deming. There was neither electricity nor indoor plumbing. "I remember," Dr. Deming wrote in a note to the author many years later, "my mother, taking my brother and me by the hand, prayed for food. . . . Our house in Powell, [from] roughly 1908 to 1912, was a tarpaper shack about the size of a freight car. Snow blew in through cracks in the door and in the windows. There would be accumulations in the morning." Sometimes the $1.25 that William Edwards earned doing chores in the local hotel was all the family had. He made ten dollars per month for years lighting the five gasoline streetlights—then four after a team of runaway horses demolished one.

In 1909, there arrived a daughter, Elizabeth, the first baby born in Powell. She, too, remembers the poverty. "We didn't have much, but nobody had anything," she said, and added, "there wasn't anything there." In time, however, as William Deming's business prospered, their situation improved, and they moved to better and better houses, each "more pretentious than the other," as brother Bob quipped.

Powell, although poor, was more peaceful than Cody, yet, in spirit, still part of the Wild West. Dr. Deming remembers his mother once waking him to see Cody in the distance, apparently on fire. They later learned that eleven saloons had gone up in smoke.

Edwards, as he was called to distinguish him from his father, was by his own account a well-behaved and studious child who earned the nickname "the professor" for his diligence. When a dozen of his peers ran away from home, albeit briefly, he was not among them. Each evening his father would ask what he had learned in Powell's one-room school that day.

One treasured family anecdote is the story of Edwards's attempt to volunteer for the National Guard, which was engaged in a skirmish on the Mexican border. The entire town had a farewell dinner for its enlistees; young Deming was among them. His sister pressed a ten-cent chocolate bar upon him, a valuable commodity at the time, but he nobly refused to take it. He left on the first leg of the journey, a train ride to Cheyenne. In short order he was back, rejected for being too young. He was fourteen at the time.

Camping and fishing were among his passions. He could always, brother Bob said, be counted on to provide fish for a meal. As a teen-ager, Edwards was "never a partier, never a girl chaser." He went to the dances but not, in a euphemism for racy behavior, "to the show."

In 1917, W. Edwards Deming took the train from Powell to Laramie to begin his education at the University of Wyoming. He arrived several days early so he could find a job. "He always worked," said Elizabeth. He became a janitor at twenty-five cents an hour and later would recount how, in his inexperience, he had spread soapy water across a floor, then left it in that treacherous state, expecting it to dry on its own. He shoveled snow, cut ice, and worked as a soda jerk. But he also sang in the choir and played the piccolo in the university band.

After he graduated in 1921, he remained a year for additional studies in mathematics, and he taught engineering—"albeit very badly. How could I do otherwise? I didn't know very much." He taught physics the following year at the Colorado School of Mines, then enrolled for a master's degree in mathematics and physics at the University of Colorado. There he courted and married a young schoolteacher named Agnes Belle in 1923. They adopted a daughter, Dorothy.

In 1924, a professor encouraged him to continue his studies at Yale. There he got his Ph.D. in physics.

In the summers, he worked on transmitters at Western Electric's legendary Hawthorne plant in Chicago, the site of Harvard researcher Elton Mayo's experiments on the relationship between working conditions and productivity. There, a workforce of forty-six thousand—most of them women—turned out telephone equipment in a sweatshop environment. Early on, the young man had been warned by a colleague to stay well away from the stairway when the whistle blew at the end of the day. "Those women will trample you to death," he said. "There won't even be an oil slick." Dr. Deming was sympathetic. "It was hot. It was dirty. No wonder they wanted to get out." Some of his ideas about management are rooted in his experience at Hawthorne, where the workers were paid by the piece and docked if it failed inspection. "Piecework," he says today, "is man's lowest degradation."

In 1927, Dr. Deming turned down job offers from private industry, including one from Bell Laboratories, to work for the U.S. Department of Agriculture in the fixed nitrogen laboratory, which had done pioneering work during World War I. He was intrigued by the opportunity to study nitrogen and analyze its effect on crops.

In 1930, after seven years of marriage, Agnes Deming died. Dr. Deming two years later married Lola Shupe, a mathematician who had come to work for him. Together they authored several papers on the physical properties of gases. His second daughter, Diana, was born in 1934 and his third, Linda, in 1942.

While Dr. Deming was at the Department of Agriculture, one of his colleagues introduced him to Walter A. Shewhart, a statistician at Bell Telephone Laboratories in New York. Shewhart, a soft-spoken but probing scholar, had developed techniques to bring industrial processes into what he called "statistical control." Shewhart had defined the limits of random variation in any aspect of a worker's task, setting acceptable highs and lows, so that any points outside those limits could be detected and the causes studied. Workers could be trained to do this charting themselves, giving them greater control over their jobs and allowing them to make adjustments on their own. Shewhart's genius, Dr. Deming would often say, was in recognizing when to act and when to leave a process alone. For several years, Dr. Deming traveled regularly to New York to study with Shewhart. Shewhart's theories of quality control would become the basis of his own work.

Elsewhere in the government, in the census bureau, a debate was raging over the new techniques of sampling that were being used in federal agencies, including in the Department of Agriculture, where Dr. Deming was becoming known as an expert. He had studied the theory of statistics with a famous British professor, Ronald Fisher, and had sought out other scholars to give lectures and seminars for himself and his colleagues.

The 1940 census was approaching. In previous censuses, every individual had been polled, a process that was "complete but abhorrent," as Dr. Deming put it, because it was so incredibly time-consuming. But the idea of sampling was extraordinarily controversial. The bureau's conservatives were mistrustful of it, but there was pressure from others for more information than could be provided by 100 percent surveys. Dr. Deming would say later that "sampling was in the air." Not long after Secretary of Commerce Harry Hopkins decided in favor of sampling, the phone rang in Dr. Deming's office. It was a request from the census bureau for him to take charge of the new sampling program. Dr. Deming accepted immediately.

Acting on his mandate, he developed sampling techniques that were used for the first time in the 1940 census. As a sideline, using what he had learned from Shewhart, Dr. Deming was also able to demonstrate that statistical controls could be used in clerical as well as in industrial operations. It could be shown, for example, that the error rate of card punchers dropped markedly with training and expertise, making it necessary to inspect only a third of their work. Dr. Deming speaks of those years at the census with relish. "We did a great many things that were novel and new."

In 1942, during World War II, his services were sought by

W. Allen Wallis, a professor at Stanford University. Wallis, later to become an undersecretary of state, inquired in a letter to Dr. Deming whether there was some way that Stanford might be able to contribute to the war effort.

Dr. Deming immediately responded with a four-page proposal for teaching the Shewhart methods of Statistical Quality Control (SQC) to engineers, inspectors, and others at companies engaged in wartime production. Wallis was enthusiastic. In July 1941, Dr. Deming taught the first ten-day course in statistical methods with the aid of Ralph Wareham of General Electric and Charles Mummery of Hoover Corporation. Wareham had studied statistical theory at the University of Iowa; Mummery was self-taught in the Shewhart methods.

They and others went on to teach courses around the country to 31,000 students, including many engaged in government procurement. Dr. Deming personally led twenty-three sessions. The national emphasis on quality led to the formation of the American Society for Quality Control in February 1946. Dr. Deming was a charter member. In 1956, the society presented him with the Shewhart Medal.

In 1946, Dr. Deming left the census bureau to establish a private practice as a statistical consultant. He also joined the faculty of New York University as a professor at the Graduate School of Business Administration, where he taught sampling and quality control. Even after his retirement in 1975, he continued to teach as a professor emeritus, traveling weekly to New York, where he kept an apartment, for his Monday afternoon course.

Following the war, Dr. Deming's services were in demand overseas. In 1946, he traveled twice to Greece for the State Department to observe the Greek elections. On the second trip, in 1947, he visited India as well, then continued on to Japan, where he had been asked to join a statistical mission planning the 1951 Japanese census. He was to develop sampling techniques for surveys of housing, nutrition, employment, agriculture, and fisheries.

In America, industry returned to the peacetime production of consumer goods, for which there was unparalleled demand and no competition. Untouched by war, the industrial heartland churned out cars, washing machines, vacuum cleaners, mixers, lawn mowers, refrigerators, stoves, furniture, carpets, and all the appurtenances for the mushrooming postwar suburbs, inhabited by a generation of prosperous Americans. The American corporation had fulfilled the promise of "scientific management," formulated by an influential industrial engineer named Frederick Winslow Taylor more than three decades earlier. Taylor had held that human performance could be defined and controlled through work standards and rules. He advocated the use of time-and-motion studies to break jobs down into simple, separate steps to be performed over and over again without deviation by different workers. Minimizing complexity would maximize efficiency—although it was as bad to overperform as it was to underperform on a Taylor-style assembly line.

Scientific management evolved during an era of mass immigration, when the workplace was being flooded with unskilled, uneducated workers, and it was an efficient way to employ them in large numbers. This was also a period of labor strife, and Taylor believed that his system would reduce conflict and eliminate arbitrary uses of power because so little discretion would be left to either workers or supervisors. Taylor and his believers held that management was a science that could be studied and applied. Hence, the evolution of the rule-bound, top-heavy American corporate structure, with its cadre of professional managers. In one way, Taylor was right. The system did produce large quantities. But it was also cumbersome and rigid and was slow to adjust to market conditions.

Quality in these postwar years took a back seat to production—getting the numbers out. Quality control came to mean end of the-line inspection. If there were defects and rework, there would be profit enough to cover them.

Although a few control charts lingered here and there for a time, particularly in defense industries, for the most part the techniques taught by Dr. Deming and his colleagues were now regarded as time-consuming and unnecessary, and they faded from use. By 1949, Dr. Deming says mournfully, "there was nothing—not even smoke."

But the lesson was not lost on Dr. Deming. As he considered what had gone awry, he realized that the wrong people were committed to Statistical Quality Control. Of course, the technical people had to be educated in the methods. They were the ones who would apply and analyze them. But without pressure from management for quality, nothing would happen.

He would not make that mistake again.

Dr. Deming and the Japanese

In 1947, Dr. Deming was recruited by the Supreme Command for the Allied Powers (SCAP) to help prepare for the 1951 Japanese census. Japan had paid dearly for its participation in World War II. Of its major cities, only Kyoto had escaped wide-scale damage from aerial bombardments, and 668,000 civilians had died. The nation's industrial base was in ruins; agricultural production was off by a third. The once-prosperous populace had gone first without consumer goods, then without food for the wartime effort. Now there was little of either. Their cities had been destroyed; many Japanese had scattered to the countryside. Morale had collapsed. They had lost confidence in themselves and in their leaders, which perhaps explains why they greeted the Allied occupation forces with so little hostility.

Under U.S. General Douglas MacArthur, SCAP made priorities of dismantling the military government and establishing a constitutional regime. When Dr. Deming arrived, two years into the occupation, little physical recovery was yet in evidence. He took note in his diary of the suffering: "Practically all of the area of heavy industry between Tokyo and Yokohama and in every big city is a complete blank, some concrete and twisted steel left. New wooden homes are springing up like mushrooms everywhere over the seared areas. The debris is practically all cleared away; what isn't being built on is in winter wheat or garden."[1] Food was scarce. A tearoom in those days he would later say, was exactly that—no more than tea was served. Rice, which was also in short supply, could not be served in restaurants. People were forbidden to sleep in the Tokyo train station because so many had died—not from cold, but from hunger. He carried candy from the Army PX with him on his travels because no food was available.

The plight of the children moved him the most. On one occasion, an American captain took him to railroad yards where twenty or thirty homeless men slept on rice mats. He saw an old man and a young boy no older than nine huddled around a charcoal burner with scarcely a flame. The boy told the captain that he had been in an institution but the adults ate all the food so he ran away. Dr. Deming wrote in his diary, "At 11:30 I crawled into my beautiful bed, wondering why some people have so many good things while others are sleeping on mats in rags, hungry."[2] Another time he visited an institution: "Miserable wretches in rags, most of them dying of hunger. Human beings wasting away. Curious mixtures of the sick with the well, old and young. Crazy people in dark cells, no windows because they'd escape. But who said they were crazy, and who wouldn't be?"[3] He used whatever authority he had to urge that the superintendent be fired.

Then and in years to come, he did not closet himself with the American colony that sprang up in postwar Japan. He delighted in invitations from Japanese hosts, and he sought to familiarize himself with the culture, frequently attending Kabuki theater and Noh plays, exploring markets and shops, visiting temples and shrines. "My method of learning is to become, so far as possible, Japanese," he wrote in 1956. His longtime secretary, Cecelia Kilian, remembers him studying Japanese by records late at night in his Washington study.

Entertainment in the early postwar years was not easy for either him or the Japanese to come by. But Dr. Deming took advantage of his privileges at the PX. He would buy such delicacies as rolls and butter, canned pork and beans, and cake and ice cream. He would arrange for a small room at a hotel and invite guests from among the statisticians he'd met during his studies.

The Japanese reciprocated. Toward the end of his first visit, he was invited to a meeting of the Japan Cabinet Bureau of Statistics, which ended in a "real Japanese dinner with geisha girls." For once, there was ample food—raw fish and eel, fish soup, sukiyaki, fresh tangerines, and sweet cakes made of beans. The geisha girls talked and entertained, dancing out ancient Japanese myths, then dancing with the barefoot guests to a squeaky phonograph. Wrote Dr. Deming, "The party was hilarious. I haven't laughed so in a long time and I never expect to enjoy a dinner so much again."[4]

Unknown to Dr. Deming at the time, a group called the Union of Japanese Scientists and Engineers (JUSE) had organized to aid the reconstruction of their country. Night after night, they would meet to talk.[5] Their meetings were lively enough. One of their number, E. E. Nishibori, was in charge of light-bulb production at Toshiba. Light bulbs were a scarce commodity, and Nishibori would travel to the countryside to swap them for two other scarce commodities, rice and sake, which the learned members would consume as they talked. But they had little idea of how to begin the task they had assigned themselves. The situation was desperate. Japan could not grow enough food to feed its people. It was clear that they needed to export goods for money to buy food. But not only had Japan lost traditional markets like China and Manchuria due to the war, but the industrial production that did exist was almost worse than none at all because it had given Japan what Dr. Deming would call a "negative net worth." MADE IN JAPAN stamped on a piece of merchandise was a synonym for junk.

Some Americans on loan from the Bell Telephone Laboratories to SCAP were aware of these meetings. Indeed, military approval was required for all new organizations, and JUSE had applied like any other. The Bell delegation thought JUSE might do well to study the Statistical Quality Control techniques used by U.S. companies during the war. Those techniques had originated at Bell, of course, under Shewhart. These good-hearted Americans sent for texts to supply the Japanese. One was Shewhart's book, *The Economic Control of Quality of Manufactured Product*, published by McGraw-Hill in 1931. The Japanese were also familiar with the Z.1, 2, and 3 pamphlets outlining standards for wartime production, published by the American Standards Association.

The JUSE members, numbering at that time fewer than a dozen, were taken with Shewhart's theories. One member laboriously stenciled a copy of the book onto mimeograph sheets, using a stylus, so that it could be circulated. In their studies, the men also read about Dr. Deming, who had worked with Shewhart. Some of them actually knew Dr. Deming, who had made a point of socializing with his Japanese counterparts during his 1947 visit. They were impressed with his knowledge and his friendliness, and they thought perhaps he would help in their recovery effort. In March 1950, JUSE Managing Director Kenichi Koyanagi wrote Dr. Deming asking him to deliver a lecture course to Japanese research workers, plant managers, and engineers on quality control methods.

As the Japanese had hoped, Dr. Deming replied that he would be happy to help. "As for remuneration," he wrote Koyanagi, "I shall not desire any. It will be only a great pleasure to assist you."[6] Dr. Deming arrived in Tokyo on June 16, 1950. His office was in the Empire House, which flew the British flag and overlooked the moat and wall around the Imperial grounds.

Conditions had improved in Japan. "The people look better than they did 3 years ago," Dr. Deming noted in the diary he kept for friends and relatives. "They looked hopeful then, and happy; but now they look really happy and their clothes are better, and they are eating much better.

"The shops are now bursting with food, textiles, house fur-
nishings, fountain pens. But prices are high. The average Japanese family must spend half its income for food."[7]

On June 19, before a standing-room-only crowd of five hundred, he gave the first in a dozen sets of lectures. They were
scheduled for as far south as the island of Kyushu. Demand was
such that it was frequently necessary to turn people away.

The response was gratifying, but Dr. Deming nevertheless was
troubled by his experience in the United States, where Statistical
Quality Control had flourished for such a brief period. Midway
through that first lecture, he would later say, he was overcome
with a sense of déjà vu. He was not talking to the right people.
Enthusiasm for statistical techniques would burn out in Japan as
it had at home unless he could somehow reach the people in
charge. He decided he had to meet with the *Kei-dan-ren*, an association of Japan's chief executives. Ichiro Ishikawa, the JUSE president, made the arrangements for a dinner with them on July 13.

An account of that dinner appears in his diary: "At 5 came Dr.
Ishikawa's dinner for the 21 presidents of Japan's leading industries. I talked to them an hour. There was a lot of wealth repre
sented in that room, and a lot of power. I think they were
impressed, because before the evening was over they asked me to
meet with them again, and they talked about having a conference
in the mountains around Hakone. The dinner was superb, American style, with knives and forks. I thought the food would never
stop coming. Fortunately the Japanese do not bring on heavy
desserts. We had lobster, fish, chicken, and steak, besides all the
other things that go with a dinner. The meeting and dinner were
held at the Industry Club, not far from my office in the Empire
House."[8]

What he told them, he would later relate in his seminars, was
this: "You can produce quality. You have a method for doing it.
You've learned what quality is. You must carry out consumer
research, look toward the future and produce goods that will
have a market years from now and stay in business. You have to
do it to eat. You can send quality out and get food back. The city
of Chicago does it. The people of Chicago do not produce their
own food. They make things and ship them out. Switzerland
does not produce all their own food, nor does England." The
Japanese, he had already noted, were putting up with poor quality in incoming materials—off-gauge and off-color. "I urged them

to work with the vendors and to work on instrumentation. A lot of what I urged them to do came very naturally to the Japanese, though they were not doing it. I said, 'You don't need to receive the junk that comes in. You can never produce quality with that stuff. But with process controls that your engineers are learning about—consumer research, redesign of products—you can. Don't just make it and try to sell it. But redesign it and then again bring the process under control . . . with ever-increasing quality.'' On a blackboard he drew a flow chart that began with suppliers and ended with consumers, which is now a staple in his seminars. "The consumer is the most important part of the production line," he told them. This, he realized, "was a new thought to Japanese management. They had hitherto sold their wares to a captive market.

"I told them they would capture markets the world over within five years. They beat that prediction. Within four years, buyers all over the world were screaming for Japanese products."

In August, Dr. Deming was invited by the Tokyo Chamber of Commerce to address an additional fifty manufacturers, and he spoke to forty-five more in Hakone. By summer's end, in addition to teaching statistical techniques to thousands of technical people, he had reached the management of most of Japan's large companies.

Although some of those men would tell him years later that they had privately thought his optimism was crazy, at the time they had been willing to swallow their disbelief. In a sense, having lost all, they had nothing to lose. The Japanese embraced the Deming philosophy, channeling the energy that had made them such a fearsome military enemy into making them a formidable economic opponent. Charts and checklists blossomed throughout their factories, giving them an almost festive appearance. On a return trip six months later, Deming was waylaid at dinner by the president of an electric materials company who unfurled charts to show how he had cut rework on insulated wire to 10 percent of its previous level. A pharmaceutical company was producing three times as much of one major product with no changes in machinery.

In the summer of 1951, *The London Express* saw fit to headline the following news: AND NOW COME JAPANESE NYLONS AND THEY ARE OF GOOD QUALITY.

"By the time I'd made several trips to Japan," Dr. Deming

reported in an interview many years later, "JUSE was able to teach hundreds of people. They had courses for people outside of Tokyo in the evening for people who were working there during the day. There were also courses for management. They trained almost 20,000 engineers in rudimentary statistical methods within 10 years."

To show their appreciation, in 1951 the Japanese established the Deming Prize—a silver medal engraved with a profile of Dr. Deming—to be given in two major categories: to an individual for accomplishments in statistical theory and to companies for accomplishments in statistical application. The award was established with proceeds from Dr. Deming's published lectures—proceeds that he refused to accept for personal use but donated to the prize. So anxious were the Japanese to win the awards that the first prizes were certificates in lieu of medals, which had not been cast in time. (Once cast, they had to be redone because *committee* was spelled with a single *t*.) Now a prestigious, sought-after award, presented in a nationally televised ceremony, the prize was awarded for the thirty-fifth time in 1985. Dr. Deming attended in person with a retinue of several dozen American businesspeople.

Dr. Deming returned in 1951 to teach more courses and attend the ceremonies. He also toured a camera factory and noted somewhat prophetically, "A year ago they made 200 cameras per month; now they are making 400, and hope it will be 500 this month and hereafter, with no increase in workers or hours—simply better control of quality."[9]

In 1960, he was awarded the Second Order of the Sacred Treasure—the first American to receive such an honor. Preparations for the ceremony included a frantic search for a morning coat large enough for his six-foot frame, a rare commodity in Japan. At the ceremony, according to his diary, "Prime Minister Kishi pinned a small emblem on my lapel. The medal itself is about 3 inches in diameter, heavy with much gold, with a certificate in Japanese, signed by the Prime Minister. The design of my medal is mirror, jewels and swords. The mirror is about the size of a dime, platinum or peladium, the jewels (rubies?) in a circle, and radial swords, all set in solid gold, in a beautiful lacquered box, a delightful work of art. I can say that nothing ever pleased me so much as this recognition. The citation stated that the Japanese people attribute the rebirth of Japanese industry, and their success in marketing their radios and parts, transistors, cameras, binoculars and sewing machines all over the world to my work there."[10]

That same year, in a pamphlet issued on the occasion of the tenth Deming Prize awards, Kenichi Koyanagi wrote touchingly of Dr. Deming: "Special mention must be made of the fact that the Deming Prize was instituted with gratitude to Dr. Deming's friendship as well as in commemoration of his contributions to Japanese industry. When Dr. Deming gave his 8-day course in 1950, Japan was in the fifth year of Allied occupation. Administrative and all other affairs were under rigid control of the Allied forces. Most of the Japanese were in a servile spirit as the vanquished, and among Allied personnel there were not a few with an air of importance. In striking contrast, Dr. Deming showed his warm cordiality to every Japanese whom he met and exchanged frank opinions with everybody. His high personality deeply impressed all those who learned from him and became acquainted with him. He loved Japan and the Japanese from his own heart. The sincerity and enthusiasm with which he did his best for his courses still lives and will live forever in the memory of all the concerned. . . . Herein, lies why we loved and respected, and still love and respect him."[11]

Back in the United States, none of this hoopla made much of an impression. Here Dr. Deming was known less for his work in Japan than as a distinguished statistician. He developed a large clientele in the trucking industry, for whom he designed most of the rate structures now in existence. His published papers—161 to date— suggest the breadth of his work, from "On a Statistical Procedure for Study of Accounts Receivable in Motor Freight" to "Changes in Fertility Rate of Schizophrenic Patients in New York State." In one offbeat study, Dr. Deming and two colleagues undertook to analyze the ability of thirty-year-old twin "idiot savants"—George and Charlie—to name the day of the week for a given date in any year, mentally calculating the answer in minutes.[12]

His varied assignments kept him on the road a great deal. The family seldom took vacations, but on weekends they would go for bike rides or day trips. On Saturday mornings, his youngest daughter, Linda, would wake to the sound of her mother at the calculator. Not only did Lola Deming perform the calculations for much of her husband's work, she edited his manuscripts as well and traveled with him several times to Japan. Meanwhile, she continued to work for the federal government until her retirement in 1967.

The Demings regularly had guests for cocktails or dinner. After his trips to Japan, there were frequent houseguests from that country. Both parents liked to work in the garden. Her father's reverence for wildlife, said daughter Linda, made a strong impression on her as a child. She remembered his concern for turtles that became disoriented after a dirt road in the neighborhood was paved. Every morning for a period, the family would troop out of the house to pick up all the turtles who were confused by the intrusion of the paved road and move them to the other side. Years later, Linda Deming Haupt laughed at the memory of the rescue mission with her father in the lead. "I can't look at a turtle without thinking of him."

He biked with his family well into his seventies. And he was, said his elder daughter, Diana Deming Cahill, an expert kitemaker, whose products were aerodynamically engineered to stay aloft when those of other children failed. He also composed liturgical music and loved to sing and play the piano.

His daughters were aware that their father was famous in Japan, and they were duly impressed by the jeweled Emperor's medal. They also realized that he was not held in the same high esteem in this country. Diana Deming Cahill remembers being "perplexed" at the dual standard. "I know it was frustrating to him," Linda Deming Haupt said. "Whether he would admit it, I don't know. He's a very proud man. But I think he hurt. It's hard to have your mission and not have anyone listen."

All that changed in 1980. Thirty years after he first taught the Japanese his methods, Dr. Deming was "discovered" in America. At a time in their lives when most men would have long since retired, Dr. Deming was catapulted into national prominence.

The person who discovered Dr. Deming was a television producer, Clare Crawford-Mason. And the discovery made her exceedingly nervous. Mason was a seasoned reporter who had covered both the police beat and the White House for the Washington *Daily News*. She also had done investigative reporting and a monthly television magazine for the local NBC television station and had helped start *People* magazine.

In 1979, she was producing a documentary for NBC with the working title, "Whatever Happened to Good Old Yankee Ingenuity?" The subject was the suddenly precarious position in which

American industry found itself, faced with the economic threat from Japan. But as Crawford-Mason well knew, "you can only explain issues through a story," and there didn't seem to be any story to tell. She found herself conducting interviews with economists that were about as exciting as "watching paint dry," and she wondered how she was going to pull a program out of it.

One day, she heard from a faculty member at American University, "There's this guy named Deming who lives out in American University Park." Deming, she was told, had done a lot of work in Japan. Crawford-Mason contacted Dr. Deming, who invited her out to talk. He spoke of his work in Japan and showed her yellowed clippings of stories the Japanese had written. Crawford-Mason didn't know what to think. He was nice, if eccentric; he reminded her of her father; but what he said, if true, was astonishing.

"He kept going on and on and on that nobody would listen to him." Not for nothing had Crawford-Mason put in all those years as a reporter. "I thought, 'Here's a good story.' "

Their first conversation led to five interviews, consuming twenty-five hours. The more they talked, the more impressed she was and the more suspicious she got. It was simply incredible. "Here is a man who has the answer, and he's five miles from the White House and nobody will speak to him." She contacted a high-ranking economics official from the Carter Administration and asked if he knew W. Edwards Deming. He didn't.

Crawford-Mason wanted to know if anybody was using his techniques. As it happened, Dr. Deming had just recently acquired a major client, Nashua Corporation in Nashua, New Hampshire, a manufacturer of carbonless paper, among other products. Nashua's president, William Conway, had contacted Dr. Deming after first hearing of him through Japan's Ricoh Company, Ltd., a manufacturer of copiers that were sold by Nashua overseas. Nashua tracked him down in March 1979, and Conway invited him to come up. They had lunch at the Nashua Country Club, and Conway decided to hire Dr. Deming. His managers thought he was nuts. "I'm still the boss," Conway told himself as he made the offer. Besides, as he would later say, "I wasn't into participative management anyway." Dr. Deming made it clear that he had to have Conway's personal commitment. And Conway said he had it.

When Crawford-Mason appeared on the scene, Nashua had

been at work long enough to have had some success stories to tell about the use of statistical methods and how the Deming philosophy changed the workplace. Being able to explain and film the methods in use was reassuring, but Crawford-Mason still felt out on a limb. "I really was incredibly nervous." What if Deming's methods were superficial or unworkable for reasons she didn't understand? How otherwise to explain why he'd been ignored for so long? Could it be, she worried, that "somebody is pulling one over on me?"

In the end, she trusted her judgment and instincts and wound up with one of the most successful documentaries in television history. "If Japan Can . . . Why Can't We?" was broadcast at 9:30 P.M. on June 24, 1980, with Lloyd Dobyns as narrator. The final quarter-hour was devoted to Dr. Deming and his work at Nashua Corporation. Nashua President William E. Conway reported that the company was saving millions of dollars and substantially increasing productivity under Dr. Deming's guidance. "If you get gains in productivity only because people work smarter, not harder, that is total profit, and it multiplies several times," Dr. Deming told the television audience. He spoke of his work in Japan and chastised Americans: "I think that people here expect miracles. American management thinks that they can just copy from Japan. But they don't know what to copy."

Near the end, the following exchange took place:

DOBYNS: Is there an attitudinal difference between the United States and Japan?

DEMING: They are using statistical methods. They have not only learned them, they have absorbed them, as Japanese absorb other good things of cultures. They are giving back to the world the products of statistical control of quality in a form that the world never saw before.

DOBYNS: Would the same methods work in the United States, could we do the same thing?

DEMING: Why, of course we could. Everybody knows that we can do it.

DOBYNS: Why don't we?

DEMING: There's no determination to do it. We have no idea what, what's the right thing to do, have no goal.

The next day, the telephone rang relentlessly in Dr. Deming's basement office. "We were bombarded with calls," recalled Cecelia

Kilian. "It was a nightmare." Many of the callers sounded desperate. "They have to see him tomorrow, or yesterday, or their whole company will collapse." Mrs. Kilian was used to working long hours for her boss. She had come to work as a part-time secretary in 1954, but before she knew it, *part-time* referred only to her working hours at Dr. Deming's office. The rest of the time she was at a makeshift office in her own home, juggling take-home work with raising two sons. There was one year when she had worked every Sunday but seven and Christmas as well.

With the turn of events following the NBC broadcast, Dr. Deming began to travel more than ever before. He was on the road constantly, not only in the United States but abroad. He made trips regularly to London, South Africa, and New Zealand, where he had clients. Mrs. Kilian bought shuttle tickets to New York twenty at a time. She saw less of him, but her work did not diminish. One day she heard from him in four states. He called as many as three or four times a day, sometimes dictating portions of his book from an airport telephone booth. He could remember page number and paragraph. He was never satisfied with his writing. "How could something be perfect a year ago and be so different today?" Mrs. Kilian asked of the constant revisions, answering the question herself: "on-the-job training." She joked that he had invented the eight-day week.

Among those who immediately enlisted his aid were the Ford Motor Company and General Motors. In the latter, he worked intensely with the Fiero Division. In the years to follow, the Dow Chemical Company and Hughes Aircraft were among the larger companies that also sought his services, which typically included abbreviated seminars for managers and workers and consultations on specific issues. He worked with many small companies as well, if he felt they were sincerely interested in change. Nor did he neglect his long-standing clients in interstate commerce. Although he did not publicly identify his clients, word inevitably leaked out.

In the meantime, attendance swelled for his four-day seminars, which were sponsored by George Washington University's continuing education program. Requests for the seminars poured in from around the country. Diane Ritter, a statistician with Nashua Corporation, took the course with about fifteen others in 1979. The group was small enough that Dr. Deming invited them back to his house for drinks. ("He makes a wicked martini.") But as enrollments of three and four hundred became common, such casual entertaining was out of the question.

In 1982, he published a book for use in his courses, *Quality, Productivity, and Competitive Position,* a large paperback published by the Massachusetts Institute of Technology Center for Advanced Engineering Study. No sooner was it finished than he was at work on a revision, titled *Out of the Crisis.** He still found time to raise tomatoes in his backyard and to have an occasional meal at the Cosmos Club, but not much more.

His brother, Robert, who had long since retired from a career as a car and automotive products dealer, managed to intercept his older brother from time to time on his travels. "I think he's radiantly happy," he said of Dr. Deming. "The work ethic is so much a part of him and to achieve success in your work—there's no substitute."

"I don't see why anyone that age has to get up at 7 A.M. and work till 7 P.M.," said his daughter Linda. "I don't like to make an appointment to see him. I wish he'd relax a little." But her efforts to get him to slow down had no effect. When she protested, he told her, "Thank you for caring, but this is what I need to be doing. I went so many years without people really knowing what I had to say."

---

* He was also the author of eight technical books and brochures on statistics and sampling, as well as 161 scholarly studies.

Chapter 2

•

The Deming "Four-Day": A Seminar Begins

One by one, or sometimes in small groups, the participants take their seats at tables that stretch across the width at one of those low-ceilinged, windowless motel meeting rooms that all look the same. For the next four days, the only change in scenery will be the color of the tablecloths.

This particular seminar is hosted by the Growth Opportunity Alliance of Greater Lawrence (GOAL) in Springfield, Massachusetts. The list of companies who have sent people is a cross-section of corporate America. They range from low-tech to high-tech. There are firms with household names and others that are little more than households themselves: AMF's Molecular Separation Division; Apollo Computers; ARCO Metals; AT&T; BTU Engineering; Campbell Soup Company; Carpenter Technology Corporation; Centronics Data Computer Corporation; CTI-Cryogenics; Digital Equipment Corporation; Dupont Connector Systems; Duracell; Fountain Plating; General Electric; General Findings; G&O Manufacturing Company; W. R. Grace; GTE Products Corporation; HBA Cast Products; Hoover Universal, Inc.; IBM Instruments; Instron; Kidder-Stacy; Kinemotive Corporation; A. J. Knott Tool and Manufacturing Corporation; Longview Fibre Company; Ludlow Packaging; Lydall, Inc.; Monsanto; National Gypsum; Norton Company; Paragon Electric; Pfizer; Procter & Gamble Company; Rohm & Haas Company; Sanders Associates; C. E. Scrymgeour; Sweet Life Foods; Telco Systems; Temptronic; Thermal Dynamics; Union Carbide Coatings; Wang;

Westinghouse; and Westvaco/U.S. Envelope Division. The dean of a college of engineering from a major eastern university is here, as well as an assistant professor of managerial sciences from a less major university. Many of the people are from the departments labeled "quality assurance" and "quality control." There are also a fair number of engineers, plant supervisors, and managers, plus a sprinkling of general managers and CEOs—15 percent, on average. Some are women; most are men.

They have come because their companies are looking for answers. Most are not quite sure what to expect from the man that they have heard so much about. They have heard that he is irascible, seemingly short-tempered, and does not suffer fools gladly. Even so, some—particularly those in management—will not be prepared for the abuse that is about to be heaped upon them, and they may leave. It is not easy, after all, to be told that the executive skills in which you take pride are misguided and shortsighted—simply wrong, in short.

When the 9 A.M. to 4 P.M. sessions end, there will be discussions that begin over drinks and last well into the night, as the participants grapple with a philosophy that seems so revolutionary. Some will be in open disagreement. Workers are not to blame for problems? Ridiculous. Others will be convinced that Dr. Deming is right but will be frustrated because the sessions are not explicit about how to use his methods.

But that is ahead of them. On this, the first day of the seminar, Dr. Deming will introduce the philosophy that revolutionized Japan. The heart of that philosophy is embodied in his Fourteen Points, and the Seven Deadly Diseases. On the afternoon of the second day, he will conduct a "bead experiment" that illustrates that workers are helpless to change the system in which they work. Much of the third and fourth days will be devoted to examples of how statistical methods can be used as a basis for taking action—or not, as the case may be.

There is an air of expectation as the hour approaches for the seminar to begin. Early birds arrived at 8 A.M. to watch a videotape of Harvard Business Professor Robert B. Reich, author of *The Next American Frontier*, whose criticisms of American management are similar to Dr. Deming's. Both Reich and Deming believe that American management, which has fallen into the hands of financiers and lawyers—"paper entrepreneurs," in Reich's words—is in dire need of reform.

A few minutes before 9 A.M., Dr. Deming advances slowly toward the podium with the cautious steps of old age. His white hair is neatly cropped in a crew cut, the way he has worn it since 1914 (and he has, he would like it noted, "all of it that he ever did.") He wears a dark suit with a seven-button vest that covers an ample paunch, attesting to his appreciation of good food.

He takes his place at the speaker's stand. On the table before him are a pitcher of water and several Danish pastries, which he does not eat. The members of the audience position their notepads. When he speaks, the no-nonsense tone of his deep, ministerial voice makes his listeners stiffen.

"You came here to learn how to change," he begins. "Not just to patch up. Not just to work downstream. It is so easy to do that, with very little help. Don't laugh it off. But we're going to do more than that, or we won't be here."

His voice is heavy with foreboding. His eyes dart back and forth across the audience, birdlike. "Imagine that it was only pessimists that talk that way. I'm no economist. I'm a statistician. My job is to find out the sources of improvement, sources of trouble. I said *source*, not downstream. That is what I have been doing. And as you go to the sources, you see that change is absolutely necessary.

"Let me tell you something. Unemployment leveling off, is it? At 7.1 percent? I know you have to understand the figures, and you can't understand the figures if you don't know how they were produced. Let me tell you something. When it leveled off before, it went to 4.1. Now we're hoping it will level off at 7.1. See the difference? Nobody mentions that. The papers don't mention that. They talk about things leveling off.

"Things will have to be changed.

"We're going to learn something here about how to go about it—what must be changed. Not that I know all of it, or can take every part of it and show just what to do."

At this point in his preamble, the microphone begins to squawk. Dr. Deming does not overlook this opportunity for a humorous aside. "I often think," he says mournfully, "every time a session like this begins, that during the session . . . with all the brains in this country that we have, all the experience and knowledge—someday somebody may be able to make a microphone and a system that will work."

His audience, discovering the man is human, laughs and relaxes a little.

He directs their attention to written materials that have been handed out to supplement his book *Quality, Productivity and Competitive Position*.

"Let's have a look at page three of the additional notes—chain reaction. You can't argue with a chain reaction. It will work."

He has placed the chart on a projector, which provides another opportunity for a comment on the quality of the equipment he is using. "I know that you can't read this. Fortunately, you have it in hand. There are several kinds of overhead projectors. This is one of the medium kind. I've seen worse ones. Bought at the cheapest price, almost. Can you blame the hotel for doing it? Don't you see that they do it because their customers can do nothing about it? We're here. We're stuck with it. Fortunately, we don't need to care much. You have it in hand. I just put it on the screen to show where we're at."

He resumes his lecture. "Chain reaction. Improve quality, what happens? Your costs go down. Half of the people here will un-

THE DEMING CHAIN REACTION[1]

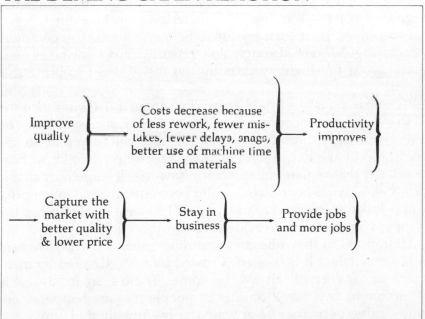

—Deming, *Out of the Crisis*

derstand that. The other half will not." His voice rises in indignation. "On the third day here, people will ask, 'Where do we stop improving quality? How do we know where to stop?' That is, where further improvement will not pay for the cost of improvement?" Dr. Deming's voice drops in feigned disapproval. "He that asks me that question will have his certificate recalled." This little witticism produces more laughter.

"But go ahead and ask. I want to make it clear that as you improve quality, your costs go down. That is one of the main lessons that the Japanese learned and that American management doesn't even know about and couldn't care less about. Interested in finance, creative accounting. That's all right. But when it means that you ignore the fundamentals of improvement, it is not right. Improve quality. Your costs go down. Fewer mistakes, fewer breakdowns."

It is, he says, very expensive to break down on delivery, and far better to look after maintenance. "Don't let the breakdown happen. . . . To say that there will never be any would be ridiculous. I didn't say there would never be any. But the frequency can be reduced and reduced more and more. To zero? No. But more and more. Continual reduction in mistakes, continual improvement of quality, mean lower and lower costs. Less rework in manufacturing. Less waste—less waste of materials, machine time, tools, human effort. Your costs go down. So many ways they go down. As costs go down, through less rework, fewer mistakes, less waste, your productivity goes up. So many ways to bring that about. . . .

"There is a missing link. I am well aware of it. I always mention it, to my point number one. It has been there from way back. You require not only a product or a service that will help man to live better. You have to put it on the market. You have to know how to sell it. I realize that you can learn how to sell something that is pretty shoddy. I know that. . . . But better quality and lower price with a little ingenuity in marketing, will create a market. Keep the company in business, provide jobs and more jobs."

He returns to the subject of unemployment. "Unemployment is not inevitable. It is created. Created by man. Created by management. There will always be some. There's an irreduceable minimum in anybody's country of people that are temperamentally—either permanently or temporarily—unsuited to work. . . . But for the most part, most unemployment is created by management. . . . Anything goes wrong—turn people out. Cut costs."

His voice rises at the thought. " 'Cut costs' means turn people out. Lost the market, turn people out. In Japan, they don't turn them out. . . . I didn't say there wasn't unemployment. I didn't say that everybody wants to stay right in that job. I didn't say that. But in Japan when any business turns down, management takes the cut. Management takes it. And the top people—four and a half times only from the lowest paid to the highest paid—they take the cut. Second step, they take another cut. . . .

"Constancy of purpose, my point number one, to stay in business. Do whatever it takes. That takes brains! Requires attention to something other than finance. And the legal department. Trying to stave off takeover, and decide whom to take over. Devoting energy to that kind of thing. 'Paper entrepreneurism,' as Professor Reich calls it, does not create wealth. It does not make the pie bigger. If you get a bigger piece of the pie, you steal it from somebody else. Isn't it better to make the pie bigger? That's why we came here. To make the pie bigger.

"There's a road map here to follow to make the pie bigger. And you can do it! You can do it. Did you ever stop to think of the power of teamwork? You don't have it. We don't have it in this country. It is every man for himself. Everybody is an individual businessman, looking out for himself. Call it rugged individualism. Better stop to think, when everybody is an individual businessman—and the American style of management creates it there cannot be teamwork. . . .

"This chain reaction, top management in Japan learned in July of 1950. . . . You can talk about quality, but if you don't know what to do about it, bring it about, quality is an empty word. I did not leave them with empty words."

Next he displays the Deming Flow Diagram.

"Draw a flow diagram. Who's your customer? What comes in? What goes out? Do you know your customer? Do you know what he needs? Almost nobody does. . . .

"What must be done about it? And don't tell me you can't do anything about it. You can. . . . Everybody here has a job in improvement. . . . You can show your top management what to do. And if you can't show your top management what to do, he's not worth working for. . . .

"Everybody wishes to do a good job, and usually knows a lot about how to do it better, how to improve. Not everybody's idea is right. Some ways that people suggest for improvement turn out to be exactly the opposite. A large part of what we learn in this seminar is what's wrong with what appear to be some wonderful ideas, generated with the best of intentions but having exactly the opposite effect of what is aimed at. . . .

"You see a little bit of what must be done to improve quality. . . . In the first place, materials come in. What are incoming materials? Whatever it is that you work with. Might be a motor . . . might be high technology . . . might be a subassembly . . . might be iron ore. . . . Whatever it is, it is your raw material, and it is somebody else's finished product that he turns over to you.

"The first step is to improve the materials and never stop improving them, and that means that you work with your suppliers. Work with them. That does not mean tramp on them, demand better and better quality. That won't do it. Quality has meaning only in terms of the customer, his needs, what he is going to use it for.

"Everybody here has a customer. And if he doesn't know who it is and what constitutes the needs of the customer, and work in

THE DEMING FLOW DIAGRAM²

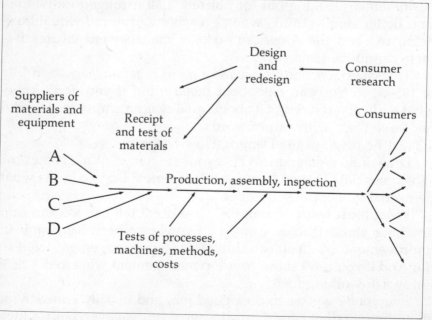

Suppliers of materials and equipment

Receipt and test of materials

A
B
C
D

Tests of processes, machines, methods, costs

Production, assembly, inspection

Design and redesign

Consumer research

Consumers

—Deming, *Out of the Crisis*

the cycle of adjustment to customers' needs and what he can produce, then he does not understand his job. We may come to a better understanding in these four days.

"Incoming materials—suppliers. I call them [in the flow diagram] A,B,C,D, and so on. Their materials come in at different spots in the production line. You require constant improvement of what comes in. Constant change to your needs. And your needs will change. That requires constant working together. Just meet specifications on an annual contract, based on the lowest price tag—those days are gone. . . . There's a better way. A flow diagram can be put down for anybody, any job, anywhere in the world, whatever it is. I didn't say it was easy. You have to stop and think.

"Improve stuff that comes in, adapt it, provide more and more what the customer needs. That requires cooperation, working together. And continual change, as requirements change. And they will change. In a continual cycle. See that upper box—'design and redesign' for the future.

"Specifications don't tell you what you need. A supplier does not know from your specifications what you need. He has to find out how you are going to use this stuff. . . . That will mean . . . continual movement toward one supplier, for any one item, so far as possible. Because for one thing, you don't have knowledge nor manpower to work with two. Not even with one. Don't tell me that you can work with two when you can't even work with one. I know, this is difficult. You have no idea what I'm talking about. How could you?

"There's a production line. And there'll be a customer. Ultimate customer, I will call him. The one that pays for your product or service. Must pay attention to the ultimate customer. Lead him. You have to tell him what he's going to need three to five years from now, and have it ready. He cannot tell you. . . .

"It is very important, very important to find out what he thinks is right or wrong about your product today. Very important to have customers that brag about buying your product or service. Just to be satisfied—that will not keep you in business. Lead him.

"People have told me—not everybody—but people have told me that they could come to this seminar only on promise that returns would come back to the company within three months. Can you think of anything more ridiculous? Maybe that will happen. I don't know. They could double or treble. That is not the aim. Your contribution will not be measurable. You won't be able to quantify your contribution. The most important figures are unknown and unknowable. You won't know your contribution in terms of dollars. . . . You'll not be able to quantify your attendance here. . . .

"The consumer—pretty important, isn't he? If nobody buys your product, the whole production line shuts down. The consumer over toward the right [on chart] is the most important part of the production line. And distinguished people have told me that is ridiculous—to put the consumer into the production line. I'd say he is the most important part of it. Without him, you don't have any production line. . . .

"Do you know that most dissatisfied customers just switch to somebody else? Your competitor, if you have one. And most of you do. And incidentally, if you're going to have a competitor, be thankful if you have a good one. . . . Nothing can do you so much harm as a lousy competitor. One that turns out product for service. He can ruin both of you—and will. . . .

"What you need are customers that are more than happy. You need customers that boast about your product. That return—repeat customers. There's the gravy. Your fixed costs are all paid. . . .

"Someone that you served in real estate, say five years ago, helped him to find the property that he really needed. Not something that he didn't need. Persuaded him not to spend too much. Saw his needs and tried to serve them. When that property comes for sale, he'll come back to the same agent. And meanwhile, tell his friends. The repeat customer, best part of any business. The one you don't have to argue with. He comes back. . . .

"Just to have the customer satisfied is not enough. Just to meet specifications—what you think the customer requires—no. That won't keep you in business. You'll have to do better than that.

"Pneumatic tires—somebody's dream. Harvey Firestone. People thought he'd gone crazy. Putting air in a tire. How ridiculous. He must have thought himself that he was crazy. All the fears that he had, but he stuck with it. If you'd asked customers in 1900 what they needed in a tire, nobody would have suggested the pneumatic tire, it was somebody's dream. . . .

"Your study of the consumer—what he finds right and what he finds wrong—and your innovation are all bound up together. It will affect design and redesign of your product for service. That will affect your incoming materials. [He refers to chart.] You may need different kinds. Maybe some at higher price. Maybe some at lower price. It will affect your processes, and it will affect your final product. A never-ending cycle. He that thinks he has come to an end, that there is no more to do, will go out of business.

"This flow diagram gives anybody an idea of what to do. Still, it is only a start.

"Top management in Japan began to see from this flow diagram what their job was. As you may remember in 1950, thirty-five years ago—people under forty-five won't remember—Japanese stuff was shoddy. Cheap in price, but worth it. They could not build up export trade that way. They were well aware of it. They'd have to change, develop a huge export market to bring in food and equipment. They could not raise their own food. Switzerland does not raise their own food. Hardest currency in the world, raises barely a third of their own food. Chicago doesn't, or Cleveland. . . .

"I put this flow diagram and this chain reaction on the blackboard at every conference with top management that first hot summer. I taught hundreds of engineers statistical methods and a lot of other methods. . . . It took fire straightaway. All top management came. Not just part of it, all of it. The twenty-one top dogs. And they came again. And they stayed with it. . . . It was spread all over in less than four years. Prairie fire. Not that they knew all of what to do. Certainly not. But they were on their way. In four years, manufacturers the world over were screaming for protection, as if that would help. Protection is the wrong way. Everybody knows it. Why do they do it? Self-defeating. Sure way to go out of business. Sure way to ruin the country. Everybody knows it. . . .

"Is it not true from roughly 1948, 1949, up until 1960, North America [the United States and Canada] was the only country that could produce what the world needed? And they couldn't produce enough of it. The demand was greater than the supply. There were talks about recession around the corner, pipelines filling up. Never happened. The demand got bigger and bigger. American management thought that they must be doing things right. All that they had to do was hold out a basket. Apples would fall into it. Any kind of management could do it. You couldn't miss. . . . Somehow or other by 1964, there was recognition that there is such a thing as competition.

"Still, there's a lot to do. By 1968, as Professor Reich says, the accountants and the lawyers became the important people in the company. Paperwork, creative accounting, make things look better, reduce taxes—but that doesn't make the pie bigger. . . .

"The lawyers became important to try to find out how to take over something, how to stave off takeover. It became pretty important. But don't you see that's defensive? That's not getting ahead. . . .

"Takeover is modern. Practically unknown in this country before 1968. It doesn't happen in Japan. There are mergers. A company may acquire others, but by mutual consent. It is not takeover. There's nothing to take over. In Japan, there's very little stock. . . . No quarterly report, no quarterly dividend. No price of the company's stock to try to maximize. There are obligations to the bank, and you jolly well better fulfill them, in Japan as in any other place.

"How to improve quality and productivity? 'By everyone doing his best.' Five words—and it is *wrong*. That is not the right answer. You have to know what to do. Doing your best won't do it. We should be thankful that not everybody's doing his best. Look at the chaos that there would be. Held down to this and that, bumping into each other, working at cross purposes. Not knowing what to do. Just doing his best.

"The system is such that almost nobody can do his best. You have to know what to do, *then* do your best. Sure we need everybody's best—everybody working together with a common aim. And knowing something about how to achieve it. Not just with what seem to be brilliant ideas, but with a system of improvement. The system of improvement consists of the Fourteen Points and removal of Deadly Diseases and Obstacles."

Chapter 3

·

An Introduction to the Fourteen Points, the Seven Deadly Diseases, and Some Obstacles

There are those in his audience, Dr. Deming realizes, who have come to learn solely about the statistical methods he taught during World War II and later to the Japanese. But, as he realized when those methods evaporated from American industry during the postwar period, statistical methods are not enough. As he so often says today, "He that starts with statistical methods alone will not be here in three years."

As a statistician, Dr. Deming's lifelong mission has been to seek sources of improvement. Given the failure of statistical methods to endure, he pondered what might have caused that failure and how to avoid it in the future. He gradually concluded that what was needed was a bedrock philosophy of management, with which statistical methods were consistent. He was ready with new principles to teach when the Japanese called him in 1950. And he continued to refine and enlarge upon them for the next three decades.

He has christened these "the Fourteen Points."[1] There were not, Dr. Deming says, always fourteen. When he first put them in writing twenty years ago, there were ten or fewer. In his work with Japanese companies, problems were absent that he would encounter only later in this country. It was not necessary to counsel the Japanese to "drive out fear," as in Point Nine, for example. Everyone was eager to work together for the recovery of the nation, and the employer was regarded not with suspicion but as a benefactor. Employer and employee were "all one family," as the relationship is often described. By the same token, his admonition in Point Twelve to "remove barriers to pride of workmanship" was not necessary in Japan. "If anybody had some ideas on improvement, there was nothing in the world to stop him. He had everybody on his side trying. It was not uphill work—batting your head against the wall to bring about improvement. There was no fear of improvement," Dr. Deming remembers.

It was in America that he became aware of the tyranny of fear, of barriers, of quotas and sloganeering. Their existence was reflected in his Fourteen Points. A few years later came an extension—a "later awakening," as he calls the "Seven Deadly Diseases." Dr. Deming is continuously honing these principles. "I learn," he says. "May I not learn?" For years, Point Seven was a mandate to "institute supervision." He has decided of late that "leadership" is a better word.

The Deadly Diseases have recently been revamped—new ones have been added and others dropped into a lesser status into a new category, "Obstacles." The Points, Diseases, and Obstacles—to be examined individually in succeeding chapters—constitute a broad prescription for reform. Each company must work out its own adaptation, suitable to its corporate culture. It is never easy. But, Dr. Deming says, what management can accomplish using the Fourteen Points "is so enormous compared to what you get otherwise."

The Fourteen Points

1. *Create constancy of purpose for improvement of product and service.* Dr. Deming suggests a radical new definition of a company's role. Rather than making money, it is to stay in business and provide jobs through innovation, research, constant improvement, and maintenance.

2. *Adopt the new philosophy.* Americans are too tolerant of poor workmanship and sullen service. We need a new religion in which mistakes and negativism are unacceptable.

3. *Cease dependence on mass inspection.* American firms typically inspect a product as it comes off the line or at major stages. De-

fective products are either thrown out or reworked; both are unnecessarily expensive. In effect, a company is paying workers to make defects and then to correct them. Quality comes not from inspection but from improvement of the process. With instruction, workers can be enlisted in this improvement.

4. *End the practice of awarding business on price tag alone.* Purchasing departments customarily operate on orders to seek the lowest-priced vendor. Frequently, this leads to supplies of low quality. Instead, they should seek the best quality and work to achieve it with a single supplier for any one item in a long-term relationship.

5. *Improve constantly and forever the system of production and service.* Improvement is not a one-time effort. Management is obligated to continually look for ways to reduce waste and improve quality.

6. *Institute training.* Too often, workers have learned their job from another worker who was never trained properly. They are forced to follow unintelligible instructions. They can't do their jobs because no one tells them how.

7. *Institute leadership.* The job of a supervisor is not to tell people what to do or to punish them but to lead. Leading consists of helping people do a better job and of learning by objective methods who is in need of individual help.

8. *Drive out fear.* Many employees are afraid to ask questions or to take a position, even when they do not understand what the job is or what is right or wrong. People will continue to do things the wrong way, or to not do them at all. The economic loss from fear is appalling. It is necessary for better quality and productivity that people feel secure.

9. *Break down barriers between staff areas.* Often staff areas—departments, units, whatever—are competing with each other or have goals that conflict. They do not work as a team so they can solve or foresee problems. Worse, one department's goals may cause trouble for another.

10. *Eliminate slogans, exhortations, and targets for the workforce.* These never helped anybody do a good job. Let people put up their own slogans.

11. *Eliminate numerical quotas.* Quotas take account only of numbers, not quality or methods. They are usually a guarantee

of inefficiency and high cost. A person, to hold a job, meets a quota at any cost, without regard to damage to the company.

12. *Remove barriers to pride of workmanship.* People are eager to do a good job and distressed when they can't. Too often, misguided supervisors, faulty equipment, and defective materials stand in the way. These barriers must be removed.

13. *Institute a vigorous program of education and retraining.* Both management and the workforce will have to be educated in the new methods, including teamwork and statistical techniques.

14. *Take action to accomplish the transformation.* It will take a special top management team with a plan of action to carry out the quality mission. Workers can't do it on their own, nor can managers. A critical mass of people in the company must understand the Fourteen Points, the Seven Deadly Diseases, and the Obstacles.

The Seven Deadly Diseases

1. *Lack of constancy of purpose.* A company that is without constancy of purpose has no long-range plans for staying in business. Management is insecure, and so are employees.

2. *Emphasis on short-term profits.* Looking to increase the quarterly dividend undermines quality and productivity.

3. *Evaluation by performance, merit rating, or annual review of performance.* The effects of these are devastating—teamwork is destroyed, rivalry is nurtured. Performance ratings build fear, and leave people bitter, despondent, and beaten. They also encourage mobility of management.

4. *Mobility of management.* Job-hopping managers never understand the companies that they work for and are never there long enough to follow through on long-term changes that are necessary for quality and productivity.

5. *Running a company on visible figures alone.* The most important figures are unknown and unknowable—the multiplier effect of a happy customer, for example.

Diseases 6 and 7 are pertinent only to the United States:

6. *Excessive medical costs.*

7. *Excessive costs of warranty, fueled by lawyers that work on contingency fee.*

In addition to the Diseases, Dr. Deming identifies a lesser category of Obstacles that thwart productivity. These include: neglect of long-range planning; relying on technology to solve problems; seeking examples to follow rather than developing solutions; excuses such as "Our problems are different"; and others.

The Fourteen Points, Seven Deadly Diseases, and some Obstacles are discussed in detail in Part Two.

Exposure to the Fourteen Points, Deadly Diseases, and Obstacles provokes strong responses, not all of them positive. Not long ago a group of line workers, engineers, and supervisors from an automotive plant attended one of his seminars. Here is what some had to say afterward. The remarks illustrate the range of reactions a company will encounter upon embarking on the Deming method.

UNION REPRESENTATIVE: "I think our plant is far from this way of management. Management is not willing to change and that's what it will take. Only when it comes close to them losing their jobs will they change."

MANUFACTURING ENGINEER: "Sounds too good to be true. Is it really going to happen, or is this just another flash-in-the-pan? I hope it happens. It will not only improve quality, it will make my job easier."

MANUFACTURING ENGINEER: " 'Drive out fear' is not applicable and cannot be achieved in the real world. Fear has always been and it will be a factor affecting employee efficiency."

TOOL SETTER: "It's the right approach. Have group meetings where the supervisor is the same as hourly workers. Everyone should have equal input. This would break down barriers between management and hourly. Everyone is good at something and should have the chance to express it to willing ears."

PRODUCT ENGINEER: "It appears that a significant portion of this philosophy depends on the response by our vendors. When and how are they going to be converted to this line of thinking?"

BUYER: "It will be hard to change the mind set, but we have to change the way we are doing business if we want to remain in business. I agree with most all of the points."

MANUFACTURING ENGINEER: "Some of the upper levels of management will not be able to change. How is the system prepared to support the people who use the new philosophy?"

JOB SETTER: "Was on supervision for a time, but gave it up as I was asked to treat 'people' in a demeaning manner and did not agree with the appraisal system."

ENGINEER/STATISTICIAN: "Are the people who could effect the most change seeing this seminar? How can we eliminate annual appraisals unless the corporation as a whole is committed to this?"

PRODUCT DESIGNER: "The concepts presented in this seminar will have to be implemented by upper-level management. We have no communication with upper management."

PRODUCT DESIGNER: "I don't believe we can 'drive out fear' because the boss will always resort to a 'power play' when the situation overwhelms him—it's an ingrained response. Since fear and trust tend to be mutually exclusive, this does not bode well for the rest of the Fourteen Points."

SUPERVISOR: "Doesn't the Fourteen Points take a lot of money? How does this fit in with our budget, manpower, and tools?"

SUPERVISOR: "How can fear be driven out between staff areas? It's at every level and every shift. Fear is implanted in everyone from hourly people to plant managers."

TOOL SETTER: "I think in most cases in the past, management says one thing on the one hand and business goes on on the other. I will do my part, but I think management has to prove its commitment to me."

TOOL CUTTER GRINDER: "Another management fad. Skepticism. Same barriers are still here. I hope this works. It will be too late for me."

TOOL SETTER: "Just how to change the company's way of thinking toward short-term profits?"

MANUFACTURING SUPERVISOR: "Salaried people have been talking about processes like this for years but upper management is so damn slow to react. Good program only if lower management can see some progress soon."

FACILITIES ENGINEER: "This evolutionary change in management style must also be accompanied by an equal change in union philosophy and style. We have a long way to go in the change of union philosophy."

MACHINE OPERATOR: "It would be good to be able to have Dr. Deming's ideas applied in the workplace. But it would take a miracle from God if they were."

Chapter 4

———•———

The Parable of
the Red Beads

In each seminar, on the afternoon of the second day, when the audience is digesting both lunch and the "new philosophy," Dr. Deming performs what he cheerfully assures his audiences is "a stupid experiment" but one, he promises, "that you will never forget." He produces the tools for the experiment: a plastic box of red and white wooden beads the size of peas; a paddle with fifty bead-size holes arranged in five rows of ten each; and a second plastic box large enough for dipping the paddle.[1]

The experiment is carried out over the course of the next hour amid much joking and laughter. But however good-humored, the bead experiment profoundly illustrates the way many managers hold workers to standards beyond their control; it also suggests the way statistics can be used to look for problem areas.

The front of the room becomes a production line, and the redoubtable Dr. Deming is in charge. "The job," he announces sternly, "will be to make white beads. Our customer will not take red ones."

From the audience, he recruits his production line, joking that "women will be considered."

These are the personnel: "We need six willing workers; we need two inspectors—we do everything the wrong way—well overstaffed; a chief inspector. We do only one thing right—the inspectors will make independent counts, not by consensus. We need a recorder. A recorder is the most important job. . . . Must be able to write and add. The recorder will record names and keep track of production."

A recorder—Paul—takes his place at the front of the room.

"You can write? Write figures?" Dr. Deming inquires with mock severity. "And can add? Take your place. You're on the payroll." In like manner, he recruits two inspectors—Bruce and John—and a chief inspector, Fred. ("You can count? Can you count to twenty? Okay. You have to have a piece of paper with you. Go get a piece of paper.")

Next, he calls for his production line. "Now, six willing workers. Educational requirements, minimal. Must be willing to work. Have one, come on up. Two. Three. Four. Five. Six willing workers. Come on up here." The workers are Dick, Pat, Bob, Steve, Horst, and Dave.

His workforce in place, Dr. Deming explains the job, mimicking all the while the authoritative manner of a foreman. "Our recorder will step onto the job. You may record at any time the names of the inspectors." He addresses the workers. "Now the six willing workers: don't associate with the inspectors. Your workplace is over here. (He motions to his right.) Our recorder will find a pen. Here, I'll lend you one of mine. Remember where you got it. You put down your own name, recorder. Inspectors, chief inspector. Our six willing workers."

Dr. Deming looks over his crew. "Now, which one of you is average man?" His eyes light on Dick. "Are you average man?"

"I guess," Dick replies.

"All right, take your place here. And all the other five are above average. (The audience laughs appreciatively.) Keep this order— the average man, what is his name? Dick? Pat. Bob. Don't go too fast. The recorder can't write very fast. Don. Horst. Wait a minute. You got them out of order. Erase it all.

"Order is very important here. Average man is first. What is his name? Next comes Pat. And Bob. Wait a minute. Don't go too fast. Steve. Horst. Dave."

The names duly recorded, Dr. Deming issues orders. "You will undergo an apprenticeship of three days. You will be on the payroll. I'll act as foreman. Since we don't have anybody here that understands the job, I'll take it on. The job will be to produce white beads.

"Now, we have some rules here. I'll tell you about them. Are you willing to put forth your best efforts? Only your best efforts?" The workers nod. "We have procedures here. Very definite procedures. There'll be no departure from procedures. You understand? No suggestions. Follow procedures absolutely. No resignations. You can get fired, but you cannot resign. Is this clear to everybody?"

Dr. Deming produces the larger of the two boxes, which contains a mixture of 800 red beads and 3,200 white beads. He holds them in his right hand. "You will observe that there are two vessels," he says. "They are of different sizes. There is a small one and a larger one. Is that clear? You will grasp both vessels on the broad side, do you understand? You will pour from the larger one into the smaller one, from the near corner, at a distance of five centimeters." He emphasizes the "five centimeters," drawing an appreciative laugh. "Our procedures are rigid," he tells the audience as he pours the beads into the smaller container and returns them to the larger one, to mix them.

"Five centimeters, then back again," he intones. "Grasping both vessels on the broad side, pour from the near corner. You will then perform a day's work. We have work standards here. Fifty per day—no more, no less. Our job is to produce white beads. Our work standard is fifty. We count red and white both. Our customer will not take red.

"After you pour the beads into the larger vessel, you will take the paddle and dip into the material. Do not shake the paddle. You will spill red beads. If a red bead goes onto the floor, halt the line." He pauses a moment before the punchline. "Everybody down on hands and knees."

Dr. Deming continues the demonstration, dipping the paddle into the larger container so that each of the fifty holes contains a bead. This is more difficult than it looks, but eventually each of the "workers" will master it. "Push the paddle, down into the bottom. Raise it, do not shake," cautions Dr. Deming.

"You think that you understand the job?" The workers nod in the affirmative.

"I purposefully made some red beads so that you can see what they look like," Dr. Deming jokes, before going on to explain the next step. "You will carry your work to inspector number one. He will call out his count. Next, to the second inspector, who will record his count. The chief inspector will compare their counts.

"You are responsible for the counts," he tells the chief inspector. "If you find any discrepancy here, one of them is wrong. And you are responsible. And you will shout with a loud voice the number. . . .

"Do you think the job is clear? Do you understand it? Do you understand there will be no departures? Our procedures are rigid, precisely as I describe them. When you are satisfied with the count, you will dismiss the willing worker. You dismiss him only when you are satisfied with the count. He will then carry his day's work and dump it back into the supply.

"Is that clear? The average man may start."

Dick grasps the larger container, pouring the beads into the smaller one, as Dr. Deming thunders, "FIVE CENTIMETERS."

Dick scoops the paddle into the large container, striving for white beads. "Are you watching?" Dr. Deming asks the other workers. "Watch him. If he makes any red beads, see how he did it. Make sure that you don't do it." He addresses the audience, in an explanatory aside. "Fear. . . ."

Dick fills his paddle, tipping it slightly so that the excess beads roll off. "Now, over to inspector number one," Dr. Deming tells him. "Record silently on a piece of paper his count. Then inspector number two. Chief inspector is responsible for the count and will announce it."

Paul announces the number of red beads in a loud voice, as instructed. "Fourteen."

Dr. Deming feigns concern. "Fourteen is the number. I'd say that we are off to a bad start." (Laughter.) He gathers his workers together. "I need to talk to you. Our customer will take only white beads. The job is to make *white* beads, not red ones. Fourteen. . . ." His voice is lugubrious. "We'll go out of business that way."

Now it is time for worker two, Pat. "Five centimeters," Dr. Deming admonishes her. "Easy, don't shake it. They'll roll off. Carry your work to inspector number one."

At the count of "Seventeen," the audience groans, and foreman Deming is even more concerned than before. "I need to talk to you," he tells Pat darkly. "The job is to produce white beads. Were you watching? Why'd you go ahead and produce red beads? I can't understand it. Next man."

This time, the count is slightly improved. Bob turns up only eleven red beads.

"Hah!" exclaims Dr. Deming, "that's what I call improvement. But not enough improvement. But that is improvement." He turns to the other workers. "Were you watching to see how he did it? All right, now let's have improvement. Improvement is what we need. Constant improvement."

Steve's count is better yet. There are just eight red beads.

"That's improvement," Dr. Deming says with satisfaction. "Continual improvement. Excellent. Now, that's what we need. More and more improvement. Every job better than the one before."

But with Horst, the count rises to twelve. And Dr. Deming chides him. "That's not improvement! Seems to be a misunderstanding."

He turns his attention to Dave, the final worker. "All right, Dave, you'll have to do very well to make up for the average man."

Dave scores nine, the second-lowest count of the day. But foreman Deming isn't satisfied. "I want to talk to you," he tells the workers. "Our procedures are rigid. No departure from procedures. The yields we're getting are very low. The variation that we are seeing is beyond my comprehension. Steve made eight. Pat made seventeen. Same procedures. Same incoming material, always 20 percent red. Our procedures are rigid, there should be no variation. Why does this number run from eight to seventeen? Incredible. Seventeen is more than twice eight." He repeats in an incredulous voice. "There should be no variation. Our procedures are fixed. Everybody works under the same procedures. Exactly the same rules. . . . As your foreman, I can only express disappointment at your performances.

"We'll proceed into the second day. Average man, go again. And as your foreman, I hope for something better."

Dick starts off the "second day" with ten red beads, an improvement over the fourteen of the day before. Dr. Deming congratulates him. "Dick, that's what I call improvement."

There are cheers for Pat, the next worker, when she draws only five red beads, the best count so far, and ultimately a record only she and Bob will match again. Foreman Deming uses Pat's example to inspire the other workers. "If Pat can make five, only five, anybody can make only five. Anything above five is incomprehensible. Our procedures are rigid. They are the same . . . over and over again. There should be no variation."

There is praise for Bob, with six. And a qualified compliment for Horst, with eleven. "That's an improvement over the day before. Mighty little, but every bit will help." He tells Dave, "You'll have to make up for the poor work of your companions." And when Dave scores eleven nevertheless, foreman Deming chides him. "You know, Dave, that you are partially responsible for the low yield that's coming out of this group." He turns to all the workers, "What we need is better performances. The management has been watching these figures. They are very disappointed about the low yield. And your foreman cannot understand the variation. Incomprehensible! . . . There should be no variation. Proceed. Remember, your job depends on your performance. You can have jobs, or you can go back on the street. Totally dependent on your performance. We can keep the place open, or the management will close it down."

When Pat brings up eight on day three, the foreman is disappointed. "Pat, I can't understand this. You made five the second day. Eight the third. This variation is incomprehensible. Doesn't make any sense. And remember this. You may not have a job for long."

At the end of the third day, he calls his workers together. "Now, listen. The management's been watching these figures. They can't understand the low yield. They've decided unless there's substantial improvement on the fourth day, they will close the place down. Your jobs are totally dependent on your performance. . . . Costs are outrunning revenues. Totally up to you. Substantial improvement. Now I hope that you enjoy your day's work. This may be your last day."

The workers continue into the fourth day. "Hard for me to see improvement there," Dr. Deming sighs, as Dave produces ten red beads. "I can't understand why there should not be zero defects." The remaining red bead count is five, nine, six, eight, and ten, respectively.

"The management has been watching the figures," Dr. Deming announces. "They are very dissatisfied with the low yield. They have decided to close the place down. You can pick up your pay on the way out. Thanks very much. I appreciate your willing work."

Paul, the recorder, has been duly noting each worker's red bead count. At the end of four days, he totals the numbers and computes the daily averages for each worker and then for the group as a whole.

Flashed on an overhead projector, this is what the complete chart looks like:

NAME	DAY				
	1	2	3	4	All 4
Dick	14	10	9	10	43
Pat	17	5	8	5	35
Bob	11	6	5	9	31
Steve	8	8	9	6	31
Horst	12	11	12	8	43
Dave	9	11	7	10	37
All 6	71	51	50	48	220
Average ($\bar{x}$)	11.8	10.2	9.6	9.2	9.2

Foreman Deming reflects on the results. "You'll observe that some of the performance is above average and some below. Can't understand it. Steve was man of the day the first day. Pat came up with seventeen. Pat's performance the first day was the worst of all. Seventeen red beads. The second day, down to five. Man of the day the second day. First day, she was the cause of all our troubles."

As Dr. Deming continues, the audience grasps the basic message: that even with identical tools, tasks, and talents, production will vary. In mimicking a foreman, Dr. Deming suggests that managers are wont to blame workers for results that are beyond their control. Moreover, given *any* number of workers, some will always be below average and some above.

Next, Dr. Deming illustrates how a simple statistical formula can be employed to establish the limits of variation. "Now let us make a little computation. The total is 220. Let's make the supposition that a red bead did not pull a red one in, or repel; or a white bead pull a white one in, that is, to the paddle, or repel it. Let's make a supposition of independence."

First, he divides the total number of red beads (220) by the number of times they were drawn (six workers times four days) for a daily average of 9.2. The daily average is referred to as "x-bar" ($\bar{x}$).

$$\bar{x} = \frac{220}{6 \times 4} = 9.2$$

Next, he calculates the average proportion of red beads drawn each day, or "p-bar" ($\bar{p}$), by determining the ratio of red beads in the count to the total number of beads that were drawn.

$$\bar{P} = \frac{220}{6 \times 4 \times 50} = .18$$

From these figures, it is possible to compute upper control limits and lower control limits using the following formula:

$$\begin{matrix} \text{UCL} \\ \text{LCL} \end{matrix} = \bar{x} \pm 3 \sqrt{\bar{x}(1 - \bar{p})}$$

or

$$= 9.2 \pm 3\sqrt{9.2 \times .82}$$

Dr. Deming's Red Bead Experiment

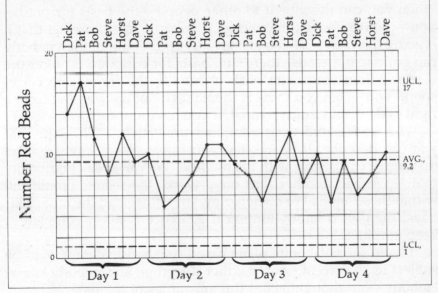

"Now," Dr. Deming says, "let's look at the results. Nobody exceeded the upper limit. Tried to. Came close. Didn't make it, though. All the lots, all twenty-four, stayed within the control limits. Pretty good sign that we have a moderately good state of statistical control. I never use the word *perfect* because there is no such thing."

A pattern might be seven or eight points in a row, or "run," either above or below average. But, Dr. Deming notes, "I see no pattern. . . . You have before you as near a constant cause system as you will run across. And look at the variation. Constant cause system means stability in the sense that you may compute the limits of variation for the future. All future? No. Let's say immediate future, on the basis of the twenty-four lots that we have. Meager information, yes, but it is twenty-four. If we had another forty-eight worth, we could combine them, to compute new limits for the future. It would probably turn out to be just about what we have now. I don't know. Nobody knows the future. Empirical evidence is never complete."

In other words, barring any change in the system that governs the bead production line, the number of red beads will fluctuate between the upper and lower control limits, but not exceed them.

"When you predict in a rational manner," Dr. Deming says, "then you can describe it to other people—the basis for prediction—then anybody can criticize. If you just say, 'I predict that it is going to rain,'. . . if you just give us your opinion, then nobody can criticize it, because there's no basis for criticism. If I offer the reasons, then you might wish to modify the formula to correspond with what you think is the behavior of nature. You have a right to do it, and a duty to do it, if you have any such knowledge.

"You understand what a rational prediction is? It is one that you can describe. It is one that you can explain. Anybody else may agree or disagree with the method. We can predict rationally that if we had another four days work, the results would fall within these limits. We do not know that. If we had the other four days, then we'd know. Empirical evidence is never complete. I keep emphasizing that.

"I have seen elaborate plans based on shoddy data. Could be subject to 25 percent error in either direction, and nobody knew. Nobody even thought about the infirmities of the data."

Next, Dr. Deming teases his audience, inviting them to consider what results they would have predicted had they not seen the experiment. Given that there were 4,000 beads—3,200 or 80 percent white and 800 or 20 percent red—would "x-bar" settle down to a certain number? Those bold enough to answer reason that if the daily production is fifty, over time red beads would settle down to an average daily count of 20 percent or ten.

And indeed, there are scattered calls of "ten" in response to Dr. Deming's query.

"What do I hear?" he demands. "Ten? You're all wrong. Look! This is important. You jumped, with no basis whatever. Sure, 20 percent of the red beads in the supply are red—20 percent of fifty is ten, yes. Why did you say you would predict that x-bar would settle down to some number? I didn't ask you what number. I said, some number. Why did you say yes? A whole chorus of yeses. Why did you do that? I don't mind the yes. I want to ask you why. On what basis would x-bar settle down? Why did you say that?"

"Probability," comes an answer. "Central limit theory."

"Probability?" thunders Dr. Deming. "We don't have any probability. Central limit theory. Wish you'd tell me what it is. I've been getting along now for fifty-five years without it. I didn't want to know what it is, but tell me. What the hell do you mean? (Laughter.) Central limit theory. Put that away. That's one of the problems that we face in teaching of statistics. Teaching people what's *wrong* and doing it very well."

Another intrepid person offers an answer: "The population would have to average out."

"What has to average out?" Dr. Deming retorts. "What's a population? I've never seen one in my life."

"The universe," comes the answer.

"Universe? Tell me what it is." Dr. Deming cautions, "I think that it is necessary to think and not to assume what you don't know. Now, let's keep going. Why, on what basis would you predict that x-bar would settle down to anything? . . .

"Before we did the experiment, as of this morning, would you have predicted that x-bar would settle down to something? No! Now that's not a matter of opinion. I'm not advancing something and asking you to examine it. It is not that kind of thing. The answer is no. You could not, should not, make any such prediction. . . .

"Now that we have a state of statistical control, we could say that x-bar would settle down to some number. We don't know what it is. We only have four days. Seems to be settling down to something. To what? Some number. Let's look at the data again. 11.8; 10.1; 9.6; 9.2; seems to be slipping downward; possibly approaching something. Don't know. Another four days would tell us something more. Would you say that x-bar would settle down to some particular number? I hear a faint yes, and that is right. I think that it would. Now, what would it settle down to?"

"Ten," comes the answer once again.

Continues Dr. Deming, "Now you say that it would settle down to ten. You're wrong again. Look, this is the place to learn. And we're learning. Why would you say it would settle down to ten? On what basis? You have no basis whatever. All the evidence that we have so far is that it does not settle down to ten. Slipping downward—11.8, 10.2, 9.6, 9.2. Why did you say ten? Wishful thinking, because you didn't learn in statistical theory what it means and how to use it. Why did you say ten?"

A member of the audience insists that "80 percent of what's in the box is red. It should be ten."

Dr. Deming replies, "It should be, but it is not! You can see very well that it is not. Why did you say ten? Because ten is 20 percent of fifty. And 20 percent of the beads in the box are red. But if you run your business that way, you'll really be in trouble. Really be in trouble."

At this point, the point is beginning to sink in. Because the average is not ten but rather appears to be somewhat lower, then there must be variables that affect the process.

"Is there more than one variable?" a man asks. "You're giving us the information that the beads are red and white. Are they also different sizes?"

Dr. Deming takes the question seriously. "Different sizes? Of course they are of different sizes. No two are alike. You know that. So what? Does that mean that you get something different from ten?

"That doesn't do it. If they don't fit in the hole, they won't be in the sample." But, he tells the man with good humor, "You put your finger on something." He addresses his audience with a smile, "Why do I have to work so hard?

"Now, let's put the question another way. . . . Think of the reasons why red would behave differently from white. Why would the proportion be not what you said? So sure of it! Nothing worse than being so sure of something that is wrong. That will really get you into trouble. . . .

"Tell me some reasons why x-bar might not settle down to ten. Could be wildly different from ten.

"Sure, the red beads are different from white. If they weren't different, how could our inspectors count the number of red beads?

"Red is different from white. No fooling. And any chemist can tell you how the two pigments differ. They feel different to the paddle. They feel different to the fingers. And the red are bigger! How do you think you make red beads? You make them all white. You lay them out on the table. Let them dry. Dip some of them into red pigment. Lay them out to dry. You now have some red beads and then some white ones. The red ones are bigger and heavier. And you try to tell me that x-bar will settle down to ten, because 20 percent of the box is red.

"The paddle is important. Paddle number one I carried for thirty years; taught Japanese engineers with it. It gave 11.3 for my average number of red beads per paddle, over hundreds of experiments. Paddle number two gave 9.6. Paddle number three, which we used today, is settling down to 9.4 or possibly 9.2.

"If you were buying coal for your factory at 9.6 percent ash and getting 11.3 percent, you would have a hard time to make ends meet. Mechanical sampling, which we use in such experiments, will never tell you what is in the incoming reservoir of material—here, the red and white beads.

"If you have moderately good statistical control, then x-bar will settle down to *something*. May take a long time, another four days. We will build up a degree of belief. You may plan on that for the future. If we had to plan for the future right now, we would say x-bar is about 9.2. But we don't know how close. We'd have to lay a plan that would allow a lot of flexibility."

As with any parable, there is a moral. The parable of the beads has several:

- Variation is part of any process.
- Planning requires prediction of how things and people will perform. Tests and experiments of past performance can be useful, but not definitive.
- Workers work within a system that—try as they might—is beyond their control. It is the system, not their individual skills, that determines how they perform.
- Only management can change the system.
- Some workers will always be above average, some below.

Having seen it once, Dr. Deming promises that you will never forget his simple "stupid" experiment. "You will be seeing red beads wherever you go."

PART TWO

THE DEMING MANAGEMENT METHOD

·

Chapter 5

•

Point One:
Create Constancy of Purpose
for the Improvement of
Product and Service

Management has two sets of problems, Dr. Deming says: those of today and those of tomorrow—on the supposition that there is a tomorrow for the company that hopes to stay in business.

The problems of today concern the immediate needs of the company: how to maintain quality; how to match output to sales; budget; employment; profits; service; public relations; forecasting. Most American companies tend to dwell on such problems, without adequate attention to the future. Because corporate managers change jobs every two or three years, their interests are short term. They live for the next quarterly dividend, without regard for whether they will be in business five years hence. But what value is a 25 percent increase in the quarterly dividend to a company that is out of business five years from now?

"It is easy to stay bound up in the tangled knots of the problems of today, becoming ever more and more efficient in them,"[1] Dr. Deming notes. But no company without a plan for the future, he emphasizes, will stay in business.

When employees are working for a company that is investing for the future, they will feel more secure and less likely to look for jobs in companies that appear more promising.

Companies may think they have a statement that declares constancy of purpose. But how often, queries Dr. Deming, do they consult it? "It is on the shelf, dust-covered."[2] He advises companies to think hard about the future, developing both a plan and methods to stay in business.

Establishing constancy of purpose means 1) innovation; 2) research and education; 3) continuous improvement of product and service; 4) maintenance of equipment, furniture and fixtures, and new aids to production in the office and in the plant.

Innovation

Innovation does not consist of the introduction of some flashy new product for the mere sake of having something new to sell. The product—or service—must have a market, able to help people to live better materially in some way.

A company that intends to stay in business can make no decisions about innovation without a plan that answers the following questions:

- What materials will be required, at what cost?
- What will be the method of production?
- What new people will have to be hired?
- What changes in equipment will be required?
- What new skills will be required, and for how many people?
- How will current employees be trained in these new skills?
- How will supervisors be trained?
- What will be the cost of production?
- What will be the cost of marketing? What will be the cost and methods of service?
- How will the product or service be used by the customer?
- How will the company know if the customer is satisfied?

As obvious as these questions seem, it is amazing how many companies forge ahead without answers.

By its very nature, innovation requires faith in the future. It cannot possibly succeed, Dr. Deming says, unless top management has "declared unshakable commitment to quality and productivity."[3]

But it is not enough merely to innovate. New products are not the salvation of an ailing company.

Put Resources into Research and Education

To prepare for the future, a company must invest today. There can be no innovation without research, and no research without properly educated employees.

Continuous Improvement of Product and Service

This obligation to the consumer never ceases. Great gains can be made through a continuous process of improvement in the design and performance of already-existing products, even ones that seem to be in trouble. The status quo will not do. Writes Dr. Deming, with a touch of irony, "It is a mistake to suppose that efficient production of product and service can with certainty keep an organization solvent and ahead of competition. It is possible and in fact fairly easy for an organization to go downhill and out of business making the wrong product or offering the wrong type of service, even though everyone in the organization performs with devotion, employing statistical methods and every other aid that can boost efficiency."[4]

Invest in the Maintenance of Equipment, Furniture and Fixtures, and in New Aids to Production in the Office and in the Plant

Clearly, a company cannot improve a product with equipment that malfunctions or introduce a new one using outdated machinery. Investment is necessary in these areas.

Dr. Deming says:

"People are concerned about the future, and the future is ninety days at the most, or nonexistent. There may not be any future. That is what occupies people's minds. That is not the way to stay in business. Not the way to get ahead. You have to spend some time on the future. And to put it off—'Nothing could happen today anyway. Could just as well put it off another day, another week, no harm done because nothing would happen anyway today.' So you put it off and put it off and nothing happens."[5]

Chapter 6

Point Two: Adopt the New Philosophy

Quality must become the new religion. Japan has introduced a new economic age of reliability and smooth operation. There are new standards. We can no longer afford to live with mistakes, defects, poor workmanship, bad materials, handling damage, fearful and uninformed workers, poor training or none at all, executive job-hopping, and inattentive and sullen service. Defects are not free.

"The cost of living depends inversely on the goods and services that a given amount of money will buy," Dr. Deming points out. "Reliable service reduces costs. Delays and mistakes raise costs."[1]

Dr. Deming illustrates this point by telling of a beer manufacturer who boasted that he had no problem with cans because his suppliers replaced those that were defective. It never occurred to him that he was paying for the defective cans, because their cost was included in the wholesale price.

By the same token American consumers accept that when there is an industrial accident—the nuclear shutdown at Three Mile Island, for example—they will end up footing the bill. They even joke about it. Who has not said, "You know who will end up paying for this."

Thus, consumers of goods and services end up paying for delays and mistakes, which reduces their standard of living.

Businesses seldom learn of their customers' dissatisfaction. Customers, Dr. Deming says, do not complain. They merely switch. How much better it would be to have customers that would boast about products and bring in new business.

Everyone can come up with a personal list of horrors of things gone wrong, and complaints unheeded.

In the post–World War II period, American-manufactured items, produced under economies of scale, dominated the market. There was no competition until Japan began to make inroads in the late 1950s.

In those days an actor named Ronald Reagan popularized a slogan for General Electric: "Progress is our most important product." That was back in the days when GE's version of progress was a never-ending selection of affordable household appliances fueled by cheap, seemingly unlimited electricity. Everybody believed in progress, which was thought to mean a constantly improving standard of living. Today, General Electric has pleaded guilty to fraud on federal contracts.

Dr. Deming suggests that we must believe in quality as we once believed in progress.

Dr. Deming says:

"Point two really means in my mind a transformation of management. Structures have been put in place in management that will have to be dismantled. They have not been suitable for two decades. They never were right, but in an expanding market you couldn't lose. The weaknesses showed up when competition came in. We will have to undergo total demolition of American style of management, which unfortunately has spread to just about the whole western world. In fact, one problem is that American companies have forced it on to their Canadian subsidiaries and subsidiaries in other countries, thus injecting disease the world over. This is a pity.

"Competition introduced a squeeze. Management offered all kinds of excuses. There was every kind of thing in this world, except the awful truth that Americans were beaten. Where they have been beaten is in the management. It has been focusing on results."[2]

Chapter 7

———————•———————

Point Three:
Cease Dependence
on Mass Inspection

"Inspection with the aim of finding the bad ones and throwing them out is too late, ineffective, costly," says Dr. Deming. "In the first place, you can't find the bad ones, not all of them. Second, it costs too much." The result of such inspection is scrap, downgrading and rework, which are expensive, ineffective and do not improve the process. "Quality comes not from inspection but from improvement of the process.[1]

"The old way: Inspect bad quality out.

"The new way: Build good quality in."[2]

As a practical matter, a certain amount of inspection will always be required, if only to find out what you are doing, Dr. Deming points out. In other words, "Don't drive in the road without your lights on."[3] Clearly, inspection—or review—is necessary to obtain data for control charts. Inspection becomes a way of finding out what you are doing.

In some cases, 100 percent inspection may be necessary for reasons of safety "or to avoid embarrassment and sometimes even for minimum total cost." He adds, "These circumstances exist where perfect conformance—or no mistakes—are beyond man's capability." A bank might properly verify all calculations of interest and penalties. But Dr. Deming cautions that "inspection must be carried out in a professional way, not by lick-and-spit methods."[4]

In all other cases, however, a company's aim should be to do away with quality by inspection.

Even inspection at various stages of production rather than at the very end is no answer. No one likes to do rework. All too often, the pile of defects grows until, in desperation, the parts are used as is.

Inspection will certainly be necessary during that period when quality is being upgraded but has not yet reached a point where inspection becomes unnecessary due to diminishing returns. It may be necessary, for example, to inspect or test incoming materials to determine which supplier provides the highest quality. Many problems can be eliminated at this stage. In general, inspection should not be left to the final product, when it is difficult to determine where in the process a defect took place.

Dr. Deming calls attention to the absurdity of "meeting specifications," the common American practice for establishing production criteria. This practice implies that anything inside the specifications may be all right, while something just outside is all wrong. It was, he says, "Dr. G. Taguchi who won the Deming Prize in 1960 who saw the absurdity of such suppositions and proposed an important improvement of principle."[5] The Japanese have learned that ever decreasing variation decreases the total cost. Two products may meet the same specifications but be so different that one will work and another will not.

Dr. Deming says:

"Down the road, there's a music store, and that music store would be delighted to sell you the score for a 140-piece orchestra—Beethoven's Fifth Symphony. Listen to the London Symphony Orchestra play it. So wonderful. Now listen to my hometown orchestra play it. Just listen to the difference. The London Symphony . . . the hometown orchestra. Same music; same specifications. Not a mistake. Both perfect. But listen to the difference. Just listen to the difference."[6]

Chapter 8

Point Four: End the Practice of Awarding Business on Price Tag Alone

So common in America, this practice has three major drawbacks. In the first place, it almost invariably leads to a proliferation of suppliers. Dr. Deming says, "Two or more suppliers for the same item will multiply the evils that are necessarily inherent and bad enough with any one supplier." As it is, he notes, even with a single supplier "there is too much variation lot-to-lot and within lots."[1] Variation causes problems in production and impairs quality. Impairment of quality snowballs, picking up worse and worse quality. (Conversely, good quality at a point also snowballs along the line, picking up better and better quality.)

"Another way to put it, defects beget defects. There's no better way to put it. Three words. Good quality begets good quality."[2]

Second, it causes buyers to jump from vendor to vendor. And third, it produces a reliance on specifications, which become barriers to continuous improvement.

"Price," Dr. Deming emphasizes, "has no meaning without a measure of the quality being purchased."[3]

A buyer will serve his company best by developing a long-term relationship of loyalty and trust with a single vendor, with engineering and other departments working together to reduce costs and improve quality.

"To work with a single supplier on development of an item demands so much talent and manpower that it is unthinkable that one could go through the development with two suppliers," Dr. Deming observes.[4]

Striking deals with the cheapest supplier is the accepted American way of doing business. Certainly thrift is an admirable quality, and costs are important. But if low cost guarantees low quality anywhere in the supply chain, then the final product, though it may be cheap, will also be of low quality. Indeed, often low quality of the final product can be traced back to problems with incoming materials.

"Cost-plus" is another pitfall, Dr. Deming notes. In this ruse, a supplier offers a bid so low that he is almost certain to get the business. Midway into production, the customer discovers that certain changes are critical. The supplier obliges, while boosting the price of the items. It is too late for the customer to make other arrangements. Hence, the "cost overruns" with which our government is so familiar. Insists Dr. Deming, "With a single supplier and a long term relationship of trust, such pillage does not occur."[5]

The buyer, merely executing company policy, is not at fault.

A price tag, notes Dr. Deming, is unambiguous and therefore appealing. Determining quality is another matter entirely, and it requires some degree of knowledge and skill. The purchasing agent must have education in statistical evidence, supplemented by experience. The purchasing agent must also learn how materials are used, in order to acquire the right information from the supplier. A raw material may meet specifications but still present problems in production. In recent history, a Boston skyscraper had a problem with windows that burst from their steel frames. It might have been laughable were it not so dangerous. Both the windows and the steel frames met specifications, but they did not work well together.

Better than the manuals full of standards by which vendors must qualify for business would be evidence of active involvement by a supplier's management with the Fourteen Points, especially Point Five on the never-ending improvement of processes. Active involvement, Dr. Deming stresses, "is not to be confused with conference room promises."[6]

Dr. Deming is the first to admit he does not have all the answers for choosing the single supplier. "It takes a lot of thought.

You have to do it, though, whether you have it all worked out or not.

"Does he have the experience? Does he have the knowledge? Does he plan to stay in business? How many suppliers has he, for one thing?"[7] But the advantages will become apparent. A supplier assured of long-term contracts is more likely to risk being innovative or to modify production processes than a supplier with a short-term contract, who cannot afford to tailor a product to the needs of a buyer. There are other advantages to long-term relationships. Accounting and other paperwork is simplified with a decrease in the number of suppliers and fewer shipping points.

Purchasing agents worry that a vendor who has an exclusive arrangement will try to take advantage of his customer. They are equally concerned that this arrangement makes the buyer too dependent on a single source. What happens if the supplier has a labor strike or a fire? These things happen, Dr. Deming admits. But customers can find alternative suppliers.

Financial people like to have several vendors to pit against each other to drive down price. This practice, Dr. Deming says, with no regard to quality and service, can actually drive good vendors and good service out of business.

Dr. Deming says:

"Purchasing should be a team effort, and one of the most important people on the team should be the chosen supplier—if you have a choice—picked on the basis of his record of improvement and of his efforts to learn and to follow the Fourteen Points.

"The team should also include the product engineer and representatives of manufacturing, purchasing, sales, or whatever other departments will be involved with the product. Other vital members of the team will be the people who have to use the equipment.

"There must be a long-term arrangement—a 'gentlemen's agreement.' There is no legal definition of long. The one thing it is not is an annual contract based on price tag. It is more powerful. With a gentlemen's agreement, you're on your own and so is he. It is far stronger than a legal agreement, which your lawyer can always help you get out of.

"A company that adopts the recommendations made here will have wide influence. The suppliers that serve one company also serve other companies, and will deliver to all of them better and better quality with better and better economy. Everybody will come out ahead.

"Ask people who do it this way. They would have it no other way."[8]

Chapter 9

---•---

Point Five:
Improve Constantly and Forever the System of Production and Service

Improvement is not a one-time effort. Management is obligated to improve continually. Quality, Dr. Deming says, "must be built in at the design stage," and teamwork is essential to the process.[1] Once the plans are well underway, changes are costly and cause delays.

Everyone and every department in the company must subscribe to constant improvement. It cannot be limited merely to manufacturing or the service delivery systems. Purchasing, transportation, engineering, maintenance, sales, personnel, training, and accounting all have a role to play.

Dr. Deming emphasizes that management must lead the way. Only management can initiate improvement in quality and productivity. Production workers on their own can achieve very little.

Removal of an irritant, or solving a particular problem, is not improvement of a process. It is simply "putting out a fire."

He tells the story of attendance at an awards ceremony. The highest award went to a man who had discovered that the labels were not on bottles of a vaccine that were ready to be shipped. Identification was still possible. A few minutes later, that would not have been the case. The man saved the company $250,000.

The second award went to a man who discovered contamination in a shipment before it went out. The shipment was of course condemned.

Those awards, Dr. Deming says, were for putting out fires, not for improvement of quality nor of the system.

Statistical thinking is critical to improvement of a system. Only by use of properly interpreted data can intelligent decisions be made. But to depend only on the use of statistics is a sure way to go out of business. A company must follow all of the Fourteen Points.

By the same token, meeting specifications does not result in constant improvement. It ensures the status quo.

"Zero defects" is the same misguided notion. As a goal, it makes no sense. There must be a method. Likewise, with "meeting the competition." "You think the Japanese are going to stand still while somebody catches up?" Dr. Deming queries.[2]

It is more appropriate, Dr. Deming suggests, to consider such questions as whether your firm is doing better than a year ago, or two years ago; whether marketing is more effective, whether customer satisfaction has increased, and whether the pride and performance of employees has improved. A company that subscribes to Point Five can answer yes to those questions.

Dr. Deming says:

"Putting out fires is not improvement. Finding a point out of control, finding the special cause and removing it, is only putting the process back to where it was in the first place. It is not improvement of the process. [Dr. Deming attributes this conclusion to Dr. Joseph M. Juran, many years ago.]

"You are in a hotel. You hear someone yell fire. He runs for the fire extinguisher and pulls the alarm to call the fire department. We all get out. Extinguishing the fire does not improve the hotel.

"That is not improvement of quality. That is putting out fires."[3]

Chapter 10

Point Six:
Institute Training
and Retraining

All too frequent are stories of workers who learn their jobs from other workers or who are forced to depend on unintelligible printed instructions. Often there is little training or none at all. Just as often, workers don't know when they have done their jobs correctly. What may be acceptable one day is unacceptable the next because, for example, a foreman may be having difficulty meeting his daily quota.

It is very difficult to erase improper training, Dr. Deming notes. It can be done only if the new method is totally different or if the person is being trained in a different set of skills for a different job.

The same kind of control charts used to determine whether a process is in statistical control can be used to chart a worker's performance. When output reaches the stable state, further training will not help the worker. This is a useful measure for determining when a worker has received enough training. There are other applications as well. A physical therapist can chart a patient's progress in learning to walk. When it reaches statistical control [a stable state], it means no more progress can be made and it is time for the therapist to move on to another patient.

On the other hand, Dr. Deming stresses that training should not end as long as performance is not yet in statistical control and there is something to be gained.

All employees will have to have some training in the significance of variation, and be taught rudimentary knowledge of control charts. When new equipment or processes are introduced, there must be retraining as well.

Dr. Deming says:

"A woman said she couldn't find out what the job was. I said, 'Well, how did you find out?' Her companions helped her. They taught her what was right and what was wrong. How could they teach her anything else but the way that they were doing it, some ways of which were right and some wrong? They didn't know; she couldn't know. It's just like taking lessons on the piano from someone who never had a lesson on the piano. He learned by himself how to play. If you take lessons from him, you will learn a lot that is wrong; you might learn some that is right. Neither pupil nor teacher will know what is right and what is wrong.[1]

"Did you know that when this happens, and it is going on all around us, the training gets worse and worse? It resembles a game everyone knows about. A number of people sit in a circle. Someone whispers words to the next person, who whispers it onward. By the time the words make first circle, they may be distorted beyond recognition. The meaning takes a random walk as it goes around. That's what you get when worker trains worker."[2]

Chapter 11

Point Seven: Institute Leadership

Leadership is the job of management. It is the responsibility of management to discover the barriers that prevent workers from taking pride in what they do. The workers know exactly what these barriers are: an emphasis on numbers, not quality; turning out the product quickly rather than properly; a deaf ear to their suggestions; too much time spent on rework; poor tools; problems with incoming materials.

Rather then helping workers do their job correctly, most supervision accomplishes just the opposite. Often supervisors, hired straight out of college, don't know the work they supervise. They have never done the job.

In America long ago and in Japan today, a foreman knew the job. There was, notes Dr. Deming, a problem with that, of course. Those who became supervisors were generally the better employees. They expected others to do as well as they. But it was nevertheless preferable to today's situation, when the job frequently is as new to the supervisor as it is to the workers.

Although not familiar with the work, these supervisors can count. Because they have no other basis for judgment, they are comfortable in a system that imposes numbers or quotas on employees. Typically, in rating people they forget that for every person who is above average there is another below.

One of Dr. Deming's favorite examples of this error in reasoning was committed by the American Historical Society, which asked its membership to rate America's thirty-seven presidents.

The Society announced with great satisfaction that half were above average. Newspaper articles on the survey trumpeted the news.

Asks Dr. Deming, "What if they'd all been below? The article said that we've been mighty lucky, considering the haphazard way in which we select presidents."[1]

The job of the manager is to lead, to help people do their jobs better. In hiring people, management takes responsibility for their success or failure. Dr. Deming contends that most people who do not do well on the job are not malingerers, but have simply been misplaced. If someone has a disability, or is incapable of doing a job, the manager has an obligation to find a place for that person.

Dr. Deming says:

"People come into a company from college, learn about the company by going in and being supervisors somewhere. Pity poor people that have such supervision. No help at all! Aren't they entitled to some help? Where is the supervisor who knows how to find who is in need of individual attention? Show me one. There is no such thing as supervision, and should not be, unless people know how to supervise.

"There is no excuse to offer for putting people on a job that they know not how to do. Most so-called 'goofing off'—somebody seems to be lazy, doesn't seem to care—that person is almost always in the wrong job, or has very poor management."[2]

Chapter 12

Point Eight: Drive Out Fear

"Most people on a job," says Dr. Deming, "especially people in management positions, do not understand what the job is, nor what is right or wrong. Moreover, it is not clear to them how to find out. Many of them are afraid to ask questions or to take a position.

"The economic loss from fear is appalling."[1]

People are afraid to point out problems for fear they will start an argument, or worse, be blamed for the problem. Moreover, so seldom is anything done to correct problems that there is no incentive to expose them. And more often than not there is no mechanism for problem-solving. Suggesting new ideas is too risky. People are afraid of losing their raises or promotions, or worse, their jobs. They fear punitive assignments or other forms of discrimination and harassment. They are afraid that superiors will feel threatened and retaliate in some fashion if they are too assertive or ask too many questions. They fear for the future of their company and the security of their jobs. They are afraid to admit they made a mistake, so the mistake is never rectified. In the perception of most employees, preserving the status quo is the only safe course.

It is necessary, Dr. Deming says, for better quality and productivity, that people feel secure. He notes that *se* comes from Latin, meaning "without," *cure* means "fear" or "care." *Secure* means "without fear,"—"not afraid to express ideas, not afraid to ask questions."[2]

Workers should not be afraid to report broken equipment, to ask for additional instructions, or to call attention to conditions that interfere with quality.

Fear, says Dr. Deming, will disappear as management improves, and as employees develop confidence in management.

Dr. Deming says:

"What are people afraid of? Afraid to contribute to the company. Better not get out of line. Don't violate procedures. Do it exactly this way.

"Why don't they complain to manufacturing about stuff that comes in already defective, hard to work with? No matter what you do, you can't turn out quality work—not within the time allowed. Why don't they say something about that?

"Look. Complain to the foreman about it, he can do nothing. Totally helpless about it. You only advance yourself on his list toward the top. And if he has to do some cutting, he begins at the top. Gets rid of the nuisance makers. Asking too many questions that he can't answer will only embarrass him. People don't complain. They don't complain. They have jobs.

"Fear takes a horrible toll. Fear is all around, robbing people of their pride, hurting them, robbing them of a chance to contribute to the company. It is unbelievable what happens when you unloose fear."[3]

Chapter 13

Point Nine:
Break Down Barriers
Between Staff Areas

To illustrate this point, Dr. Deming likes to tell the parable of the shoes. It seems that the technical staff of a shoe factory designed a shoe they thought would be a surefire hit. They made eight prototypes for the sales force, and sure enough, the sales people returned with orders for thousands of pairs. A success story? No. There were so many orders the factory couldn't fill them. The designers and sales had never consulted manufacturing.

The plant manager put his foot down. The sales force had to tell the wholesalers they couldn't fill the orders.

Probably every company or organization in America can tell stories that illustrate what happens when departments have different goals and do not work as a team to solve problems, set policies, or map out new directions.

Purchasing departments, for example, usually place orders based on written specifications. Buyers do not understand how the materials they buy are used, with the result that when problems occur or defects arise, they do not always know about them. Or, as is often the case, they may be the ones held responsible.

Designers are forever coming up with products that give engineers headaches. And engineers all too frequently are persona non grata on the production line.

People forced to administer policies that they had no hand in drafting and with which they may disagree do so half-heartedly and without uniformity, angering customers.

People can work superbly in their respective departments, Dr. Deming says, but if their goals are in conflict, they can ruin the company. It is better to have teamwork, working for the company.

Having been perfected in Japan, "just-in-time" production is enjoying a surge of popularity in this country. In this system, supplies arrive as they are needed, so that money and storage are not tied up in inventory. But just-in-time will not work without teamwork.

People in manufacturing and sales have a difficult time accepting the just-in-time method. The plant manager may be afraid of running out of parts. Sales and service people like to have a full inventory on hand so that customers don't have to wait. Working out the kinks and allaying these fears involves the cooperation of all departments.

With regard to just-in-time, Dr. Deming makes two points. In the first place, he says, this practice is "sheer nonsense unless the process is stable. Unless it is stable, nobody knows who is going to need what or when he'll need it."

By stable, Dr. Deming means in statistical control.

Second, he observes, "many American manufacturers are trying to start with just-in-time, unaware that this process is years off. Just-in-time is focused downstream. It's a natural occurrence. It is the end result of getting things right in the first place."[2]

Dr. Deming says:

"Is it management's job to help staff areas work together? To promote teamwork? Sounds great, but it can't be done under the present system. In spite of the system, you will find teamwork. But when it comes to a showdown under the present system and someone has to make a decision—his own rating or the company's—he will decide for himself. Can you blame him? People work in the system. Management creates the system."[3]

Chapter 14

Point Ten:
Eliminate Slogans,
Exhortations, and Targets
for the Workforce

Slogans, Dr. Deming says repeatedly, never helped anybody do a good job. They "generate frustration and resentment."[1]

Safety slogans like, "Don't skate on an oil slick"—an actual example in an American factory—make as much sense as road signs that say "Falling rock," as if you could somehow dodge a rock shower in a car going sixty miles per hour. In Japan, notes Deming, factories simply don't have oil slicks.

American slogans are imaginative. "Zero defects." "Do it right the first time." These have a lofty ring, Dr. Deming says. "But how could a man make it right the first time when the incoming material is off-gauge, off-color, or otherwise defective, or if his machine is not in good order?"[2] In short, management fails to provide the means to the ends it proclaims.

Implicit in such sloganeering is the supposition that employees could, if they tried, do better. They are offended, not inspired by this suggestion. Forced to work with improper or malfunctioning equipment, poor lighting or ventilation, in awkward work spaces under incompetent supervision, they perceive slogans and exhortations as signals that management not only doesn't understand their problems, it doesn't care enough to find out.

Dr. Deming places numerical goals in the same category. A

goal without a method for reaching it is useless, he says repeatedly. But setting goals without describing how they are going to be accomplished is a common practice among American managers.

Moreover, Dr. Deming adds, "it is totally impossible for anybody or for any group to perform outside a stable system, below or above it. If a system is unstable, anything can happen. Management's job, as we have seen, is to try to stabilize systems. An unstable system is a bad mark against management."[3]

Dr. Deming says:

"You can beat horses; they run faster for a while. Goals are like hay somebody ties in front of the horse's snout. The horse is smart enough to discover no matter whether he canters or gallops, trots or walks or stands still, he can't catch up with the hay. Might as well stand still. Why argue about it? It will not happen except by change of the system. That's management's job, not the people's."[4]

Chapter 15

Point Eleven:
Eliminate Numerical Quotas

Quotas or other work standards such as "measured day work" or "rates," Dr. Deming maintains, impede quality perhaps more than any other single working condition. "I have yet to see a work standard that includes any trace of a system which would help anyone do a better job," he says.[1] Indeed, as work standards are generally used, they guarantee inefficiency and high cost. They frequently contain allowances for defective items and scrap, which is a guarantee that management will get them.

Consider a quota that is set to the average output of a group of workers. Half will be above it and half below. Peer pressure, notes Dr. Deming, holds the upper half to the average rate, while those below cannot make the average rate. "The result is loss, chaos, dissatisfaction, and turnover," he says.[2] Sometimes, Dr. Deming notes, management will purposely set a work standard on the high side to weed out people who can't meet it. When rates are set for the achiever, the demoralization is even more intense.

Moreover, he contends, once workers have completed their quotas for the day, they quit working and linger around till the end of the shift.

He cites the example of the airline reservations clerk, who is under a directive to answer twenty-five calls an hour, while being courteous and not rushing callers. Sometimes the computer is slow in providing information. Sometimes it is entirely unresponsive and she must resort to directories and guides. Yet there is no leeway in the twenty-five-call mandate. What is her job? To take twenty-five calls or to satisfy the customer? She cannot do both.

Even more devastating is piecework. People are paid for the number of items they turn out, whether or not they are defective. Never was the old adage "Haste makes waste" more thoroughly ignored. He puts incentive pay in the same category because it also encourages people to turn out numbers rather than quality. Seldom are the costs of rejects, rework, or downgrading factored into the equation.

In some cases, workers are docked for the defective items they turn out. But wouldn't it be preferable not to make them in the first place? And how can managers be so sure that it is the worker who is at fault?

A proper work standard would define what is and is not acceptable in terms of quality.

The same is true for numerical goals assigned to management. All too often, a company will announce such goals out of the blue and with no plan. To decrease costs of warranty by 10 percent next year, for example, or to increase sales by 10 percent or to increase productivity by 3 percent are examples of nonsensical goals. Dr. Deming likes to quote Lloyd S. Nelson of Nashua Corporation on this subject: "If they can do it next year with no plan, why didn't they do it last year?"

He tells the story of seven men who discovered a way to save their company $500—a minuscule amount, but they took great pride in their plan. The company wisely recognized their accomplishment. The $500 was unimportant. But the figures that couldn't be measured—the enhanced feelings of loyalty and pride in their company at having their ideas accepted—ultimately would be worth a lot more. A system that fosters an atmosphere of receptivity and recognition is far preferable to one that measures people by the numbers they turn out. Moreover, Dr. Deming adds, "the quality will snowball from that stage onward."[3] Rather than assigning quotas to a job, Dr. Deming suggests studying the work and defining the limits of the job. To speed the work, refer complicated or nonroutine matters to a specialist.

Dr. Deming says:

"Where are the hangups? Study the records. What is taking the time? What is the difference between people who have been there three years versus two years? Maybe you can learn something.

There will be a distribution of results. They will not all come up to the average. No matter what, half of them will be below. The problem is to improve the system and find out who is having the trouble.

"Isn't it clear? Numerical quotas—so many per day; a plant manager—so many per day. If he fails to meet it, he fails. No regard for what is a day's work. No possibility to improve. Do you think a plant manager will report 7,000 when the quota is 5,000? That he will report 5,500 when the quota is 5,000? No. Put them under the counter. May need them for a rainy day.

"It may rain tomorrow."[4]

Chapter 16

•

Point Twelve:
Remove Barriers to Pride
of Workmanship

When Dr. Deming takes on a corporate client, he insists that there be a meeting of workers without supervisors present, which is recorded so that management can listen or watch it at a later time. Dr. Deming skillfully leads the workers into dialogue. Before long they are voicing their frustrations at being unable to perform the jobs the way they would like. The workers, it is clear from these meetings, understand very well that as quality improves, so too does productivity. They understand very well that their jobs, more than those of management, depend on the acceptance of their product or service on the marketplace. Yet they are powerless to change things. Often managers are shocked when they hear what is wrong.

Workers complain that they do not know from one day to the next what is expected of them. Standards change frequently. Supervisors are arbitrary. They are seldom given feedback on their work until there are performance ratings or raises, and then it is too late.

Under Dr. Deming's questioning, workers reveal that they never really learned to do their job. They were trained, perhaps, by another worker, or told to read the instructions.

They report that equipment doesn't work right and their calls for help are answered belatedly, if at all. Maintenance is slipshod and seldom permanent. Supplies may be defective, but no one wants to hear about it.

Another source of discontent is inspection that turns up defects but contains no clues on how to prevent them. Sometimes inspectors themselves aren't sure what is right, or whether their machinery makes accurate measurements.

Finally, workers complain about supervisors whose only interest is in getting the work out, not the quality of the work.

During a strike one manager found out firsthand what his employees had to put up with. When salaried employees took over the jobs of striking hourly workers, the department manager learned for the first time of machines that needed maintenance, repair, and replacement. Production doubled when he tuned up the machines. He resolved immediately to begin a system whereby employees could report trouble with machinery and materials in a fashion that would bring prompt attention. How many companies can say they have such a system?

People today are regarded as a commodity, to be used as needed. If not needed, they are returned to the market.

In his rounds of American companies, Dr. Deming has observed that managers work long hours and willingly cope with many vexing situations but shy away from the problems of the people that work for them. To deal with "people problems," they are wont to establish "employee involvement" programs. Quality Control Circles are the current vogue. Dr. Deming calls such quick-fix solutions "instant pudding." They are, he says, a "smoke-screen," a way for a manager to pretend to be doing something about a problem. Such programs demonstrate a notable tendency to fade away because management never invests employees with any authority, nor does it act upon their decisions and recommendations. Employees become even more disillusioned.

Dr. Deming says:

"In a meeting of two hundred factory workers, a man said to me, 'It is a matter of communication.' I hear that word a dozen times a day—communication. I said, 'Tell me about it.' His machine had gone out of order and would make only defective items. He had reported it, but the maintenance men could not come for a long time. Meanwhile, he was trying to repair it himself. The foreman came along and said to run it. 'In other words, he told me to make defective items.'

" 'Where is my pride of workmanship?' he asked me. 'If the

foreman would give me as much respect as he does the machine, I'd be better off.'

"He didn't want to get paid for making defective items.

"Talk about motivation. People are motivated. All people are motivated. Everyone? No. There are exceptions. Some are beaten down so often, so many times, that they have lost, temporarily at least, interest in the job."[1]

Chapter 17

Point Thirteen: Institute a Vigorous Program of Education and Retraining

It is not enough to have good people in your organization. They must be continually acquiring the new knowledge and the new skills that are required to deal with new materials and new methods of production. Education and retraining—an investment in people—are required for long-term planning.

As productivity improves, fewer people will be needed in some cases. Some jobs may be added, but others may disappear. There will be fewer inspectors, possibly, for example. But quality must not cost jobs. A company, Dr. Deming emphasizes, "must make it clear that no one will lose his job because of improvement in productivity."[1]

Education and training must fit people into new jobs and responsibilities. There will be a need for more education in statistics, maintenance, and how to deal with vendors. Purchasing departments will change character and require different skills.

Education in simple but powerful statistical techniques will be required at all levels.

Dr. Deming says:

"How do you help people to improve? What do you mean by improve? If you ask me, I would say that I find a general fear of education. People are afraid to take a course. It might not be the right one. My advice is take it. Find the right one later. And how do you know it is the wrong one? Study, learn, improve. Many companies spend a lot for helping their people in this and that way. In arithmetic, geology, geography, learning about gears.

"You never know what could be used, what could be needed. He that thinks he has to be practical is not going to be here very long. Who knows what is practical?

"Help people to improve. I mean everybody."[2]

Chapter 18

Point Fourteen: Take Action to Accomplish the Transformation

Management will have to organize itself as a team to advance the thirteen other points. A statistical consultant will be required. Every employee of the company, including the managers, should acquire a precise idea of how to improve quality continually. The initiative must come from management.

How to begin? Follow the Shewhart Cycle. In Japan, it is called the Deming Cycle because it was Dr. Deming who introduced it. Some refer to it as the "PDCA Cycle," for "Plan, Do, Check, Act." Today it is a staple of the planning process. Explains Dr. Deming, "The Shewhart Cycle was on the blackboard for top management for every conference beginning in 1950 in Japan. I taught it to engineers—hundreds of them—that first hot summer. More the next summer, six months later, and more six months after that. And the year after that, again and again."[1]

Step 1: The first step is to study a process, to decide what change might improve it. Organize the appropriate team. Perhaps people from purchasing, or the supplier, or the product engineer. What data are necessary? Does the data already exist, or is it necessary to carry out a change and observe it? Are tests necessary? Do not proceed without a plan.

Step 2: Carry out the tests, or make the change, preferably on a small scale.

Step 3: Observe the effects.

Step 4: What did we learn? Repeat the test if necessary, perhaps in a different environment. Look for side effects.

THE SHEWHART CYCLE[2]

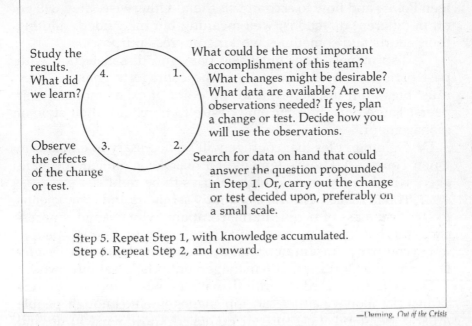

Study the results. What did we learn?

4.   1.

What could be the most important accomplishment of this team? What changes might be desirable? What data are available? Are new observations needed? If yes, plan a change or test. Decide how you will use the observations.

Observe the effects of the change or test.

3.   2.

Search for data on hand that could answer the question propounded in Step 1. Or, carry out the change or test decided upon, preferably on a small scale.

Step 5. Repeat Step 1, with knowledge accumulated.
Step 6. Repeat Step 2, and onward.

—Deming, *Out of the Crisis*

In addition to the use of the Shewhart Cycle, Dr. Deming says, to accomplish the transformation it is vital that everyone begin to think of his or her work as having satisfaction for a customer. There are internal as well as external customers. Ask yourself, he says, who is the person who receives your work? Whom must you satisfy? Many people cannot identify their customers and therefore cannot determine precisely what their jobs are. Everyone has a customer and must know who it is.

In following his Fourteenth Point, Dr. Deming recommends the following plan for action, for which he credits Phyllis Sobo, a Philadelphia consultant:

"1. Top management will struggle over every one of the above

Thirteen Points, the Deadly Diseases, the Obstacles. They will agree on their meaning and on the direction to take. They will agree to carry out the new philosophy."

Dr. Deming stresses that "it is not just constancy of purpose, but consistency as well."[3] It is important, he says, for people to work together with a mutual understanding of the foregoing Thirteen Points and how to accomplish them. Otherwise, they will go off in different directions, well-meaning but misguided, diluting their efforts and sometimes working at cross-purposes.

"2. Top management must feel pain and dissatisfaction with past performance and must have the courage to change. They must break out of line, even to the point of exile amongst their peers. There must be a burning desire to transform their style of management."

Dr. Deming notes that courage will be necessary to embark on a new course. Acknowledgment of a mistake is difficult for managers who have been paid high salaries to be right.

"3. Top management will explain by seminars and other means to a critical mass of people in the company why change is necessary and that the change will involve everybody. Enough people in the company must understand the Fourteen Points, the Deadly Diseases, the Obstacles. Top management is helpless otherwise."

Dr. Deming regards a critical mass as vital. Just as workers cannot act alone, neither can top management. Enough people must understand the Fourteen Points to know what to do and how to do it. It may also be useful to form a critical mass of companies in any given area to learn from each other and bring other companies into the fold.

"4. Every activity is a process and can be improved. Everyone belongs on a team, to work in the Shewhart Cycle, to address one or more specific issues, for example: constancy of purpose, constant improvement of product and service; designs for future product and service; purchase of materials; marketing; removal of the annual rating; removal of barriers to pride of workmanship on the factory floor."

Use of the Shewhart Cycle, Dr. Deming says, will lead to "continual improvement of methods and procedures."[4] It can be applied to any process and can also be used to find special causes detected by statistical signals.

Chapter 19

The Seven Deadly Diseases and Some Obstacles

Dr. Deming once told the U.S. Agency for International Development to "export anything to a friendly country, except American management."[1] Management in the United States, he says, suffers from deeply entrenched diseases that are potentially fatal unless corrected.

Dr. Deming makes a distinction between the serious and the not-quite-as-serious. The former he enumerates as the Seven Deadly Diseases; the latter are merely Obstacles.

To overcome these diseases will require, Dr. Deming says, no less than "a complete shakeup of Western style of management."

The Seven Deadly Diseases

1. *Lack of constancy of purpose*

If constancy of purpose—the first of the Fourteen Points—is essential to stay in business, its absence spells doom for a company. A company that is without constancy of purpose does not think beyond the next quarterly dividend and has no long-range plans for staying in business. Dedication to the new philosophy must be widespread throughout the company. It is not sufficient to announce intentions to improve quality, even repeatedly. Employees in many companies have been exposed to a succession of plans for improvement. They have seen programs come and go, often coinciding with the term of the chief executive officer. A new president, a new program. Disenchanted and disillusioned, they require proof that the company is serious this time. One way to demonstrate commitment is with money. Such concrete activities as spending money on training and equipment, or shutting down operations when something is wrong can help convince employees. Management must take the time to explain the Deming method in full.

2. Emphasis on short-term profits

Today's corporations are controlled by financial wizards and lawyers who airily manipulate figures but do not make substantial changes in production and quality. They are subservient to stockholders and committed to giving them ever-increasing quarterly dividends. Stockholders who depend on dividends for income need to be assured that their company will still be in existence, and still be producing dividends, some years hence. It is common for companies to ship products on the last day of the month, without regard to quality, merely to inflate the figures.

Emphasis on short-term profits is fed by fear of unfriendly takeover or, says Dr. Deming, "the equally devastating leveraged buyout.

"Must American management be forever subject to such plunder? Where is the Securities and Exchange Commission?" wonders Dr. Deming.[2]

He finds an ally on this subject in Harvard Prof. Robert B. Reich. Writing in *The Atlantic*, March 1983, Reich said "Paper entrepreneurialism is both cause and consequence of America's faltering economy. Paper profits are the only ones easily available to professional managers who sit isolated atop organizations designed for a form of production that is no longer appropriate to America's place in the world economy. At the same time, the relentless drive for paper profits has diverted attention and resources away from the difficult job of transforming the productive base."

"Paper profits do not make the pie bigger," Dr. Deming is fond of saying. "They give you a bigger piece. You take it from somebody else. It doesn't help the society."[3]

3. Evaluation of performance, merit rating, or annual review

The popular management by objective (MBO) programs and management by the numbers fall in this category. "Management by fear" would be a better name, suggests Dr. Deming. The effects, which are twofold, are devastating.

First, performance evaluations encourage short-term performance at the expense of long-term planning. They discourage risk-taking, build fear, undermine teamwork, and pit people against each other for the same rewards. On a team, it is difficult to tell who did what. The result is a company composed of prima donnas, of sparring fiefdoms. People work for themselves, not the company.

Such evaluations, Dr. Deming says, leave "people bitter, despondent, dejected, some even depressed, all unfit for work for weeks after receipt of rating, unable to comprehend why they are inferior. It is unfair, as it ascribes to the people in a group differences that may be caused totally by the system that they work in."[4]

He notes that merit ratings tend to increase variability of performance, as people with lower ratings attempt to emulate those with higher ones.

An insidious side effect is that they also increase reliance on numbers, Dr. Deming maintains. Because they measure short-term results, there is a tendency to consider only evidence that can be counted. The number of designs an engineer turns out, for example, with no consideration of their quality. Merit ratings also depend on the subjective judgment of supervisors. One's rating may vary wildly, depending on the boss.

Some supervisors dread making the judgments. One popular system requires them to assign ratings from one to five, with a certain number of people at each level. Even when there are only five workers, one must be rated at the top and one at the bottom.

The greatest accomplishments of man, Dr. Deming says, have been accomplished without competition.

"Look at Moses. He had no competition. Two hundred years ago Sebastian Bach was writing the rules of harmony for all time. Why did he do it? Pride of workmanship.

"People ask how I grade my students. I give them all 'A.' How do I know who will be great? They may turn papers in, I don't care when. Some of those papers are good enough, more than good enough, to be chapters in a book. I give my students no time limit. Not forever. It is all right with me. Just tell me what you're doing. Give me an outline of some kind. I give the 'A.' And what do I get? Great papers. Only one student has ever failed me. He was in trouble. He needed counseling. I didn't know it at the time. I gave him 'A.' He never delivered. One failure in all those students. Pretty good record, I'd say. How do I know what they will do in future years? Who am I to judge?"[5]

Dr. Deming feels very strongly about the damage done by performance ratings. In his speech at the December 11, 1985, Deming Prize awards in Japan, Dr. Deming cautioned his listeners against infection with American diseases. He talked at length about performance ratings. His audience, of course, was familiar with the use of control charts to determine statistical limits.

"The ratings of people in a group by any numerical system whatever, whether it be based on a single measure or whether it be a composite or weighted index, whether it makes sense or not, will divide the people of a group into three groups. A) People outside the control limits on the bad side; B) people outside limits on the good side; C) the people between limits.

"Group A requires individual help. Group B, if there's anybody there—there may not be anybody in A or B—but if there is, they require individual attention. Now, people in between the control limits must not be ranked. That is wrong, for the same reason that it is costly, devastating to try to discover the reasons why a point within control limits is higher than another one, or lower than another one. Differences within levels between the limits come from the system itself, not from the people there. Everybody in group C should receive the same increase in pay or the same bonus. There is no rightful distinction between them. The differences come from the system. They must be ascribed to the system, not to the people.

"The job of the leader is to shrink the control limits, to get less and less variation in a process, or less and less difference between people."[6]

4. Mobility of top management

Business schools are dedicated to the idea that you can train a good manager in universally applicable techniques. But how can managers be committed to long-term change when they are constantly building up their résumés? How can managers really know a company when they are there for only two or three years? In Japan, executives move through the ranks in a progression that takes decades to reach the top.

Dr. Deming quotes J. Noguchi, managing director of the Union of Japanese Scientists and Engineers, as saying, "America cannot make it because of mobility of American management."[7] Says Dr. Deming, "Mobility from one company to another creates prima donnas for quick results."[8] "People require time to learn to work together."[9] Mobility of labor in America, he adds, is almost equally as serious a problem. The principal cause is dissatisfaction with the job.

5. Running a company on visible figures alone ("counting the money")

Visible figures are important, of course. There is a payroll to meet, vendors to pay, taxes to pay, and pensions and contingency funds to support. But, says Dr. Deming, in a formulation for which he credits Lloyd S. Nelson of Nashua Corporation, the figures that are "unknown and unknowable" are even more important.

It is impossible, for example, to measure the effect on sales of a happy customer or the gains in quality that result from ridding a company of the Deadly Diseases. Only in time will these results become apparent.

Dr. Deming says that two of the Seven Deadly Diseases are beyond the scope of his present discussion. These are:

6. Excessive medical costs

For some companies this is their largest single expenditure.

7. Excessive costs of warranty, fueled by lawyers that work on contingency fees

The United States is the most litigious country in the world.

And Some Obstacles

• *Neglect of long-range planning and transformation*

Even where long-range plans exist, they are frequently neglected because of so-called emergencies. Often, company policies that are essentially frivolous take up the time of top-level management. Policies on attendance and promptness can consume large amounts of executives' time whereas in a climate of good management they would not be issues.

• *The supposition that solving problems, automation, gadgets, and new machinery will transform industry*

Americans love new technological toys, but these are not solutions to deep-seated quality and productivity issues.

• *Search for examples*

Companies tend to look for solutions to problems used elsewhere that they can copy. This is a hazard. Examples by themselves teach nothing, Dr. Deming stresses. It is necessary to know why a practice succeeds or fails.

• *Our problems are different*
This is often offered as an excuse.

• *Obsolescence in schools*
Dr. Deming is referring to schools of business in America that teach finance and creative accounting, that operate on the theory that management skills can be taught, not learned on the factory floor.

• *Reliance on quality control departments*
Quality belongs in the hands of management, supervisors, managers of purchasing, and production workers. They have the most to contribute. But quality departments, wielding figures that show what happened in the past—not what will happen in the future, which they cannot predict—often mystify managers to the point that they continue to leave quality in the department's hands.

• *Blaming the workforce for problems*
Workers are responsible for only 15 percent of the problems, the system for the other 85 percent. The system is the responsibility of management.

• *Quality by inspection*
Companies that depend on mass inspection to guarantee quality will never improve quality. Inspections are too late, unreliable, and ineffective.

• *False starts*
The wholesale teaching of statistical methods—without a corresponding change in company philosophy—is one such false start. Another false start, very popular these days, is the QC Circles, Dr. Deming says. (QC stands for Quality Control.) The idea is appealing. "The production worker can tell us a lot about what is wrong and how improvements can be made."[10] But, Dr. Deming notes, "A QC Circle can thrive only if management will take action on the recommendations of the Circle."[11] When the management has no interest in participation, as is often so, QC Circles simply disintegrate. Too often, the establishment of QC Circles, Employee Involvement Groups, and Employee Par-

ticipation Groups is only somebody's hope to rid himself of the problems of people. Moreover, QC Circles cannot solve problems of management, which are the real problems.

False starts, however, provide temporary comfort. They make it appear as if something is happening. Dr. Deming calls them "instant pudding."

- *The unmanned computer*

Although a computer has its place, Dr. Deming says, it can also serve as a repository for data that is never used. Too often, purchasing a computer seems to be the "thing to do." There is no real plan for its use. People are confused and intimidated by computers. Often they are never properly trained to use the equipment.

- *Meeting specifications*

This is the accepted way of doing business in America, but it is not sufficient if quality and productivity are to improve.

- *Inadequate testing of prototypes*

Often prototypes perform beautifully in the laboratory, but exhibit all sorts of problems in production.

- *"Anyone that comes to try to help us must understand all about our business"*

Dr. Deming frequently takes on clients in businesses with which he is not intimately familiar. It is possible, he notes, to know everything about a business except how to improve it. "Help toward improvement can come only from some other kind of knowledge."[12]

Chapter 20

Doing It with Data

"In God we trust. All others must use data."

If there is a credo for statisticians, it is that. Critical to the Deming method is the need to base decisions as much as possible on accurate and timely data, not on wishes or hunches or "experience."

A training manual for Komatsu Ltd., a Japanese competitor of Caterpillar Tractor Company, puts it this way:

"The first step in quality control is to judge and act on the basis of facts. Facts are data such as length, time, fraction defective and sales amount.

"Views not backed by data are more likely to include personal opinions, exaggeration and mistaken impressions.

"Data volume has nothing to do with the accuracy of judgement. Data without context or incorrect data are not only invalid but sometimes harmful as well. It is necessary to know the nature of that data and that proper data be picked as well."

Dr. Deming's views on statistical methods are twofold. First, they are essential to the transformation of American business. Only with the proper use of statistical methods can people minimize confusion in the presence of variation. Statistical methods help to understand processes, to bring them under control, and then to improve them. Otherwise, people will forever be "putting out fires" rather than improving the system.

But he emphasizes that to rely on statistical methods alone is not nearly enough. There may be immediate gains, then nothing. They are mere tools, albeit valuable ones, for workers executing a blueprint that must come from top management.

Nothing has caused him to alter this view. Here is how he put it in a speech he made at the 1960 Deming Prize awards:[1]

"What statistical methods do is to point out the existence of special causes. A point beyond limits on a control chart, or a significant result in an experiment or test, indicates almost certainly the existence of one or more special causes. Points in control, or showing no significance, indicate that only common causes of variation remain. . . .

"When you find most of the special causes and eliminate them, you have left common causes of variability, which may be any of several types—poor light, humidity, vibration, poor food in the cafeteria, absence of a real quality program, poor supervision, poor or spotty raw material, etc. Common causes are more difficult to identify than special causes are. Moreover, the removal of common causes calls for action by administration at a high level. Workers and foremen cannot change the lighting, nor write new contracts for raw materials, nor institute a quality program, yet these are examples of common causes of variation and of poor quality."

Some of the most useful statistical tools are neither difficult nor complicated to master. The level of mathematics necessary is no more than a seventh or eighth grader might learn. Several of the basic tools are merely ways of organizing and visually displaying data. In most cases, employees can collect the data and do much of the interpretation, and they are happy to do so because it gives them more responsibility.

Writes Dr. Deming, "Education in simple but powerful statistical techniques is required of all people in management, all engineers and scientists, inspectors, quality control managers, management in the service organizations of the company, such as accounting, payroll, purchase, safety, legal department, consumer service, consumer research. Engineers and scientists need rudiments of experimental design. Five days under a competent teacher will suffice as a base. . . .

"Only a teacher with the equivalent of a master's degree in statistics, and who has worked years in industry, is qualified for this teaching."[2]

It is the intent of this chapter not to teach statistics but merely to introduce some of the basic tools and to illustrate how they can be used in problem solving. Indeed, some of the charts that companies find helpful do not employ statistical methods but are merely ways for groups to organize their thoughts.

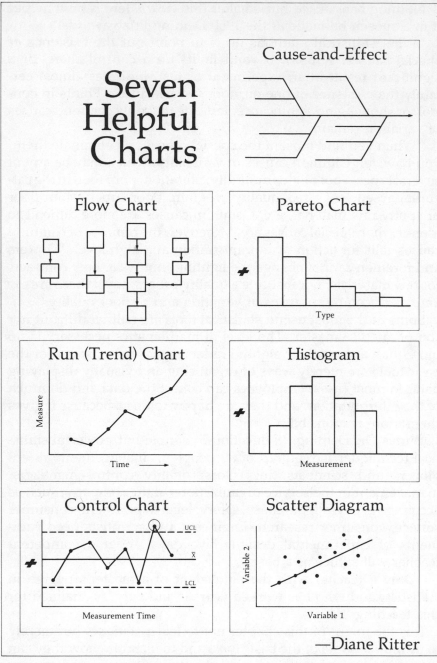

Seven Helpful Charts

Cause-and-Effect

Flow Chart

Pareto Chart

Type

Run (Trend) Chart

Measure

Time

Histogram

Measurement

Control Chart

UCL

X̄

LCL

Measurement Time

Scatter Diagram

Variable 2

Variable 1

—Diane Ritter

To demonstrate these tools simply, and to show how they can sometimes be used together, the theme of getting up and getting to work with which most of us are familiar has been used as an illustration. In addition, the Growth Opportunity Alliance of Greater Lawrence (GOAL) has been kind enough to provide actual examples drawn from various companies, which have been published in its pocket-size *Memory Jogger*.

Cause-and-Effect Diagrams

Also known as the "fishbone" diagram because of its shape, or the Ishikawa diagram, after its originator, Kaoru Ishikawa, cause-and-effect diagrams are used in brainstorming sessions to examine factors that may influence a given situation. An "effect" is a desirable or undesirable situation, condition, or event produced by a system of "causes." In teaching this tool, the Japanese often use as the effect "a perfect plate of rice." Americans have used "bitter coffee." Minor causes are often grouped around four basic categories: materials, methods, manpower, and machines. Different groups may be used.

Let us suppose that you are late for work more often than you would like to be. Your morning routine begins with your alarm clock going off, and it ends when you arrive at your desk. Many things happen within that period of time. Your spouse and your two school-age children have their own schedules, which may conflict with yours. Sometimes the television offers something worth watching. Loading the dishwasher takes time. There are frequent telephone calls because people know it is a good time to catch you. You are not always able to drive to work. Your spouse may need the car, or it may be in the shop. You have a choice of riding with a neighbor, which requires advance notice, or you can take the train or a bus, which means buying a ticket or having the correct change. If you drive, parking can be a problem, and so can weather.

You invite your family to join you in a brainstorming session. All of you are surprised at how complicated a seemingly simple process is and at how many variables it has. Through discussion, everyone now becomes aware of the problem and hopefully takes an interest in helping out. Helpful suggestions include taking turns loading the dishwasher, scheduling car use, not turning on the television, getting a bigger kitchen clock, and so on.

Cause-and-Effect: "Late for Work"

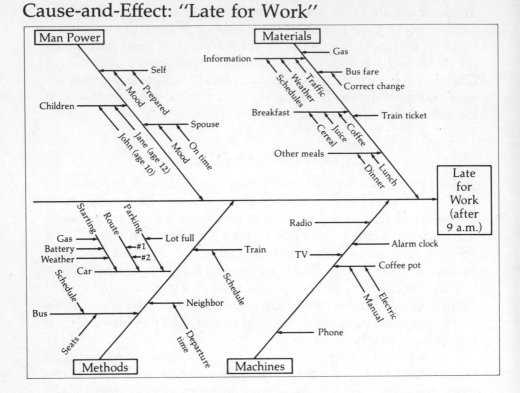

Ishikawa, whose *Guide to Quality Control* was written for Japanese workers and is now the most widely read book on basic statistics for quality in the United States, outlines these benefits from cause-and-effect diagrams:

1. The creation process itself is educational. It gets a discussion going, and people learn from each other.

2. It helps a group focus on the issue at hand, reducing complaints and irrelevant discussion.

3. It results in an active search for the cause.

4. Data often must be collected.

5. It demonstrates the level of understanding. The more complex the diagram, the more sophisticated the workers are about the process.

6. It can be used for any problem.[3]

In an actual case, a hospital used a cause-and-effect diagram to examine the reasons why patients were receiving meals that were different from the orders they had placed. Afterward, the hospital staff targeted some of the causes for data collection.

Cause and Effect: "Wrong Hospital Meals"[4]

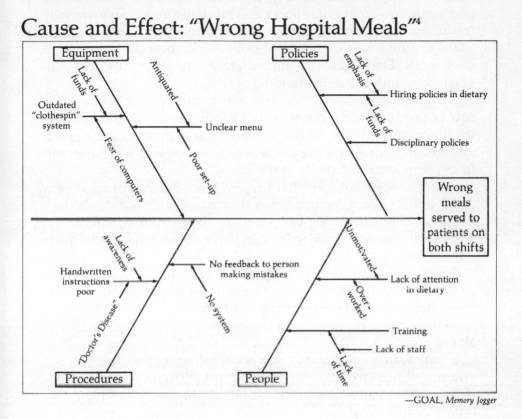

—GOAL, *Memory Jogger*

Flow Charts

Often the first step a team looking for ways to improve a process takes is to draw a flow chart of that process. A process cannot be improved, the reasoning goes, unless everyone understands and agrees on what the process is. The flow chart is an extremely useful way of delineating what is going on. One way to begin is to determine how the process should work, then chart the way it does work. Doing this can immediately turn up redundancy, inefficiency, and misunderstanding.

Vernay Laboratories, Inc., an Ohio manufacturer of precision rubber products and a client of Dr. Deming, decided to streamline its billing procedures. Vernay asked three people in the department to flow chart the way it worked. The result was three different flow charts. No one really knew.

One management consultant reports that he always asks managers to flow chart the operation they oversee. It is astonishing, he says, how often they must ask for help from subordinates. They really do not know who is responsible for what under their administration.

People in administrative or service operations where the flow of information is not always as visible as in a manufacturing process find flow charts particularly valuable.

A flow chart of your morning routine could begin with the alarm.

If you wanted to concentrate on eliminating the "no" loops, you might use two alarms, work out a bathroom schedule, prepare clothes in advance, get a second car, or rent a parking space on a monthly basis.

One manufacturer of printed circuit boards charted the process from the arrival of new materials to the shipping of finished products. It revealed three separate steps devoted to rework. If those could be eliminated, it would simplify the process and save money.

Flow Chart: "From Bed to Work"

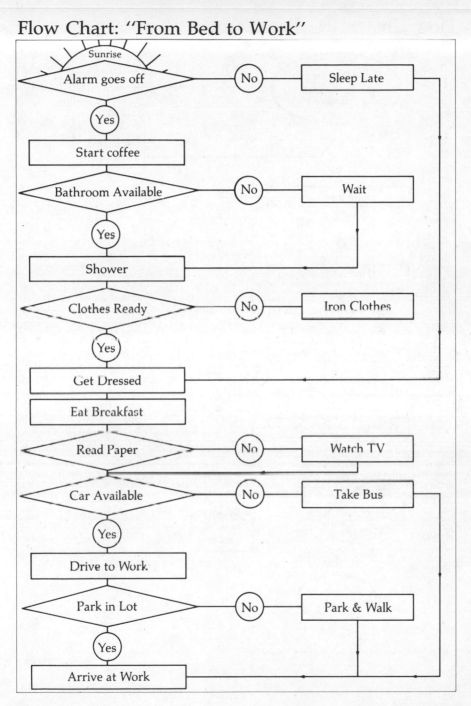

Flow Chart: "P.C. Board Flow"[5]

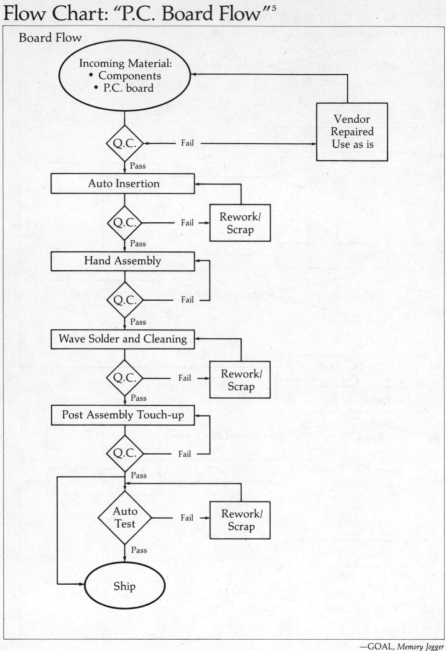

Board Flow

Incoming Material:
• Components
• P.C. board

Q.C. — Fail — Vendor Repaired Use as is

Pass

Auto Insertion

Q.C. — Fail — Rework/ Scrap

Pass

Hand Assembly

Q.C. — Fail

Pass

Wave Solder and Cleaning

Q.C. — Fail — Rework/ Scrap

Pass

Post Assembly Touch-up

Q.C. — Fail

Pass

Auto Test — Fail — Rework/ Scrap

Pass

Ship

—GOAL, *Memory Jogger*

Pareto Charts

Pronounced *pah-ray-toe*, these are among the most commonly used graphic techniques. People will speak of "doing a pareto" or say, "Let's pareto it." This chart is used to determine priorities. The pareto is sometimes described as a way to sort out the "vital few" from the "trivial many."

Suppose, in our continuing example of a morning routine, you would like to leave the house at 8:15, arriving at work by 8:45, so as to have a fifteen-minute period in which to relax—or a cushion against being late—before work begins at 9 A.M. More often, you leave by 8:30 A.M. and barely make it. You decided to keep track of the things that interfere with your departure for sixty days. You are sure that waiting for the bathroom is a major cause. And you know that getting caught up in reading the paper is a delay. So is the pesky garage door, which occasionally sticks. Sometimes you can't resist hitting the snooze alarm.

In your research, you might use a checklist, a good way of collecting data.

Here are some possible results.

Conditions That Might Cause Lateness
(*Some days have more than one occurrence*)

CAUSE	NUMBER OF TIMES
Reading paper (more than ten minutes)	45
Bathroom delay	20
Snooze alarm	8
Garage door	3
Having to iron	1
Other reasons	9

These incidents could be displayed on a pareto chart.

Pareto Chart: "Conditions That Might Cause Lateness"

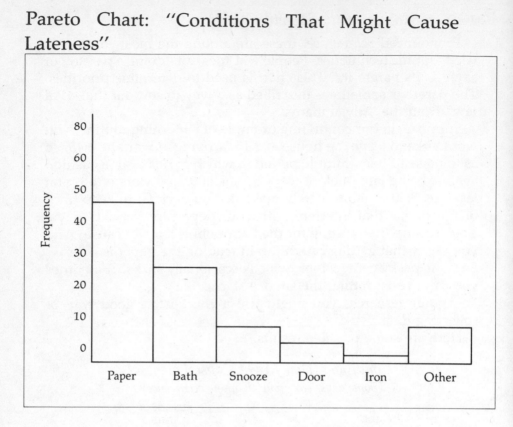

As a result, you might make some changes. Switch to an afternoon paper. Get up earlier. Buy a clock without a snooze alarm.

At the printed circuit board plant, management organized a safety campaign at the employees' request. A team gathered data on accidents, then used a pareto to diagram the findings. Eye injuries were more common than any other. The team then researched causes and again made another pareto chart. The largest number of eye accidents occurred during the process of clipping the wire leads of components after they were soldered to the printed circuit board. In this fashion, pareto charts can be used to narrow down problems.

Pareto Chart: "Types of Injury"[6]

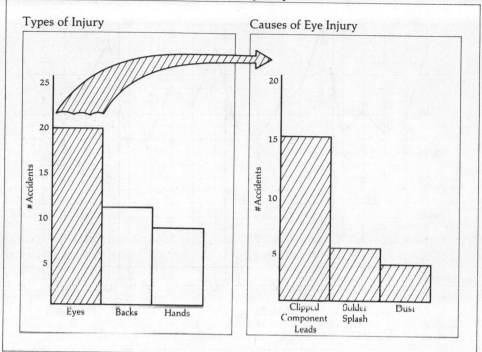

—GOAL, *Memory Jogger*

Run Charts

A run chart is perhaps the simplest of the statistical tools. Data are charted over a period of time to look for trends. Sales per month over a period of a year is a typical use.

A run chart could be used to track the number of minutes it takes to get to work. You discover that it always takes longer on Monday, and accordingly you allow more time.

Run Chart: "Getting to Work on Time"

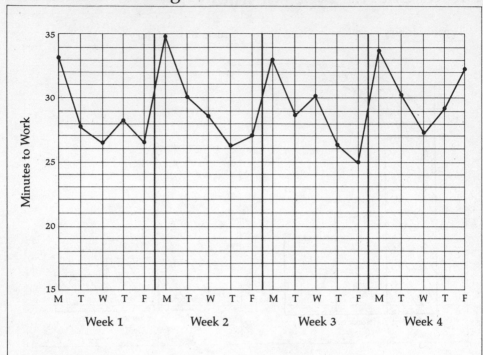

A hospital found that its emergency room was often either overstaffed or understaffed. It took the data it already had on emergency room cases and made a run chart. Admissions had been highest during January, July, September, and December. One might speculate that holidays and weather were a factor. The hospital decided it needed more information, investigating past years to see if the same pattern existed. It also used the run chart as a guide for conversations with the admissions staff.

Run Chart: "Emergency Room Admissions"[7]

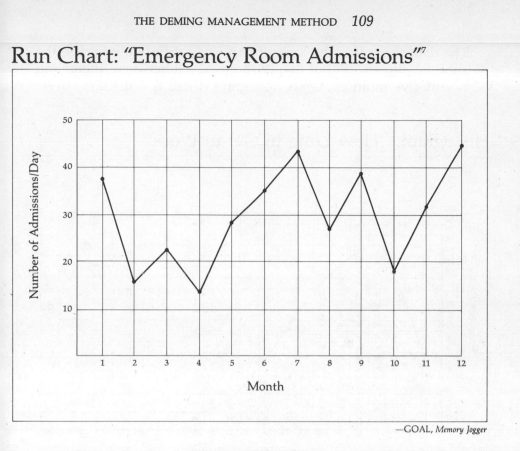

Number of Admissions/Day

Month

—GOAL, *Memory Jogger*

Histograms

A histogram is used to measure how frequently something occurs. Suppose, for example, you are wondering just how much time you should allow for the drive to work. On good days you can make it in fifteen minutes. Every so often, you hit a traffic jam, and it takes forty-five minutes. What is "normal"? Clearly, not the average of the two. To find out, you might—if you're really committed to this project—collect data for, say, a hundred working days.

Hypothetical Commuting Times

15 16 20 15 18 17 20 18 17 19 23 20 21 21 16 15 17 21 17 17
18 16 22 25 17 16 19 19 18 17 25 18 16 17 17 16 15 22 20 17
16 15 18 17 17 16 19 18 19 20 24 27 17 19 22 16 18 21 20 24
18 22 22 18 17 18 19 17 21 24 18 15 19 20 23 22 19 18 17 21
32 22 18 20 21 19 20 24 16 17 18 20 22 20 20 19 18 15 19 20

The data show that the longest trip was thirty-two minutes; the shortest, fifteen. All but two of the trips fell between fifteen and twenty-five minutes. On a histogram, there is a distinct curve.

Histogram: "How Long to Get to Work"

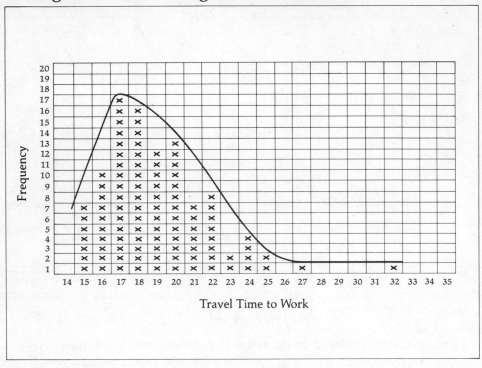

A print shop was receiving complaints about the quality of its finished product. Some customers thought the print wasn't dense enough. The shop measured the density over a period of time, then organized the results by frequency on a histogram to see where the bulk of the measurements fell.

Histogram: "Print Density"[8]

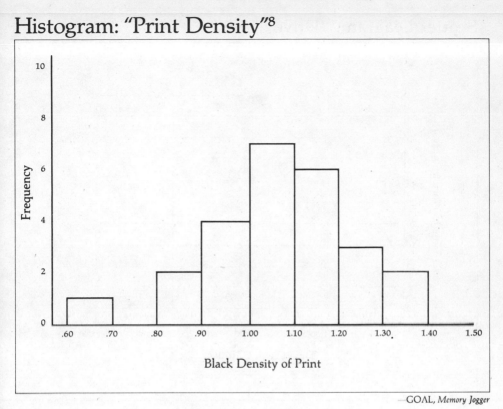

Black Density of Print

—GOAL, *Memory Jogger*

Scatter Diagrams

A scatter diagram is a method of charting the relationship between two variables.

Continuing our example, suppose your office has just instituted flextime. You may come to work anytime between 7:30 and 9:30 A.M. and leave eight and a half hours later. You would like to choose your hours to minimize drive time.

Over the next month, you leave the house at various times between 7 and 9 A.M. and record how long it takes you to get to work. On a scatter diagram, the two variables show a distinct relationship.

Scatter Diagram: "Drive Time"

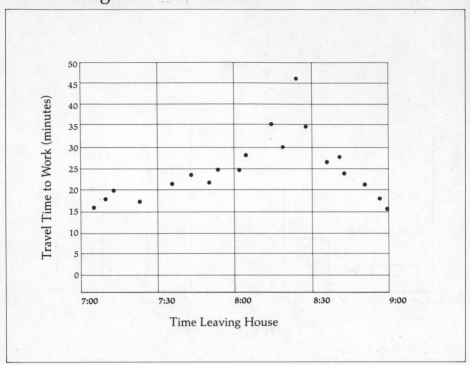

Leaving before 7:30 or after 8:30 greatly shortens the trip. You much prefer leaving later, and it eases competition for the bathroom. You tell your boss you will work from 9:30 A.M. to 6 P.M.

A manufacturer wanted to know whether there was a correlation between shelf life and the stability of his product. A scatter diagram showed that indeed there was.

In business, a scatter diagram might be used to chart the relationship between a worker's training and the number of defects, between moisture content and durability, between light levels and computer errors.

Scatter Diagram: "Active Ingredient Stability"[9]

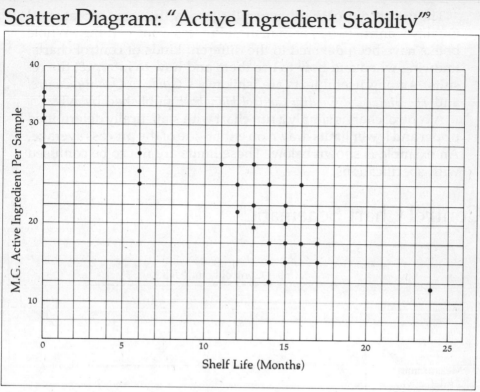

—GOAL, *Memory Jogger*

Control Charts

Dr. Deming often talks about the need to use control charts to analyze processes. The purpose, he emphasizes, is "to stop people from chasing down causes." Properly understood, a control chart is a continuing guide to constant improvement. Control charts are easy to use and certainly not beyond the capabilities of most workers. But even experts, notes Dr. Deming, on occasion "find them extremely difficult to interpret."

Writes Dr. Deming on this subject, "The production worker requires only a knowledge of simple arithmetic to plot a chart. But he cannot by himself decide that he will use a chart on the job, and still less can he start a movement for use of charts.

"It is the responsibility of management to teach the use of control charts on the job [ongoing] where they can be effective."

He sounds this cautionary note: "Proliferation of charts without purpose is to be avoided."[10]

The use of control charts generally goes by the name of Statistical Quality Control (SQC) or Statistical Process Control (SPC). Whole books have been devoted to the different kinds of control charts, knowing when and how to use them and how to interpret the results. Among useful texts are Ishikawa's *Guide to Quality Control* and *The Statistical Quality Control Handbook* published by AT&T.

A control chart is simply a run chart with statistically determined upper and lower limits drawn on either side of the process average. An example is shown below. These limits are not to be confused with specifications.

Control Chart Schematic[11]

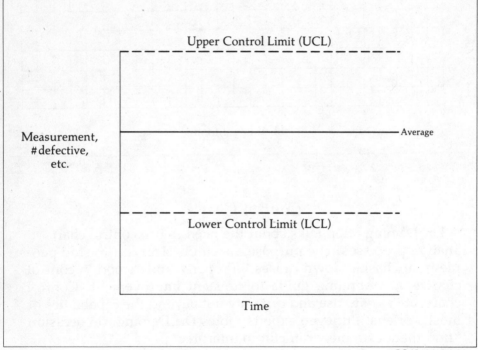

—GOAL, *Memory Jogger*

The upper and lower control limits are determined by allowing a process to run untouched and then analyzing the results using a mathematical formula. Every process has variation. The more finely tuned the process, the less deviation there is from the average.

There are two kinds of variation. The first is that which results from many small causes: minor variations in the worker's ability, the clarity of procedures, the capability of the machinery and equipment, and so forth. These are "common causes" and can often only be changed by management. The other form of variation is usually easier to eliminate. A machine malfunctions; an untrained worker is put on the job; defective material arrives from a vendor. Dr. Deming calls these "special causes." They show up on control charts as points outside the limits.

The formula for the control limits is designed to provide an economic balance between searching too often for special causes when there are none and not searching when a special cause may be found. A system can best be improved when special causes have been eliminated and it has been brought into statistical control. At that point, management can work effectively on the system, looking for ways to reduce variation.

Once a system is in control, control charts can be used for monitoring so as to immediately detect when something goes wrong—a "special cause." Line operators can record the data and take action—shutting down the line, if need be. A point need not be outside the limits to indicate action. Abrupt shifts or distinct trends within limits are also signals for investigation.

Control charts come in two broad varieties, to be used depending on the nature of the data. One is for data that can be measured: lengths, temperatures, volume, pressure, voltage. The other is for data that can be counted: defective components, typographical errors, mislabeled items.

Control Chart: "Commuting Times"[12]

Step 1			Commuting Times (min.)—A.M.							

					WEEK					
	1	2	3	4	5	6	7	8	9	10
	55	90	100	70	55	75	120	65	70	100
	75	95	75	110	65	85	110	65	85	80
MINUTES	65	60	75	65	95	65	65	90	60	65
	80	60	65	60	70	65	85	90	65	60
	80	55	65	60	70	65	70	60	75	80
$\bar{X}=$	71	72	76	73	71	71	90	74	71	77
$R=$	20	40	35	50	40	20	55	30	25	40

Step 2

$\bar{x} = 74.6$
$\bar{R} = 35.5$
$n = 5$

Step 3

$UCL_{\bar{x}} = \bar{x} + A_2 \bar{R}$
$= 74.6 + (.58)(35.5)$
$= 74.6 + 20.59$
$= 95.19$

$LCL_{\bar{x}} = \bar{x} - A_2 \bar{R}$
$= 74.6 - 20.59$
$= 54.01$

$UCL_R = D_4 \bar{R}$
$= (2.11)(35.5)$
$= 74.90$

$LCL_R = D_3 \bar{R}$
$= 0$

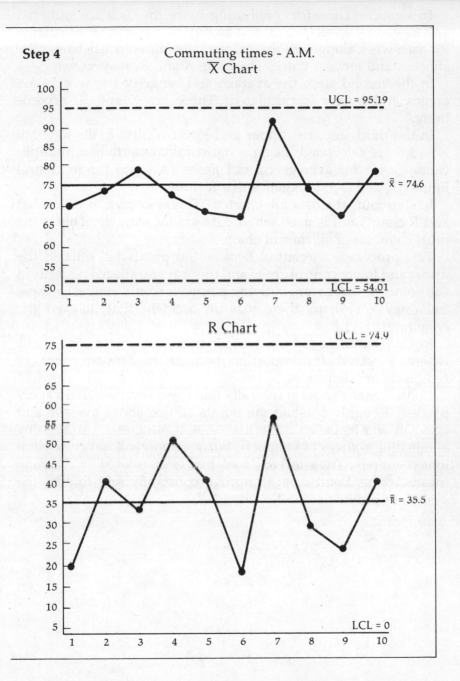

Step 4

Commuting times - A.M.
$\overline{X}$ Chart

UCL = 95.19

$\overline{\overline{x}}$ = 74.6

LCL = 54.01

R Chart

UCL = 74.9

$\overline{R}$ = 35.5

LCL = 0

In a control chart for commuting times the data are gathered and logged by week (1, 2, 3, and so on). The average is calculated for each week along with the "range": the difference between the shortest and longest times. These are $\overline{X}$ and R, respectively.

In the second step, the average and range of the weekly averages and ranges is calculated. These are $\overline{\overline{X}}$ and $\overline{R}$, accordingly.

In the third step, the upper and lower control limits for both $\overline{X}$ and R are calculated, using a statistically determined multiplication factor for average control limits (A_2) and range control limits (D_3 and D_4), plugged into a formula.

In step four, the data are charted. This is known as an "X-bar and R chart" and is used when data are measurable. This is the most common of all control charts.

This process is in control because no points fall outside the upper and lower control limits and there are no special patterns in the points. If there were outlying points, it would suggest a "special cause." Perhaps there was an accident that delayed the commuter.

In Dr. Deming's red bead experiment, he uses a "P" chart, where "P" stands for proportion, because the data are counts of red beads or "defectives."

Control charts show graphically that there is variability in every process. Roughly one-half the points will be above average and one-half will be below. One may seek to minimize variation by eliminating sources of variation, but variation will never be eliminated entirely. The effort to do so, however, is what Dr. Deming means by his Point Five. "Improve constantly and forever the system of production and service."

PART THREE

MAKING
DEMING
WORK

Chapter 21

•

The Deming Prize

QUESTION: *"How long will it take the United States to catch up with Japan?"*
DR. DEMING: *"Do you think Japan is standing still?"*

"Do not apply for the Deming Application Prize just for the sake of the prize. Apply for the purpose of promoting your TQC."

—KAORU ISHIKAWA

In 1975, an executive contingent from Nashua Corporation, which makes carbonless paper and memory disks, visited Japan's Ricoh Company Ltd., whose copiers Nashua was marketing in overseas countries. When the group returned, one vice-president complained of their treatment to William Conway, then president of Nashua. He would later recount the story with great amusement.

It seems that when the Nashua delegation arrived, on a Wednesday, their Japanese counterparts were too busy to meet. They were furiously engaged in preparations for something they called the "Deming Prize." The Americans had no idea what they were talking about. On Thursday, the Japanese apologetically explained that they were still too busy to meet, for the same reason. Finally, on Friday at 9 P.M., the waiting Americans were invited to discuss business—at 10 P.M. that evening. The meeting lasted for several hours. But once again, on Saturday the Japanese were tied up. The Nashua delegation was able to squeeze in one more meeting—on Sunday afternoon—before their departure.

On hearing this story, Conway's curiosity was piqued. "Prize?

121

What the hell is the Deming Prize?'' he wanted to know. The Nashua vice-president told Conway that as far as he could tell ''it was all about statistics and charts, and geez they're all nuts, they're all crazy. They're all working on it.''

Asked Conway, ''Who's working on it?''

''Everyone,'' replied the vice-president. ''The president of Ricoh is involved, . . . sales managers, administrative people, engineers, manufacturers, everybody's working on the Deming Prize.''

The incident lodged in Conway's mind—all those Japanese feverishly working toward some mysterious industrial award. (Ricoh did, in fact, go on to win that year.) Eventually, Conway's acquaintance with that odd, unforgettable outbreak of Deming Prize fever would lead Nashua to Dr. Deming in the late 1970s.

A Japanese firm in quest of the prize is like an athlete in training for the Olympics. Like gold medalists who literally embody the finest training, talent, and performance, the Deming Prize winners are in the forefront of Japan's quality movement. Among companies familiar to Americans, the prize has been won by Toyota, Nippon Electric, Fuji Xerox, Yokogawa Hewlett-Packard, and Rhythm Watch Company.

The Deming Prize was established in 1950 by the Union of Japanese Scientists and Engineers (JUSE) with proceeds from reprints of Dr. Deming's lectures, which he donated to the Japanese quality effort. Awarded each year with great fanfare, the prize is actually several in number. There are two categories: the Deming Prize for individuals, and the Deming Application Prize, which has subcategories for large and small companies, divisions, and factories.

Beginning in 1950, prizes were awarded to companies adept at using the new-found statistical tools of SQC, or Statistical Quality Control. Soon, however, Japanese firms began to move beyond that narrow application. By the late 1970s, quality had evolved into an all-encompassing approach consistent with Dr. Deming's Fourteen Points, which the Japanese call Total Quality Control, or TQC. Today, Japanese companies are judged on the quality, if you will, of their TQC.

Credit for originating the term goes to an American, Armand V. Feigenbaum, in a 1961 book, *Total Quality Control: Engineering and Management*. Many Japanese prefer to speak of Company-Wide Quality Control, or CWQC. But the meaning is the same.

When the Japanese speak of quality, they do not mean merely the performance of a product or service. Today, wrote the influential consultant Kaoru Ishikawa in his book *What is Total Quality Control?—The Japanese Way*, "quality means quality of work, quality of service, quality of information, quality of process, quality of division, quality of people, including workers, engineers, managers and executives, quality of company, quality of objectives."[1]

TQC, Ishikawa wrote, is "a thought revolution in management."[2] Their never-ending quest for improvement, however, has begun to take the Japanese to points beyond TQC, which is still performance-oriented. Many state-of-the-art companies are exploring what is called Quality Function Deployment (QFD).

QFD evolved for two reasons: first, because problems had developed in Japanese companies in which everyone was working assiduously on TQC. Education and organizational changes had assured that every cell in the corporate body had a quality mission. But they were not always coordinated. As a result, there was duplication of effort; on some occasions, nothing got done because people assumed that someone else was doing it. To coordinate individual quality functions, the Japanese developed an elaborate system of tables and flow charts.

In the second place, although the Japanese had become experts on improving manufacturing processes, they were impatient with the amount of time it took to work out the kinks when a new product was introduced. Once again, they came up with a detailed system of tables and charts to enable designers and engineers to identify potential problems and correct them even before manufacturing began.

Both of these are QFD systems. Quality Function Deployment was a logical outgrowth of the movement Dr. Deming started in 1950, when he stressed the need for a top management structure devoted to never-ending improvement (Points One and Fourteen).

Companies in the vanguard of quality methods are also using the analytical tools of Genichi Taguchi, a contemporary of Dr. Deming who studied classical statistics in England prior to World War II. He found them too theoretical for use in manufacturing, and on his return to Japan he developed a more practical approach for use in the design engineering phase to counteract long-standing problems that were expensive and difficult to eliminate. If varying atmospheric temperatures, for example, caused film to deteriorate in production, it might be easier to design a film that wouldn't be affected rather than try to control the temperatures. One might say that the Taguchi method concentrates not on the cause but on the effect. Taguchi has won the Deming Prize for individuals four times.

There is good reason for these highly refined methods for achieving quality to seem threatening to the United States. Most American companies are not even in the SQC stage but depend instead on an erratic system of rules, regulations, and inspection for quality.

Three to five years is generally considered the length of time it takes a Japanese company to reach a stage of TQC worthy of consideration by the Deming Prize committee. Formal application for the Deming Prize seldom takes place until that amount of time has been invested.

Generally, a company will seek at least one prior "quality diagnosis" by JUSE consultants whose services are available for that purpose. This diagnosis points out areas in which the company must improve if it hopes to qualify. Qualifying is an honor and, by the same token, failing to do so is an even greater dishonor.

The deadline for application is May 31. The winners are announced in late October, and the prizes are awarded the following month. The prize committee, overseen by JUSE, is composed of university professors and distinguished experts. Divided into survey teams, the judges may spend as long as five or six days on a site, reviewing the claims made in an application.

In the best Japanese fashion, judges are armed with checklists covering the following points:

- *Policy and planning*. What is the company policy on quality and Statistical Quality Control? How are policy and objectives established and communicated, and how are the results assessed? What is the relationship between short- and long-range plans?
- *Administration*. What is the chain of responsibility? How is power delegated? How do divisions relate to each other? What is the role of committees? How are staff people used? How effective are Quality Control Circle activities?
- *Education*. What are the company's educational activities, including those in the area of quality control and statistical methods? How widespread are they and what is accom-

plished? What education is there for QC Circles and for sub-contractors? What suggestion system is in place?

• *Information*. What are the sources of information? How is it communicated, and with what speed? What statistical analysis is applied?

• *Analysis*. What is the quality of analysis in terms of the problems tackled, the methods used, and the results?

• *Standardization*. How are standards set, revised, and applied? How are statistical methods used? What has been accomplished?

• *Control*. What is the control system for quality, cost, and quantity? How well are statistical methods used? What have been the contributions of QC Circles? How good are the control system and activities?

• *Quality assurance*. What are the procedures for new quality development? For safety and preventing product liability? For process control and improvement? For using statistical methods and evaluating quality?

• *Effects* What are they and how are they measured?

• *Future plans*. How deep is the understanding of the company's present position? What is planned to alleviate problems and to promote the company's interests? What are the long-range plans?

Only companies that score at least seventy of a possible hundred points qualify for the Deming Prize. No company is considered without an ironclad management commitment to quality, a large and productive system of QC Circles and an employee suggestion system, widespread use of statistical methods, a long-range plan for continuing improvement, education for employees and subcontractors, and a strong customer orientation.

Despite Japan's vaunted reputation for quality, conversion to TQC exacts an effort so encompassing that many companies are unwilling to make it until pressed.

Kayaba Industry Ltd., Japan's leading manufacturer of hydraulic equipment, turned to TQC when an attempt to raise prices after the 1973 oil crisis was greeted with a strong backlash. Customers complained that the company's quality warranted decreases rather than increases in price.

Startled into painful self-examination, Kayaba embraced TQC in January 1976. That first year, according to a case study by

GOAL, the company conducted an inventory of problems, examining every area of the business. "This means they looked at product planning, product development, product design, production, preparation, manufacturing, sales and service and administration. They reviewed history, they looked at failures. They looked to see whether they were caused by poor systems, lack of training, lack of commitment to implementation, of worker inconsistency in observing rules. They sorted out all causes of problems and went to work at eliminating them."[3]

That same year, an individual accountable to the president was put in charge of Kayaba's TQC effort and given a staff. The TQC staff sought advice from other companies. Long-existing but less-than-productive QC Circles were revitalized.

In 1977, Kayaba developed a structured TQC plan and expanded the teaching of statistical methods and other quality techniques at certain key plants. Employees were taught to use control charts and process control analysis.

In 1978, Kayaba went companywide with TQC and began to work "upstream"—proceeding backward in the distribution systems—on the development phase of its products, using simulation technology to identify quality and technology requirements for new products that surveys showed customers wanted, a rudimentary form of QFD. That same year, Kayaba sought a JUSE diagnosis. As a result, the company began to concentrate as well on its administrative systems, teaching the PDCA (Plan, Do, Check, Act) Cycle.

In 1979, Kayaba began to see results in the form of increased sales. Meanwhile, there was a painstaking analysis of its competitors' products, looking for ways to improve its own.

In 1980, Kayaba won the Deming Prize. Although there was rejoicing, this was not a signal that the job was done. Indeed, the improvement continued. Between 1978 and 1982, the number of QC Circles doubled to six thousand while suggestions rose from fewer than ten thousand to more than fifty thousand.

Kansai Electric Power, Japan's second-largest utility company, undertook a similar course to win the 1984 Deming Prize. At the outset, Kansai scarcely seemed like a company in dire need of improvement. It held the record for the fewest and shortest power failures in the world, and it charged the lowest rates among Japan's nine electric power companies. Nevertheless, the two oil crises in the 1970s signaled to Kansai that greater improvement was desirable, particularly in the performance, reliability, and expansion of its nuclear power base. Theirs was the first TQC effort in the electric power industry. And it would indeed take a "thought revolution" to accomplish. As the president announced at his 1982 introduction of TQC, it meant that "you give up the way you were accustomed to conceive things in the past, the way you were accustomed to deal with things in the past."

Like Kayaba, Kansai Power established a TQC Promotion Office. In this case, its chairman was the president. In other words, the company's highest executive himself took charge of the drive for quality. Committees were established for quality assurance, standardization, and purchase control.

By 1983, each branch and district office had its own TQC promotion office and staff. In 1984, the final year, a quality audit office was established to evaluate progress. It remained a permanent fixture. Meanwhile, the president conducted two of his own quality audits, a technique Ishikawa recommends for enlightening the chief executive and impressing people with his commitment.

In the area of education, Kansai developed TQC programs for all twenty-four thousand employees, beginning with courses for managers in 1982 and culminating with a general employee course in 1984. QC Circles, which in the past had been preoccupied with safety and health issues, were given manuals and case studies as a guide for extending their activities to quality. Although participation was voluntary, peer pressure to join was strong. By 1984, there were 18,223 members in 2,306 Circles. After a review of rules and standards, Kansai eliminated those that were either obsolete or pointless and developed new ones appropriate to TQC.

Environmental and safety issues merited special attention. An increased use of low-sulfur fuels and an expanded tree-planting program were TQC activities in that arena. By 1984, service interruptions and job-related accidents had decreased, and there had also been a fourfold reduction in annual costs. Kansai also cited improved employee morale, a spirit of teamwork, and a heightened sensitivity to the market and the customer.

In the early years, companies engaged in mass production claimed the Deming Prize. Of late, however, others have sought the honor. In 1979, Japan Steel Works' Hiroshima plant became the first "made-to-order" plant to take the prize.

One of Japan Steel's five plants, the sprawling Hiroshima works turns out complex industrial machinery used in plastics and chemical processing. The market for such machinery was by its very nature unpredictable. Japan Steel never knew long in advance, how many, what kind, or how large orders would be. Each order required an individual design, and trial production was uneconomical. Moreover, the products were in continual use by technically advanced customers, who found themselves in a highly competitive marketplace. The Hiroshima plant was under pressure to produce sophisticated, reliable, durable machinery. Meanwhile, the plant had its own competition from others in the business. In 1977, Japan Steel targeted Hiroshima for a test of TQC.

Canadian-born Tsotumu "Dutch" Nakayama was general manager of international liaison at the time. Like everyone else at the plant, he was intensely involved in the effort. The company's intentions, as he outlined them in a 1985 interview, were fivefold.

- To establish a policy with clear-cut goals.
- To make lines of responsibility clear.
- To make the QC Circles more active.
- To educate all levels of employees.
- To carefully audit the entire company, not to find fault but to pinpoint problems and correct them.

Beginning in 1977, the Hiroshima plant imported JUSE consultants at least twice monthly. Dormant QC Circles were activated. An employee suggestion plan was put in place. Suggestions were graded from A (the best) to F (honorable mention), and each received a corresponding monetary reward. Under a standing order, all suggestions had to be evaluated within a month. Suggestions per employee rose from 5.6 a year in 1978 to 17.6 in 1981 and 28.5 in 1984 as TQC continued.

In 1978, Dr. Deming paid a visit to the plant—an event that had a "catalytic" effect, according to Nakayama. People threw themselves into the effort, working long hours into the evening. No department was spared the effort. In Nakayama's department, a QC Circle of female clerical employees noticed that overseas facsimile transmission of charts took longer—and was thus more costly—when graph paper was used, because each line had to be duplicated. They suggested that line drawings be used instead.

A QC Circle of four young switchboard operators decided to deal with complaints from callers that telephones were not being answered promptly—in four rings or less, the point at which a caller-survey disclosed that people become annoyed. The operators collected data on calls for each department. They discovered that the engineers were the major transgressors. When they posted the statistics, there was an immediate improvement in phone-answering by the dilatory engineering department.

Perhaps the greatest contribution of TQC, Nakayama said, was that it "made everybody think for themselves and study for themselves." Rules and regulations could not bring improvement. They only preserved the status quo.

As an example, he told a story of a machine shop foreman who was disturbed that a piston rod took fifteen hours to finish, in part because a dozen scratches routinely appeared during the process and required repair. At that, the finish was still somewhat less than desired.

This problem was so much on the foreman's mind, Nakayama related, that a solution came to him one day when he "was standing on a train platform. He saw two men running, one from each direction, to catch the train. They collided midway.

"The foreman asked himself why they collided. They collided, of course, because they were coming from opposite directions. If they had been coming from the same direction, they wouldn't have collided.

"It occurred to the foreman that the machining of the piston rod represented a similar situation. The grinder was moving one way and the piston another. If they rotated in the same direction, he reasoned, there would be no 'collision.' The result would be a smoother finish. He eagerly tested his theory by reversing the direction of the piston rod. He was correct. Not only did the process take less time because there was no repair work, but it produced a smoother finish."

Such improvements proliferated throughout the Hiroshima plant. Although each alone might seem small, the cumulative impact was substantial. Between 1978 and 1981, the cost of defects and claims as a proportion of sales dropped from 1.57 to 0.4. Production rose 50 percent, while the number of employees dropped from 2,400 to 1,900. As a result of a safety campaign that was part of TQC, the accident rate dropped from 15.7 to 2.3 per million man-hours, with a corresponding decrease in the absenteeism rate due to accidents. Finally, machine time decreased dramatically.

In 1979, the Hiroshima plant was awarded the Deming Prize for a factory. Male employees received a tie clip with a replica of the medal; females got a pendant. Dr. Deming sent his congratulations, which were inscribed on a waist-high stone monument: "Dependable quality and efficient production by JSW make better living for men everywhere. I congratulate JSW for Deming Prize 1979 for quality and efficiency by statistical methods."

Well satisfied with the achievements in Hiroshima, Japan Steel went companywide with TQC, and in 1983 the entire company captured the Deming Prize.

Chapter 22

•

Shifting Gears:

Ford Motor Company, Dearborn, Michigan

In June 1980, when NBC aired its White Paper that featured Dr. Deming, "If Japan Can . . . Why Can't We?" the Ford Motor Company was in serious trouble. The oil embargo of 1973 had fueled the demand for small foreign vehicles, and although the energy crisis had eased by the end of the decade, Americans continued to buy Japanese cars in ever-increasing numbers because of their superior performance. It was clear that the nation's second-largest corporation had to change to survive.

In 1978, Board Chairman Philip Caldwell announced that quality would henceforth be the company's primary focus—"Job One," Ford called it, using the phrase that described the first new model car off the line. Also in 1979, Ford promulgated an immensely significant document referred to as *Q101*, a manual of quality specifications for suppliers. Neither of those events, however, by itself could create better cars nor halt the slide in profits. The year Dr. Deming came to the attention of American industry was the year Ford lost $1.6 billion.

A copy of the NBC White Paper ended up in Ford's library of corporate self-help films, where a number of executives saw it. Six months after it aired, William E. Scollard, then general manager of the automotive assembly division, borrowed the tape over the Christmas holidays. He remembers being mystified that anyone as prominent in Japan as Dr. Deming was so anonymous in the United States.

131

After seeing the tape, Scollard phoned the Ford quality department. "Who is this Dr. Deming?" he wanted to know. He asked them to get in touch with the quality expert.

Dr. Deming, suddenly the object of much attention in corporate America, did not abandon his prerequisites merely because Ford was calling. He would work only where there was a commitment from top management, and he refused to come to Detroit unless his presence was requested by the president of the company.

Ford, as formal and hierarchical as a monarchy, was not the kind of company where Scollard could telephone the president of Ford and say, for example, "Why don't you call this guy?" He was momentarily stumped. But then a vice-president in the North American division where Scollard worked, James K. Bakken, was transferred to world headquarters to head up an assortment of support operations, including quality. Bakken, who also had seen the film, agreed to intercede with Ford President Donald E. Petersen. As a result, Dr. Deming came to Ford in the spring of 1981 to meet with Petersen and other high-ranking officials.

By all accounts, according to a series of interviews for this chapter, Petersen and Dr. Deming got along famously. Dr. Deming's ideas were so alien to the ways the automotive industry operated, however, that Scollard for his part was still puzzled. "Frankly," he said later, "I had trouble understanding what his philosophy was and how it worked. And at his age he's not too patient." Scollard wanted to see the techniques in use. A Ford contingent subsequently visited Nashua Corporation, which had been featured in the White Paper. There, employees were routinely using control charts, and Scollard began to understand what was meant by SQC. Next, Ford made arrangements for courses at the University of Tennessee under a Deming-endorsed professor, David Chambers. This quest for statistical knowledge ultimately led to an association with Kaoru Ishikawa, the distinguished Japanese quality consultant. Ishikawa, at Ford's request, gave several seminars in Dearborn similar to those he had given at Toyota.

In November 1983, Scollard and a group of seventeen CEOs from Ford's major suppliers visited Japan, touring plants and attending various quality award ceremonies, including the Deming Prize. Meanwhile, back at world headquarters, arrangements were made with Petersen's endorsement to retain Dr. Deming as Ford's chief quality consultant. Said Bakken in an interview, "Deming just seemed to fit into what we thought that we ought to be doing about changing the philosophy in terms of our approach toward quality."

Dr. Deming, for his part, told Bakken that he would be "delighted to work with Ford Motor Company," and that his vision was to take a few large companies, who would by the strength of their work with their supply base, "create a bonfire that would create a prairie fire that would consume all America and turn it all around."

If Dr. Deming could work wonders with Ford, whose founder had introduced continuous assembly lines more than sixty years ago, he could do it anywhere. Ford was quintessentially American in its approach to quality. The company typically manufactured products to specifications, then sorted out those that didn't conform.

"There is nothing wrong with that system," Bakken said, "except that it never leads to improvement in the process—and it's expensive. You put those two things together and it's not particularly the kind of process you'd want in place."

The difference between how the Japanese made things and how Ford made things was painfully demonstrated when Ford's Batavia plant couldn't keep up with transmission orders. The company subcontracted to Mazda in Japan for additional transmissions. Discovering that customer response was better for cars with Japanese transmissions, Ford engineers investigated. They matched ten Japanese transmissions against ten of their own. Although all conformed to the blueprint, there was less piece-to-piece variation in the Mazda transmissions. Indeed, when the inside dimensions of a bore failed to register any differentiation on his gauge, one worker called for a gauge repairman.

The truth was, however, that the Japanese transmissions were simply more uniform. The distribution curve of the Japanese units occupied only 27 percent of the distance between specification limits. The distribution curve of the American units was 70 percent of those same limits. The Japanese transmissions not only were quieter, they also had warranty costs ten times lower than those made in America.

Ford subsequently made a training film about the incident. That in itself revealed a change in attitude. Time was when the company might have preferred to keep bad news quiet. But that was before Dr. Deming became its principal consultant.

Since then, under the rubric "Quality is Job One," Ford has made some fairly dramatic improvements. In five years, warranty repair frequencies dropped by 45 percent, and "things gone wrong" reported by new car owners similarly decreased more than 50 percent. In the same period, Ford's share of the U.S. car market rose to 19.2 percent, the highest it had been in five years. Total sales of cars, trucks, and tractors in 1984 were 5.7 million, up 700,000 over 1983, though still less than the record of 6.6 million in 1978. There were record profits of $4.3 billion before taxes. On the eve of his retirement as chairman of the board, Caldwell was able to report that operating costs had been reduced by more than $4.5 billion since 1979. In other words, Ford was spending $12 million less a day than it had been five years earlier.

What had happened?

After Dr. Deming met with Petersen, he began visiting Ford several days per month, holding abbreviated seminars for top executives, visiting various operations, meeting with hourly workers, engineers, and supervisors, and making recommendations for changes corresponding to his Fourteen Points.

He suggested a permanent position in statistical methodology and recommended a former student who had worked with him on several projects, William Scherkenbach, then an independent management consultant. Scherkenbach liked the idea of hands-on experience with a company as influential as Ford. In personal discussions with Petersen and Scollard (who had been promoted to vice president for manufacturing operations), Scherkenbach was impressed that they were "willing to make the investment, even though they were losing money at the time." His was an open-ended assignment to work on Dr. Deming's principles. He reported directly to Bakken.

Scherkenbach thought it was of primary importance to identify which Ford people had had statistical training, so they could train others. A query to the Ford computer produced only a handful of names, however, so Scherkenbach conducted a companywide survey, asking that people with a statistical background identify themselves. This time there were 1,300 résumés. The large response reflected, in part, the fact that Statistical Quality Control, or Statistical Process Control—the terms were used interchangeably—were becoming buzzwords, the "in" thing. Most of those who responded were not qualified. About a hundred of the résumés, however, seemed fairly credible to Scherkenbach. Indeed, he would say later that he was amazed that so many people with statistical skills had found a place in the company. He invited them to the next Deming seminar.

Meanwhile, a steering committee composed of vice-presidents and general managers was established under Bakken to promote Dr. Deming's principles and statistical methods. In addition, a statistical methods council, whose members were statisticians from various Ford operations, was formed under Scherkenbach to support the steering committee. Edward Baker and Peter Jessup, two Ford statisticians who had assisted Dr. Deming during his visits, became the nucleus of the statistical methods office, which by the end of 1982 had grown to include a half-dozen of Ford's best statisticians. They had been evaluated for their understanding of the whole Deming philosophy as much as for their skill with SQC.

Statistical methods were also getting a boost from Petersen, who took a one-day fast-track course. Whenever Petersen inquired about SQC on his rounds, the phones in Scherkenbach's office would ring off the hook. Joked Scherkenbach, "Although Deming says you have to drive out fear, the president of Ford Motor Company only has to ask you once."

Dr. Deming's Fourteen Points and Seven Deadly Diseases became the basis for a reexamination of Ford's philosophy by top corporate officials. They labored for three years to "adopt the new philosophy," as Dr. Deming directs in Point Two. Finally, the following "Mission," "Values," and "Principles" were announced by Henry Ford II in a speech to senior management in November 1984.

> *Mission.* Ford Motor Company is a worldwide leader in automotive and automotive-related products and services as well as in newer industries such as aerospace, communications and financial services. Our mission is to improve continually our products and services to meet our customers' needs, allowing us to prosper as a business and to provide a reasonable return for our stockholders, the owners of our business.
>
> *Values.* How we accomplish our mission is as important as the mission itself. Fundamental to success for the Company are these basic values:
> —People. Our people are the source of our strength. They provide our corporate intelligence and determine our reputation and vitality. Involvement and teamwork are our core human values.

—Products. Our products are the end result of our efforts, and they should be the best in serving customers worldwide. As our products are viewed, so are we viewed.

—Profits. Profits are the ultimate measure of how efficiently we provide customers with the best products for their needs. Profits are required to survive and grow.

Guiding Principles.
—Quality comes first. To achieve customer satisfaction, the quality of our products and services must be our number one priority.

—Customers are the focus of everything we do. Our work must be done with our customers in mind, providing better products and services than our competition.

—Continuous improvement is essential to our success. We must strive for excellence in everything we do: in our products, in their safety and value—and in our services, our human relations, our competitiveness and our profitability.

—Employee involvement is our way of life. We are a team. We must treat each other with trust and respect.

—Dealers and suppliers are our partners. The Company must maintain mutually beneficial relationships with dealers, suppliers and our other business associates.

—Integrity is never compromised. The conduct of our Company worldwide must be pursued in a manner that is socially responsible and commands respect for its integrity and for its positive contributions to society. Our doors are open to men and women alike without discrimination and without regard to ethnic origin or personal beliefs.

Under Dr. Deming's prodding, Ford also reexamined the way it conducts performance appraisals.

After canvassing the vice-presidents of the principal Ford divisions on major inhibitors to improvement, Petersen declared that the company's personnel evaluation constituted "a possible barrier to continuous improvement and quality performance." He continued, "There is untold waste of human resources with traditional evaluation systems.

"The waste results from excessive internal competition, not getting to the root causes of problems, and reinventing the wheel—to name a couple of situations where teamwork should pay dividends."[1]

Describing efforts to change the appraisal system in the magazine *Quality Progress,* Bill Scherkenbach elaborated on some of its evils. One was the way performance appraisal systems increased variability. "The same system that puts a person above average one year might put him below average the next. Nobody really likes to be classified as below average. The people ranked below average may emulate those ranked above average or otherwise change what they are doing to get a better rating. As a result, about half of the people may be trying to change to become above average, and so the variability of the outcomes of the organization can increase to twice what it would have been if all of the employees just continued doing what they were doing."

Another drawback was, as Dr. Deming pointed out, that performance appraisals focused on short-term results. "I have seen a division manager meet his objectives but in the process severely compromise his or his successor's future chances of any real improvements," Scherkenbach continued in the magazine.

Ford's old rating system had had ten categories, ranging from a low of Unsatisfactory up to Outstanding High. The new system, Scherkenbach said, "would reflect the fact that there are only three possible positions: outside the system on the low side, in the system, and outside the system on the high side." Data and theory showed that no more than a total of 11 percent of all employees would be outside the system.[2]

Since Dr. Deming has become associated with Ford, these additional changes have taken place on a companywide basis:

• *Hold for quality.* In a change long advocated by the United Autoworkers Union, production plants now close down for two weeks in summer rather than remain open with short-term hires or workers on staggered vacation schedules. In the past, Ford had resisted such a halt to production, which would mean the loss of 100,000 to 200,000 vehicles. But quality had also been lost because workers were filling in on jobs other than the ones for which they were trained.

• *Suppliers as partners.* Ford invited the chief operating officers of major suppliers to attend Deming seminars, then conducted seminars for engineers and quality control people. *Q101* was revised after Dr. Deming and suppliers criticized the document as too prescriptive and too punitive, emphasizing quality detection rather than quality prevention. Inspectors began to work with suppliers to improve quality in accordance with Dr. Deming's principles.

• *Three-year operating budgets.* Instituted in North American plants, these replace the annual budgets, to allow long-term planning. In the past, half a year might go by in which the new operating budget was still in preparation. People were tied up in negotiations rather than designing, manufacturing, and marketing automobiles.

The most significant change was not so much the introduction of Statistical Quality Control—Ford had been one of the American companies to use statistics for a decade after World War II—but the fact that support for quality emanated from the very top of the corporation, as Dr. Deming said it must. There had always been people concerned about quality at Ford. Now they had license to practice what they had preached.

These were people like John A. Manoogian, who was recruited to head the quality program for North American Automotive Operations. He had begun his career at Ford in 1940 as a drafting apprentice. In 1979, when the offer came, his career had included posts as general manager of the automotive assembly and transmission divisions, and he was also in charge of yet another division—climate control, where heating and air-conditioning systems were designed and manufactured.

Manoogian at first said no to the quality post. "I was very, very skeptical that the company was serious, simply because of historical actions, when they talked about quality. Nobody ever said they didn't want quality, but it was very obvious . . . they just didn't have the emphasis on it that I thought it deserved. Consequently, I said to myself, 'I don't want to be associated with a failure. And I obviously cannot succeed without the help and support of corporate management.' "

He declined the job four times in succession, each time delivering his regrets to a different vice-president. Finally, he found himself on the carpet in Caldwell's office. In a three-hour discussion, he told Caldwell he didn't want an ill-defined job with no authority in which he was supposed to convince people to do things on their own. He said he thought the company paid only lip service to quality. He boldly pointed out that not only had management commitment and involvement been missing in the past, but the incentives and the appraisal systems, which were intended to motivate people to do a good job, were cost-oriented, not quality-oriented. As a consequence, people who wanted to be successful had no reason to devote themselves to quality. Caldwell listened carefully. He repeatedly pledged that this time it would be different. He assured Manoogian of his full support.

The next morning, after a final weak protest, Manoogian said he'd do it. Dr. Deming's arrangement with Ford coincided with Manoogian's own efforts to foster teamwork and statistical methods. But it was one thing for John Manoogian to call for changes. It was another for an outsider to do so, particularly one of Dr. Deming's stature. "I think he provided an awareness of why it is so important to embrace the concepts he believed in," Manoogian said.

Today, Dr. Deming can have the satisfaction of knowing that Ford has started the "prairie fires burning." Bakken refers to Ford's six guiding principles as a "Deming digest," and he calls the quality expert "more than just a consultant." Dr. Deming is, Bakken elaborates in a continuation of the western metaphor, "our mentor, a catalyst, our conscience, and on occasion a burr under our saddle that keeps us riding tall." For his part, Petersen recently referred to himself as a "Deming disciple," adding, "We at Ford are committed to his operating principles, particularly to the ethic of continuous improvement and the involvement of all employees."

"Team Taurus": Driving Toward Quality

In 1980, the same year that Ford lost money for the first time since going public in 1956, the board of directors approved a $3.25 billion expenditure to develop a new car line. The board insisted that it be a quality car, designed with customers in mind. But it also had to be competitive in price. It was a bold decision in the face of multimillion-dollar losses that would continue into 1981 and 1982 before the company finally showed a profit.

Eventually christened the Ford Taurus and Mercury Sable, the cars were front-wheel drive, six-passenger, family vehicles. In their evolution, Ford would put to the test many of the practices Dr. Deming endorsed. Indeed, it would be the first new car with quality as the goal.

The man in charge was Lewis C. Veraldi, vice-president for luxury and large-car engineering and planning. He was a home-grown product who had come to work for Ford as an engineering file clerk in 1949 after graduation from the Henry Ford Trade School. He had strong views on how the design process should work. As it was, designers designed a car on paper, then gave it to the engineers, who figured out how to make it. Their plans were passed along to the manufacturing and purchasing people, who respectively set up the lines and selected the suppliers on competitive bids. The next step in the process was the production plant. Then came marketing, the legal and dealer service departments, and then finally the customers.

In each stage, if a major glitch developed, the car was bumped back to the design phase for changes. The farther along in the sequence, however, the more difficult it was to make changes.

In manufacturing, for example, "we wouldn't see the plans until maybe a year before production started," Veraldi said. "We would go back to engineering and say can you do it this way. They'd say, 'Go peddle your papers. It's already tooled. I can't afford it.'"

Above the desk in Veraldi's spacious office, which accommodates a big white semicircular sofa and a conference table, hangs a framed poster entitled in futuristic beige letters "Team Taurus." In the center are the letters CPDG, for Car Product Development Group, which was responsible for "overall direction, design, development control and final approval." Radiating from the center in pie-shaped sections are the departments: engineering, manufacturing, service, purchasing, legal, sales and marketing, management review, and support. Each section is filled with clusters of circles, boxes, and hexagrams, representing review committees, various organizations and operations, and Taurus staff.

The traditional way of designing a car would require a sequential flow chart. The circular schematic represents the process for Taurus/Sable. It is also in happy agreement with Dr. Deming's principles, particularly Point Nine, "Break down barriers between staff areas."

"With Taurus," Veraldi said, "we brought all disciplines together, and did the whole process simultaneously as well as sequentially. The manufacturing people worked right with the design people, engineering people, sales and purchasing, legal, service, and marketing.

"In sales and marketing we had dealers come in and tell us what they wanted in a car to make it more user-friendly, to make it adapt to a customer, based on problems they saw on the floor in selling.

"We had insurance companies—Allstate, State Farm, American Road . . . [tell us] how to design a car so when accidents occur it would minimize the customer's expense in fixing it after a collision." One of the problems mentioned by insurance companies was the difficulty in realigning a car that had suffered front-end damage. As a result, Taurus and Sable have cross marks engraved on a suspension tower under the hood to define the center of gravity as an aid in front-end alignment.

Team Taurus included Ford's legal and safety advisers, who advised on forthcoming trends in the laws so "we could design for them rather than patching later on."

"Stop buying on price tag," Dr. Deming said in Point Four. In a radical change from the way Ford and most American companies do business, Ford moved a long way in that direction. The common way of doing business is to choose the lowest bidder on advertised specifications. For Taurus, the company identified its highest quality suppliers and sought their advice in the beginning stages. In return for their contributions, Ford pledged to make them, as far as possible, the sole supplier.

One of those companies was A. O. Smith of Milwaukee, a family-owned corporation whose major division made automotive subframes, the steel structures on which were mounted the engine, the transmission, and the control arms for the wheels. The company was the world's largest manufacturer of car and truck frames. In 1980, Ford sought Smith's advice for the NGLC ("Next Generation Large Car").

From beginning to end, as described by Executive Vice-President Paul Smaglick, the working relationship was dramatically different from prior associations. "They were giving us problems. We were giving them solutions." Usually, he said, the reverse was the case. Smith would receive designs, then point out the problems and changes that needed to be made—a time-consuming and costly process.

In the past, too, Ford had done the drafting. But Smith offered to have its own drafting department, which was staffed by experts on that particular part of the car, do the drafts and give them to Ford for approval. "There was a willingness to accept each other's experts" that had not existed before, Smaglick said.

A. O. Smith was still asked to submit a bid for the job. Had the company not been selected after putting so much work into the embryonic design, he said, "we would have been bitterly disappointed." Smith was, however, awarded the contract in January 1982, more than three years before Job One. The contract was for five years rather than the usual one, and it contained a notable feature: Price reduction was built in over the term of the contract, on the supposition that Smith would be able to improve productivity over time. The supposition was not unwarranted. Strong forces were at work to improve productivity at A. O. Smith. One was pressure from Ford itself.

Although there were signals from all the car companies about quality, Ford "did much more in the way of inviting vendors in," Smaglick said, and Ford was, moreover, "more demanding." Ford offered seminars, including ones with Dr. Deming, and gave their vendors feedback on what was required.

In addition, Smaglick said, there was clear evidence that Statistical Quality Control was "coming back into favor and had profound power to help improve quality and productivity." Smaglick hired a husband-and-wife team of statistical consultants and trained hundreds of employees.

Finally, in 1982, four top Smith executives took it upon themselves to visit automotive plants in Japan. They summed up their observations in thirty-three conclusions, many related to the technical aspects of the business. But on a general note, they reported that "wherever we went, much emphasis was placed on the close relationship between the Japanese auto industry and its suppliers. It was frequently referred to as an 'arms around' versus an 'arms length' relationship." They further concluded that "nothing we saw was an original invention of the Japanese; they learned from us. By fanatical attention to fundamentals, the student has surpassed the teacher. We must recognize how right we were and they are—before they have and we haven't."

At Ford, the response from Smith and other vendors to the Team Taurus approach was gratifying. One lighting firm developed louvered interior lights that cut down on reflection on the driver's side when on elsewhere in the car. Another firm produced a carpet in which all the fibers lay in the same direction for uniform appearance. A plastics company came up with an optional fold-out tray for tailgate parties for the station wagon. Said Veraldi, "Those are the little attention-to-detail items that we've never done before."

The attention to detail even extended to the owner's manual. One complaint had been that it would not lie flat when opened, a hindrance requiring the owner to hold the manual down with one hand (or some other part of the body) while trying to work on the car. The Taurus manual lies flat.

There was training for 6,000 people from product engineering in fifty-nine new technical courses; for 1,200 people in eighteen flexible manufacturing courses; for 5,000 in robotics; for 2,700 in statistical methods; and coaching in statistics and employee involvement for 5,100 suppliers. A major part of the research was conducted on other cars. Seeking to be Best in Class (BIC) in a number of significant categories, Team Taurus bought highly rated cars and took them apart, just as they had been put together, evaluating some four hundred features and deciding whether to match or exceed them. In 80 percent of the four hundred design elements, including such diverse items as the size and shape of the hood release, seat-belt comfort and operation, forward visibility, and fuel cap removal, Taurus now rates itself number one.

In addition, Veraldi said, "we went to all the stamping plants, assembly plants and put layouts on the walls. We asked them how to make it easier to build. We talked to hourly people." In all, Team Taurus collected 1,400 suggestions and incorporated 550 of them. It's "amazing," he said, "the dedication and commitment you can get from people. . . . We will never go back to the old ways because we know so much of what they can bring to the party."

In another departure, prototypes were built nine months before the first cars would come off the line and tested by potential new car buyers, resulting in more changes for the better. The traditional way of making changes was to produce the car and wait for customer complaints. "That's stupid, isn't it?" Veraldi observed, "because the first three months, customers get something that is less than good."

The prototypes were also taken to suppliers so that their workers could see the car. In the past, said Veraldi, "the supplier would make the part, fit it to a gauge, and ship it to a plant. . . . The workers had never seen the final product they make in a car. All they do is they see a molding, or an engine, or a door. They would never see the result of their efforts in a car."

After seeing the car, one Tennessee woman, who worked on window modules, posted a sign on her machine that identified what parts were visible and had to be trimmed. When the car came to A. O. Smith, the employees got the day off to look it over. Two hundred workers at a plant that supplied exterior moldings signed a poster pledging their commitment to quality as a thank-you for what is now called "the must see before" program. Framed, the poster hangs on Veraldi's office wall.

"The next program we have is going to have a lot more than what Taurus has had, because the people have seen the benefits of this program," Veraldi pledges. One of the benefits, even before the first car came off the line, was a $400 million savings in the $3.25 billion budget.

Ten years ago, Veraldi said, "we wouldn't have had the total management support for improved quality. . . . If you don't have the support of the top guy, it isn't going to happen.

"Having that . . . I could go to anybody else and say, 'Hey, Caldwell and Petersen'—they were the top guys at the time—'and the board of directors approved this, they said we're going to have a team.' . . . I could use those names to get people to join up. Before, if it was just a missionary like myself going out, you might not have made it. . . . Isn't it logical? If you work together, you should end up with something better than if you work apart?"

Windsor Export Supply—Where Paper Was the Product

In October 1984, at the request of the statistical methods office, Dr. Deming paid a visit to a Ford installation called Windsor Export Supply, situated directly across the Detroit River from Detroit itself in the small, clean Canadian city of Windsor.

Housed in an eight-story building, which was one of the city's largest, Windsor Export Supply is the overseas supply arm for parts from North American plants. Functioning like a company within a company, Windsor Export's 250 employees take orders from Ford's foreign manufacturing and assembly plants—most of them in South America, with a few in Australia and Europe—as well as outside suppliers. In response to orders, Windsor purchases parts from Ford supply plants, arranges for their shipment, and collects payment. About 150 Windsor employees were then members of the United Autoworkers Union (UAW).

Over the years, Windsor Export had come to occupy a somewhat enviable position within Ford. Being headquartered "across the river" distanced Windsor from the Ford complex in Dearborn some fifteen miles away, albeit in a fashion that was more psychological than geographical. As long as customers were satisfied and Windsor showed a profit, the folks at Ford world headquarters had pretty much left the operation alone.

As a place of employment, it offered a great deal of stability. Managers found the conditions pleasant, with the advantages of working for a large, successful corporation, absent the sense that someone was always looking over their shoulders.

In the early 1980s, however, things weren't looking so good, even for Windsor. Overseas sales were slipping, thanks to competition from Japan. In addition, some of Windsor's former customers had turned the tables and were now supplying the United States. Finally, the devaluation of the dollar hurt. Sales were down nearly 40 percent. Even so, by cutting back on the payroll, Windsor managed to stay in the black, which was more than could be said for Ford as a whole.

Lionel Rivait, who had been with Ford thirty-five years and for the last ten had run the parts control department that placed orders with North American suppliers, was typical in his optimism. "I thought things were going extremely well." Not only was Windsor doing better than the rest of Ford, but computers were making it more efficient. "We were getting our systems in line. We were well on the road to becoming paperless."

Unknown to Rivait, higher forces were at work. Across the river, Ford management was worried. They sought Dr. Deming's counsel. The day Dr. Deming arrived, he first spent an hour with the top thirty-two people at Windsor. Rivait later chuckled at the memory. "He really got my attention by saying 85 percent of the problem is management. He intended to have a shock effect, and it worked." In short, Dr. Deming let them have it. The managers, surrounded by higher-ups from world headquarters, took the abuse in silence.

The following day, Dr. Deming met with Windsor's two hundred nonmanagerial employees. He finds it valuable to hold such sessions, which are videotaped and later shown to supervisors. Dr. Deming draws the workers out on the things that keep them from doing their jobs right (barriers to "pride of workmanship") and on what they feel is expected of them. Often managers are shocked at the things that are wrong and are also surprised at how much people care.

No one had been quite sure what to expect at a meeting with Windsor employees. Perhaps they would respond differently from people who worked in a factory. But that was not the case. As Harry Artinian, from the statistical methods office, said later, "If you took the white shirts and ties off those people and put them in overalls, you'd hear the same words."

Years of rage and frustration boiled to the surface. The employees complained that there was no incentive to do a better job and no recognition for a job well done. They said they often didn't know what happened to their work after it was done. Dr. Deming later described their mood as verging on "mutiny."

One of those who spoke up was Wayne Richard, a short, compact man with a lot of energy who had once worked for Rivait. The pair had not got along. Richard's job was to make sure customers got the most up-to-date version of the part they had ordered. He sometimes saw ways he thought the process could be improved, but he had learned that it was futile to make suggestions.

By the time Dr. Deming arrived, Richard was thoroughly disillusioned. "At certain times," he explained later, "I would strive to point out things that were woefully wrong and suggest methods we could use to correct them, like calling our customers in Brazil and saying, 'You're doing this wrong. Here's how you should do it.' " It seemed to Richard that "he'd [the manager would] be very interested in any kind of change." Not so. "At the time, nobody listened to you."

There was also the larger issue of how to increase sales to offset the losses. To do so, it appeared that Windsor would have to supply installations other than just Ford's, which would require a charter change to be okayed by world headquarters. But Windsor management hadn't yet made any moves in that direction, and workers like Richard couldn't understand the inertia. A runner, he worked out his frustrations in marathons—thirty in one year. "Why should I try to excel or save the company or make it a better company?" he asked himself. He even thought sometimes that it might be a good thing for him if Windsor went under. Maybe it would motivate him to get another job, one that would lead somewhere. "I'll be very honest with you. I thought, 'Maybe I can go out and do something worthwhile.' "

When Dr. Deming invited the workers to speak up, Richard's voice was edged with anger. He announced that he wished supervisors, particularly his own, were in the room "so I can tell them what's wrong. . . . Because they still don't know what's wrong, and I'd be willing to guarantee you, I'd bet money, that they won't a year from now."

Richard may have been right about his supervisors, but he was wrong about things changing at Windsor. In less than a year after Dr. Deming's visit, so much had improved that manager Rivait and worker Richard were, if not good friends, at least respectful of each other. And Windsor seemed to have reversed its decline.

Dr. Deming's visit was in some ways the turning point in an effort that had begun some months earlier. The person who was most aware of Windsor's plight was John McRae, the manufacturing and supply director for Latin American automotive operations who had newly been given responsibility for export operation. Statistician Ed Baker was also interested. Although Baker worked in the statistical methods office, he was assigned to Latin American operations. Baker not only wanted to help Windsor, he also felt that it was of critical importance to show that the Deming philosophy, so often associated with manufacturing, could be adapted to a service operation.

"The majority of people at Ford—about two-thirds—are support people that don't directly produce in the plant," he explained later. "They don't fabricate or assemble. They design. They do market research. They purchase. They schedule." If Ford were to change in a major way, then those kinds of people would have to be involved. McRae, who was sympathetic to Deming's techniques, gave Baker the okay to begin the education process at Windsor.

Part of Baker's job wherever he went in the mammoth Ford organization was to convince managers he could be helpful. "It's not easy," he said. "It's not like people say, 'Hey, guys. Come in and really make us productive and show us how to reduce costs and reduce waste to make everybody effective.' We don't get those calls." It helped, however, to have support at the top. "Petersen keeps talking about it, so people at least have to give the appearance of being on the bandwagon."

At Windsor, Baker discovered that he had an ally within the organization—the young statistician in Windsor's finance organization named Harry Artinian whom he would later recruit for the statistical methods office. Baker needed all the help he could get, with the entrenched Windsor management, many of whom were nearing retirement. "They had a great self-image," explained Baker, "which they deserved in terms of the Ford system. You talk to their customers, the material gets there on time and in good shape. They innovated in a couple of areas in packaging and shipping—roll on, roll off. It's hard to come into an organization like that and say we're going to change.

"Windsor didn't have problems in the traditional sense. No one was saying to them, 'Your customers are unhappy.' But they had a lot of hidden costs. And they were faced with having to be competitive enough to go outside the Ford system and get business."

There was also the nature of the operation itself. Unlike a manufacturing operation, Windsor had no physical product that proceeded step-by-step from one work station to another. The output was "software"—invoices, reports, designs—that traveled via hand, mail, or computer, destined for unknown places and purposes.

As Artinian put it, "It may go out of your department, it may go upstairs, it may go out of the building to somebody else." The employee never knew whether the work was satisfactory or not. "Your definition of doing a good job is if you don't get a grief call." The question, as Baker saw it, was "how to turn Deming's philosophy into action when people don't produce hardware—when there's not something tangible." In other words, if you were going to use statistics, you had to figure out what to measure. It was not always clear.

"At least in the plant, they've got good accounting systems to show all these things . . . to know where the waste is. They know they have so much scrap, so much rework, so much extra inventory. You can pinpoint it. You can't even begin to do that on the administrative side of business."

He had some ideas, though, about where to start. One was to do flow charts. "Look at the process flow. You might call someone an 'expediter' or a 'clerk' but discover that the person's an inspector. Stuff is coming in, and that person is checking and storing and reallocating. It's exactly analogous to what an inspector in the plant is doing. Not adding value at all. Checking on somebody else's work."

Windsor posed another problem to its would-be reformers in that it was a bureaucracy. "Part of a bureaucratic system," Baker said, "is shifting the blame. You're taught to be helpless in a bureaucratic system. . . . You really don't realize or believe in your own power because you've been told so often it's not there. It's really hard in a bureaucracy. People that want to change feel there's so little they have control over directly."

As flow charts would show, the procedures that had developed over the years were often clogged with obstacles. "They had all this demarcation, all these barriers, and you can't get the information going that way. It not only takes a long time, but the information's been distorted," Baker said.

There would also have to be a change in what Artinian called "management by exception." Artinian explained that typically "the manager doesn't have time to know what's going on, line-item by line-item, so he only looks at those items that pop out, that are unfavorable to the budget, without really understanding what caused them. He's not really looking at the process, but looking at the outcome. . . .

"So therefore you have people who try to do everything possible to make sure those exceptions don't show up. If they occur, then all your resources are directed toward explaining what happened. It doesn't solve the problems. And it leads to thinking that absence of variances—if those things don't occur—then everything's all right. Nothing could be further from the truth because there's still tremendous waste and inefficiency in the system."

With McRae's approval, Baker and Artinian set up a two-day training session in basic statistical concepts for forty Windsor employees, preceded by a half-day management seminar. Baker had learned from experience not to "do training unless it's going to lead to something. . . . I was doing that for a few years, and I try not to do that anymore. Training has to be part of an organization change strategy." Their strategy was to emerge from the training with project teams fired up and ready to go.

Although the participants didn't realize it, they had been carefully chosen by Artinian with that strategy in mind. He wanted representation from most departments, particularly ones where he knew there were problems; but more than that, he also wanted people who were in an internal supplier-customer relationship, even if they had never thought of it that way.

Baker's presentation included the basic concepts of internal supplier-customer relationships, Statistical Process Control, and also a three-hour group discussion during which the groups talked over the new ideas.

The reaction exceeded Artinian's expectations. "I'd worked there for about six years, and many of these people in these groups talked with each other on a daily basis. They'd be talking about Tiger games. They'd be talking about anything except work. Now all of a sudden, when they were taught these concepts and they could place themselves in one of these boxes—I'm a 'producer,' there's the 'customer'—it was really amazing. They started thinking of work-related situations in which they were having problems and they said, 'What about such-and-such a report?'

'What about this?' All of a sudden, all the tables are talking. . . . I'm walking around and they're talking, and they're not talking about anything except work. It was like all this energy was released all at once." Baker and Artinian had hoped to get one good project from the training. Instead, there were half a dozen. Everyone was eager to try out the new techniques.

A month later, a new operations manager arrived from world headquarters with a mandate to rescue Windsor from its downward slide. His name was J. Robert Linklater, and he had started with Ford in 1957 with a degree in business. He had worked his way up the supervisory chain of command, holding various positions at both world headquarters and in operations. Most recently, he had been in international operations as the supply director in Venezuela, where he had literally been on the receiving end of Windsor Export.

As it happened, Linklater had attended a one-day Deming seminar several years earlier at world headquarters. Given Dr. Deming's scorn for managers with business school degrees, it was perhaps not surprising that Linklater had been more insulted than impressed. "I saw one lecture of his and didn't want to go back," he said.

Still, as it became clear that the corporate hierarchy was serious about the Deming doctrine, he realized he could not discount it. When Linklater got the Windsor assignment, he found himself looking over Dr. Deming's Fourteen Points once again. This time something clicked. "I said, 'That's got to be the key.'"

He began a round of small meetings with the entire staff, fifteen people at a time, in which he laid the groundwork for the Deming philosophy and announced an open-door policy.

It was going to take more than that to motivate people. He knew it and they knew it. Windsor had already had its share of crash courses in improvement, among them Kepner Tregoe "Executive Problem Analysis and Decision Making" and "Teleometrics," a course designed to make managers more "people-oriented." Employees called them "charm school" courses because nothing substantial changed afterward. There had even been open-door policies before. But, as George Brooks, a supervisor, put it, "Behind every open door was a closed mind." When Brooks showed some training films, he was chastised for taking employees off the job. Linklater figured he had a year to show proof of a turnaround at Windsor. Much sooner than that, in November, he would have to make a budget presentation that would outline his plans. In short, the heat was on.

An in-house manager for special projects, Michael R. Moulder, was appointed to work full-time on the effort. Linklater and Moulder had worked together in Venezuela and gotten along well. Moulder began to work with the project teams. It was not long before Windsor began to show results.

One successful project involved the freight audit system. Several years earlier, Ford had instructed its manufacturing divisions to farm out auditing functions to take advantage of state-of-the-art techniques. Windsor had contracted with a bank to do the job. Problems began almost immediately after the change. The Ford computers in Oakville, Ontario, spewed out pages of queries, and each had to be answered by Windsor staff. As payments sometimes took months to straighten out, past due bills mounted. The whole thing was a nightmare.

The project team that tackled the problem included both supervisors and workers from the traffic department, as well as parts control, accounting, and the Ford accounts payable office in nearby Oakville, which actually issued the checks. Their first step was a flow chart. This helped people understand how paper and information flowed into the system. The chart also highlighted instances of waste, cost, redundancy, and other areas for improvement.

The team collected data on the time that elapsed between the date the Windsor traffic department received an invoice and the date Oakville issued a check. Using control charts, they found that the system was actually stable in that the number of days did not exceed upper and lower control limits, but that the limits seemed far too high. The average was fourteen days. Compounded by delays in mail service, the process could take thirty-five days.

Next, the team used a cause-and-effect diagram to identify several reasons why the bills were being rejected from the computerized system. High on the list were keypunch errors of either codes or dollar amounts; misfiling that led to payment in the wrong currency; missing carrier codes that occurred when a list had not been updated to include new carriers; and lost or misplaced bills.

Efforts to resolve these problems with the bank were unsuccessful, so Windsor reclaimed the auditing function, making a number of changes to correct the problems. The process was simplified, both in the number of steps and in the geographical distances over which information had to flow. As a result, the number of days required to process an invoice dropped from fifteen to six, and the proportion of rejected bills was reduced from 34 percent to less than 1 percent.

In another project, involving roll on/roll off shipments, Joe Abela, a material handling engineer, had collected figures showing a downward trend since 1980 in the cubic feet of space occupied in each van as it departed from a Florida port for its overseas destination. The vans were packed by a subcontractor "pack plant" that had held the Ford contract for decades. After taking Baker's statistical methods training and charting the operation, Abela saw that it was out of control, alerting him to look for special causes. He became the leader of a team to investigate the problem. The team discovered almost immediately that the subcontractor was not using the special rack slides designed to load the van properly. It did not help matters that the pack plant charged on a per-van basis and that its workers correspondingly were paid by the number of vans they loaded.

When Linklater made it known that the contract was in jeopardy unless the situation improved, the pack plant manager responded to an invitation to attend a Ford-sponsored statistical seminar. On the trip north, the manager complained to Abela that his problem in filling the vans was partly caused by late-arriving engines from Ford manufacturing plants in Canada. Because the engines were so heavy, they had to be loaded first into the bottom of the vans, with more lightweight material on top. The ship left on Wednesday. If the engines were not there by Monday, packing had to proceed. That meant that the first vans were filled with lightweight materials. When the engines finally arrived, everything else was packed. And the remaining vans could be only partially filled with engines because of weight limits.

From the traffic department representative on the team came the information that engines for domestic use generally had a higher priority with the engine plant than did those going overseas. As a consequence, Windsor's export orders sometimes left as late as Friday night. If U.S. customs was closed, the delivery trucks would have to wait till Monday to continue their journey. That was why they were often late in arriving at the Florida pack plant.

All this information began to add up. There was not one but several interrelated reasons for lightly filled vans. It was like pieces of a puzzle. Many people had been aware of one piece; not until the people worked together as a team could they assemble the whole puzzle.

Windsor subsequently was able to negotiate earlier shipping schedules from the engine plant, whose management had not been aware of the problems, while the pack plant began to use the rack slides correctly. The figures on space use shot up from a per-van average of 2,256 cubic feet to 2,311 the month the changes were put into effect, and the improvement continued. The more van space was filled, the fewer vans were necessary. Projected yearly savings were $83,000.

Yet another problem tackled by a project team disappeared almost as quickly as it was recognized, thanks to communication between departments. A heavily computerized department was experiencing considerable difficulty with response time. Even though the computer system was designed for peak capacity, workers at video display terminals would wait helplessly as minutes passed by, repeatedly hitting the command keys to elicit a response. After consultation with the systems department, the first step of the project team was to gather data on response time. Suddenly, response time improved. The problem had been that as workers continually punched the command keys, they were unwittingly reentering the data, causing the data to queue up and overload the system. When they ceased doing that to measure response time, they discovered there was no problem after all.

With the projects in full swing, Linklater's open door, and Dr. Deming's visit, Windsor had come alive, that was for sure. But it wasn't all positive. The workers were watching each move Linklater made. If their new man were serious about the Deming philosophy, they were sure heads would roll among their bosses. After all, a good number of them had taken advantage of the open-door policy to tell him exactly what was wrong and with whom.

The managers, for their part, felt threatened. They had been schooled to be authority figures. Now they were regarded negatively for being authoritarian. Control seemed to be seeping into the hands of their troops. Workers were running off to meetings without seeking permission. Improvements were being made without their approval. They didn't know what to do. They were still supposed to be in charge, but, as Rivait put it, "you didn't dare say no for fear of being thought 'negative.' "

Feeling both left out and threatened, the middle managers were angry. Windsor held its first Christmas party in some years—the story was that parties had been discontinued after a former manager had got drunk and chastised lower-level staffers in the presence of their wives and husbands—but no managers came. As Moulder put it, "You have a situation where the guy at the top [Linklater] is enlightened—spreading the gospel—the people at the bottom want to get turned on, and the guy in middle management is apprehensive and unconsciously acting as the inhibitor."

Baker knew you were supposed to work from the top down, but he later defended the decision not to do so on the grounds that, quite simply, "we didn't have the time. We weren't going to wait five years for Windsor to go out of business." But he did hold private sessions to listen to managers complain and to try to reassure them.

Meanwhile, workers were disappointed when it became clear that some of the managers they disliked so much weren't going to be fired. Some were even disenchanted enough to drop out of the project teams. But Linklater had come to quite another decision. No one would be fired. He would bring along those managers that he could. Some were slated for retirement. And he would put some pressure on the holdouts. The project teams would now be responsible to their respective managers. And the managers would be measured for their MBOs (Management by Objective, a performance rating system) by how well the teams did. Maybe Dr. Deming was against MBOs, but while Ford still had them, perhaps they could serve a useful function.

Eight months after he attended the Deming seminar, Wayne Richard found that his position at Windsor had undergone considerable change. Initially, he had been an active member of a project team that streamlined his job and sped up the ordering process. Then he had a new job altogether. In a push for new business, Windsor had bid on and won a Ford parts-and-accessories export operation in Newark, New Jersey, which was closing down its other operations for lack of business. Moving the operation to Windsor provided thirty-one new jobs, which was welcome news since Windsor was scheduled to lose forty-three in 1985.

From beginning to end, the move reflected a new spirit of teamwork among employees, union leaders, and management. The head count reduction, for example, was scheduled for January; the new hires for July. Under usual procedures, both changes in manpower would have taken place as scheduled. There would have been a season of upheaval as forty-three workers left and others readjusted to the changing workload; then openings would have been posted for thirty-one new jobs and workers would have returned to fill them. The paperwork would have been enormous; the negotiations with the union, interminable.

Instead, Linklater and UAW Local 240 President Leonard H. Campbell negotiated an arrangement under which Windsor would allow the forty-three to stay on until July, when the thirty-one new jobs would be available, while the union would be flexible on its rules regarding seniority and job postings. Observed David Cooper, who was in charge of industrial relations, "Things that were contractually written, like seniority lists. They just pushed them to the side and said, 'What's the best way to do it?' It was very significant in that there was some trust there. Both parties were sticking their heads out a little."

Campbell would say later that he knew that it was "politically risky" to take a less-than-doctrinaire position on job posting and seniority, two issues unions consider critical to their membership. On the other hand, "I sure didn't want to go against something that would save jobs." Besides, he was impressed at how Windsor was struggling to turn things around. At Ford's invitation, he had attended a four-day Deming seminar. As a matter of policy, he never opposes reform programs, knowing that "if they're going to flop, they're going to flop by themselves, because upper management doesn't get behind them. Then they blame the unions." He wasn't going to set himself up that way, but he had liked what he heard from Dr. Deming. He saw how the project teams improved the negative attitudes people had toward Windsor. "Deming is something that has pulled the people together in an environment that was otherwise very gloomy and dark. . . . There's continual improvement. I just see it getting better and better."

As far as Campbell could see, as a union president there was one drawback to his cooperation. "It has a tendency to look like the union is in bed with management. If it looks like that, it looks like that, but it sure does get us a lot of things we want. I sit back, I smile, and say, 'This is great. It makes my job easier.' "

After the agreement was reached, Windsor employees assigned to the new jobs traveled to New Jersey to study the system and transport it intact to Windsor. In the past, managers would have handled the move. Said Baker, "They would have gone down there, handed it out very procedurally by the steps, and told employees, all right, 'Do A, B, C, D, and E.'

"For years," he continued, "people would come into Windsor about eight in the morning, sit at their desks, never go anywhere. Now you have people commuting to Newark to learn the job. These people have discretion. You give them a budget, and you say, 'You go, you learn the job.' "

And once again, there was flexibility from a union that might once have said, "Our people don't want to travel. And if they do travel, they want overtime."

As it happened, one of those selected for the Newark detail was Wayne Richard. The assignment was not a promotion, nor did it carry the promise of more money—two missing ingredients he stewed over before saying yes. "Why," he asked himself, "should I bust my ass for this place when I can sit back in a nice easy job where I have full control and my boss doesn't know a thing about what I do?"

On the other hand, he had to admit that "we're going to be able to make all the changes and all that. There is a bit of incentive there along with the challenge." The fact was, he was hooked on the new Windsor. "It makes me want to come to work in the morning when before I didn't. . . . I know I've got a challenge. Something's going to happen rather than the old dull, dull, dull." He was also looking forward to making the new operation more productive. From his point of view, the system was totalitarian and antiquated. "We're going to Dr. Deming that all to pieces," he pledged. "We're going to cut, chop, slash, change systems. . . . It's going to be good for us and good for business."

To his surprise, Richard was also finding the newly appointed manager of the Newark operation receptive to new ideas. His new boss was an old boss, Lionel Rivait, who had also been transferred. Rivait, by his own admission, had become "a convert" to Dr. Deming. He had been heavily influenced, he said, by sitting in on the meetings where the workers seemed so unhappy. "I remember an individual who got up and said, 'I have all kinds of good ideas, but no one will listen to me.' " Rivait couldn't get it out of his mind. The man worked for him.

"He [Dr. Deming] was saying there were no lines of communication between management and workers. And I think there should be. It was true of me. I must admit that in all the years I've been here, we decided how the job was going to be run, how we would handle the job, and we went out and provided direction or procedures how to do the job that way."

It meant a whole new style of supervision—or leadership, as Dr. Deming would say. Rivait could no longer order people to do things. "You have to stop yourself and say, I'm going to get a group of people together and ask them, 'How would you handle that?' " It might take more time, but there was also an advantage. He was no longer the only person responsible for a decision. Indeed, he would say later, "I find it a lot more comfortable on myself."

If Rivait needed convincing that the new style worked, the Newark operation did it. "By sending these people to Newark for training and by giving them some latitude as to how they could conduct the job—the whole training process—they have become such a highly motivated group, it's just amazing how they've changed. . . . Some of these people—Wayne Richard was one, who had a lot to say at that initial meeting—these people are just doing an outstanding job."

Rivait might have thought Richard had changed. But for Richard, it was the other way around. Said Richard of Rivait, "I don't mind working for the guy. I know all the information. He's got to play ball with me. . . . I think the guy's changed."

Chapter 23

———•———

Spreading the Deming Word:

Growth Opportunity Alliance of Greater Lawrence, Lawrence, Massachusetts

One day in October 1980, four months after NBC had broadcast its White Paper, the telephone rang in Dr. Deming's basement office. Dr. Deming himself took the call.

The caller was Bob King, manager of industrial relations for a Lawrence, Massachusetts, textile firm named Malden Mills. Lately, he had been involved in a coalition of labor and management to rescue the aging industrial city of 65,000 from high unemployment and low productivity.

"Dr. Deming," King said, surprised to find himself reaching his target on the first call and slightly at a loss for words, "I saw the NBC White Paper, and I understand you've done some work in Japan."

"What do you mean, *some* work?" Dr. Deming replied.

King experienced a moment of trepidation but forged ahead, explaining that the city of Lawrence had formed a coalition of companies to improve quality and productivity and that the coalition had decided to seek out Dr. Deming for help.

Dr. Deming, King would later recall, said he would help "if you're serious."

King by now realized that Dr. Deming would not look favorably on anyone who wasted his time. "I think we're serious,"

King replied, "but I'll speak again to the people who are involved."

Several weeks later, King was back on the phone, and the first Deming seminar was arranged for the group known as GOAL, the Growth Opportunity Alliance of Greater Lawrence. Although no one could have foreseen it at that time, Lawrence and its environs would become a hotbed of Deming activity as a result of that phone call and would be a resource for others here and abroad.

Lawrence, Massachusetts, was a worn-out former textile town, most of whose mills had come to a halt. Located thirty-five miles north of Boston, the greater Lawrence area, and to some extent the city itself, had attracted a few high-tech firms. But back in 1979, when the city had elected a new mayor, Lawrence P. LeFebre, unemployment was still widespread.

LeFebre immediately sought to change the economic climate. He had heard that in Jamestown, New York, a coalition of government, industry, and labor leaders had worked together to turn labor strife into labor harmony. As a consequence, new companies were sufficiently encouraged to move into the Jamestown area. That was the sort of thing LeFebre would like to accomplish in Lawrence.

The new mayor approached Malden Mills, a family-owned textile firm that was the city's largest employer. Malden had managed to survive the decline of the textile industry because of its strong customer orientation and diversified manufacturing processes. Moreover, the company had foreseen the decline of the U.S. apparel industry and had switched much of its production to upholstery materials.

Malden's industrial relations director, Bob King, was immediately intrigued by LeFebre's proposal. He had been thinking of starting an Employee Involvement program for the company's 1,800 workers, and LeFebre's ideas seemed to be in sync with his.

The price of enthusiasm is involvement. King became cochairman of the group that took the name of GOAL; it included firms not only in Lawrence, but also in nearby Methuen, Andover, and North Andover in Massachusetts, and North Salem, New Hampshire.

Following the Jamestown model, GOAL tried to set up labor-management committees in each participating company. But the group failed to realize that, unlike Jamestown's, few of the participating GOAL companies were unionized. Without a formal labor structure, the committees were difficult to establish. And those plants that were unionized were generally divisions of larger companies, which meant that any arrangement was subject to negotiation on a national level. In short, it was a more complex situation than they had imagined. At the end of two years, only Malden had an ongoing Employee Involvement program. The organization was having an identity crisis.

In April 1980, King attended a conference on management at which NBC was taping a talk by Joji Arai, head of the Japan Productivity Center's Washington office. King learned that a White Paper was in the works, and he made a point of watching when it aired in June. He was so impressed that he suggested that the somewhat dispirited members of GOAL focus on quality and productivity rather than labor-management relations. And he called Dr. Deming.

Consulting his schedule, Dr. Deming said he could give his four-day course in February 1981. He invited King to attend an earlier one in January in Nashua, New Hampshire, so he could become familiar with the arrangements.

King was captivated. The climate was right. Companies responded with alacrity to the invitation to attend the GOAL-sponsored Deming seminar. Registration drew 180 people from thirty companies. Malden had the largest contingent with thirty-five, including the president and those who directly reported to him. There were sizable delegations from Honeywell Information Systems, Western Electric (then still a division of AT&T), Digital Equipment Corporation, and New England Power. When the local newspaper ran a story on the eve of the seminar, people called the next morning begging to come.

The seminar took place in the ballroom of the Salem Inn, Salem, New Hampshire, a modern motel located in a cluster of woods at an exit of Interstate 93. The Salem Inn would also be the site of the first meeting of the Deming Follow-Up Steering Committee, as the group that met afterward to discuss how to proceed called itself. However awkward, the name stuck, and it is the tag under which the group meets to this day.

At the beginning, only a half-dozen or so people signed up for follow-up. The small number reflected the reaction of those attending the seminar. As usual, Dr. Deming had managed to turn some people off with his sharp criticism of top management and his spirited defense of workers. But the half-dozen who wanted to pursue his ideas were excited.

There was one hitch. Almost all were from high-tech companies. Bob King remembers worrying that cooperative activities would violate antitrust laws. He was equally concerned that these companies—competitors, in a sense—would not be candid about internal matters relating to the quality effort. He need not have worried. "What became apparent," he said, "was that there was something about quality that made it possible for people to talk about programs to improve it without giving away any trade secrets."

Moreover, the representatives from the different companies needed each other in their struggle with new ideas and techniques. The steering committee was a support group in those early days. "When people went back to their companies," King said, "they went back to the same situation they had left. They had ideas about making fundamental changes in their companies for the better, and uncertainty about how to do that, and also some fear of initiating change and taking the risk involved with that."

For the next three years, the steering committee met biweekly to exchange stories and advice. One member of the group, he recalled, compared the experience to going to church on Sunday, then going back to your company to preach the new religion.

The first issue the committee addressed was the need for statistical training. Clearly, they needed someone to coach them in the statistical tools Dr. Deming talked about. "Dr. Deming felt it was a pilot project for the nation," King said, "and so we should use the best." Dr. Deming provided a list of just five statisticians, one of whom was from South Africa. GOAL contacted two, David Chambers, a University of Tennessee professor of statistics, and Paul Krensky, a nationally known consultant who was, as it happened, located not far away in Lexington, Massachusetts. Both offered courses through GOAL during the spring and summer of 1981 and continued to do so thereafter.

As Dr. Deming returned again and again for seminars, the steering committee grew in size. At one time, it numbered as many as seventy people. The organization was run by volunteers, whose companies gave them time to participate.

One problem was reaching top management. GOAL began to schedule CEO breakfasts with speakers on various subjects. From time to time, Dr. Deming himself would put in an appearance. Next, as companies began to have success stories to tell, GOAL put together a case study program in which a number of companies would gather for a day or an evening to describe their experiences.

GOAL—at first just King and a secretary—began to expand. Michael Brassard was assigned to GOAL by the Massachusetts Quality of Work Life Center, which was studying the relationship between Employee Involvement programs (EI) and mental health. Brassard was gradually reaching the conclusion that such programs actually did very little for workers' mental health. Indeed, workers would typically join with great enthusiasm, then grow frustrated after a year or two when very little had changed. It was just as Dr. Deming said in his debunking of EI. In Brassard's experience, the workers weren't allowed to deal with real issues "because management won't bring them those issues. They don't want to share power." It was not difficult to convert Brassard to the Deming method. He became GOAL's staff trainer and also a consultant.

A statistician, Diane Ritter, joined the staff. And Larry LeFebre, who had lost his bid for reelection as mayor, began to handle marketing for a growing number of GOAL courses. Malden Mills donated rent-free space in a small building on company property. GOAL became, in effect, a Deming resource center, with written materials, videotapes, and educational programs. A 1984 effort to establish a Deming Prize modeled on Japan's failed, however, for reasons that are instructive. Although there were more than twenty entries, the prize committee found that none was worthy of the award. GOAL substituted an annual conference, featuring presentations by Deming users.

GOAL set three priorities for spreading the Deming message in the final half of the 1980s. The first—and most important—was to help establish areawide Deming efforts such as their own. The second was to establish a Supplier Institute to help larger companies, who may, in King's words, have been "beating up" on their vendors, instead set up quality and productivity programs. Many small companies had had neither the time nor the money to free individuals for participation in GOAL-sponsored seminars.

Finally, GOAL had as another goal the translation of materials on quality written in Japanese. Explained King, "One of the absolute absurdities of this whole thing is that the Japanese have been implementing Deming for thirty-five years and no one is interested in how they did it. As a result of that, almost none of it is available in English. They have the most fantastic tools and methodologies and promotional materials to get people to implement Deming's Fourteen Points."

Chapter 24

————•————

Deming to the Rescue:

Malden Mills, Lawrence, Massachusetts

The first company to benefit from GOAL's involvement with Dr. Deming was Bob King's employer, Malden Mills. Just a few months after the NBC White Paper, the economy plunged into a recession, and Malden found itself teetering on the edge of bankruptcy. Said King dryly, the threat of bankruptcy "provided some incentive for the company to be concerned about quality and productivity."

Malden had four divisions at the time: flock, woven, cloth, and fur. All were affected to some extent by the recession, but fur, which manufactured a synthetic high-pile luxury fabric, bore the brunt of the impact.

The fur market was risky anyway. Half of the end product—coats and jackets—was sold in a three-week period following Labor Day. At Malden, orders from the cut-and-sew shops came in between March and July, but the division produced fabric year-round. There were hints early in 1981 that something was amiss. The orders just weren't coming in as quickly as usual. But the company figured that the problem was high interest rates, which made buyers reluctant to carry inventory for any longer than necessary. The company anticipated a rush of last-minute business. But that year, the orders didn't come in at all. Consumers simply weren't buying fur, fake or otherwise. By July, fur manufacturers were engaged in an all-out price war. Several of

163

Malden's competitors went out of business, and Malden itself lost millions. In September 1981, the company filed for protection under Chapter 11 of the bankruptcy law.

As fate would have it, Malden's financial woes coincided with the appearance of W. Edwards Deming on the Lawrence scene. Malden sent thirty-five people to the first seminar. One of them was the manager of the flock division. He decided to launch an all-out drive for quality lest the demise of the fur division drag down the entire company. The flock division was ripe for the Deming method. "Without knowing Dr. Deming," King said, "the division had been working on many of his ideas as being good management ideas for three years before meeting him—improving supervision, driving out fear, breaking down barriers between departments, eliminating barriers that stand in the way of people doing a good job."

That work had begun in the late 1970s, when the flock division had been plagued with a staggering annual turnover rate of 250 percent, as well as with high absenteeism. Even under the best of circumstances, Malden Mills's flock lines can be an unpleasant place to work. For twenty-four hours a day, sixty-inch-wide rolls of backing traverse the heavy machinery on the flock lines, where they are coated with adhesive and bombarded with tiny nylon fibers that rain down from a half-dozen overhead hoppers. The fibers pass through an electrically charged metal field that straightens them as they hit the adhesive. While still on the line, the fabric is cured in a drier. Afterward, it is washed, printed, and washed again.

Clouds of fine white fibers billow from the four lines of roaring machinery that produce the velvety upholstery fabric that is popular in both appearance and price. Fibers coat everything in sight, including the workers, sticking to their hair and clothing. Powerful foreign odors, similar to mold but stronger, assault the nose. In summer, when the air conditioning sometimes fails, temperatures on the flock lines have been known to rise to 110 degrees. It is difficult to hear and sometimes even to see.

But the noise, the fibers, and the heat go with the territory, so to speak. King did not believe they were the causes of the unhappiness manifested in turnover and absenteeism.

At the time, he was Malden's director of industrial relations. He decided to survey employees to ask not "What is wrong?" but the less threatening "Why are people leaving?" A number of problems surfaced. The workers said they had trouble meeting numerical goals that seemed to have no basis in reality and that they didn't understand the work standards or how people were allowed to bid on jobs.

The workers complained that the plant was so cluttered, they had difficulty reaching the bolts of fabric. Indeed, "there were a lot of problems that would just fall under the category of barriers to doing their job right," said King. "They would put the fabric on carts, some of the wheels were broken, it was tough to push them around. They couldn't get as much done because of these things."

And they were particularly bitter about the bonus system, which was intended not so much to give rewards as to force people to work on weekends to produce the needed volume. Recalled Marshall Hudson, manufacturing manager at the time, "The bonus appeared to be designed so the only time you could get it was by working on a Saturday. Up until Friday, by the end of your shift, you were just ready to make big money, but in order to do it, you had to get in here on Saturday—which was the intent—to entice people in here on Saturdays and Sundays."

When management decided to address some of these problems, there was a rapid change for the better. Many of the simpler problems, like the broken carts, were cleared up on the spot. A supervisor training program to teach human relations skills was introduced. And workers were given the training they needed to do their jobs. Turnover was reduced tenfold to 25 percent, and absenteeism dropped from 6.5 to 2.5. Supervisor employee relations seemed on the mend when the recession hit in 1981.

The job of introducing the Deming method was assigned to Hudson, the number-two man in the flock division. He was an industrial engineer who had been at Malden twelve years.

Hudson considers himself a "people person." As he sat through Deming's seminar, he was less interested in the statistical approach than in the Fourteen Points and other material relating to workers. He did, however, like the emphasis that using statistics placed on facts. "I seized on the philosophy of facts versus opinions. If you assemble and document facts, it will sell a project better, or a request for a capital expenditure, if you can back up what your recommendation is."

He also could definitely relate to Dr. Deming's "85-15 Rule," which said that 85 percent of the problems were the fault of management, and only 15 percent were the fault of workers. That had been a foreign notion at Malden. Hudson was forever being told to straighten out the people on the floor who were causing problems. It frustrated him that he never knew for sure whether they were really at fault. But he had felt trapped into playing the role of the tough boss.

He also knew that yelling and screaming didn't solve the problem. "You can go out and get everybody worked up to a fever pitch! 'If I see one more of those defects, you're all in deep trouble.' Everybody looks for the defect and pretty soon you don't see them. But as you go away, and your attention is diverted somewhere else, pretty soon the defect comes back. Because you never really solved the problem. . . . If it doesn't resurface, you're lucky. It's like a noise in your car. It just stopped making the funny noise and nobody knows why it did, but thank God it did. However, there is almost always a reason for the noise, and it comes back to haunt you."

Statistics, he realized, offered the potential for finding out what was really causing the problems. For statistical training, Malden sent a number of its people to six-week seminars sponsored by GOAL. In the once-a-week sessions, they studied statistical techniques in the morning, then returned to the plant to work on a project using those same techniques. "They had great successes almost immediately," recalled King. "They saved $2 million the first year, in a $45 million division on an investment of about $50,000 in training and consultant fees. They continued to expand in succeeding years, until at one time they had as many as thirty-five project teams working on different aspects of Dr. Deming's teachings."

In flock, Hudson's first formal step was to organize a steering committee that would choose projects for teams to work on. The committee also assigned a project leader, helped pick the team, and provided the necessary resources. There were guidelines and a system of record-keeping. Once assigned to a project, the team was to report twice monthly on its progress. On completion, the team would file a final project report that included a section on what controls had been put in place so that the problem wouldn't resurface. "There was an effort to make it participative," Hudson said, "not top down. For example, when we made out a project assignment sheet, we would sit with the project leader and come to a common understanding.

"The steering committee met once a week and would review

three projects on a rotating basis with the project leader. It was low pressure, low key—not to criticize but to assist. We were door-openers. People ask, 'Was this dictatorial?' We knew enough by then not to dictate."

As an illustration, Hudson explained how a project on "blade scrapes" was handled. As the backing traversed the flock line, the phenomenon known as "blade scrapes" occurred at a point after a nozzle had fed adhesive back and forth across the backing. The coated backing passed under a stationary blade, at a set distance from the backing, that smoothed the adhesive to a uniform thickness to receive the flock fibers. Occasionally, for reasons no one understood, a lump of foreign matter would lodge behind the blade. It could be a little hardened ball of adhesive, lint from the backing, or flock fibers that had dropped from the ductwork above. Whatever the composition of the lump, it created a line on the backing where there was no adhesive. Thus, the flock wouldn't adhere, and a section of defective material was the result. The operator had a small spatula with which to dislodge the lump—if and when he noticed it. The defect level, or product known as "seconds," due to blade scrapes averaged .5 percent.

A four-person team was assigned to the project on January 19, 1983. It consisted of the manager of the flock lines department, a "colorist" who worked with adhesives, a second-shift supervisor, and an industrial engineer. Its stated purpose was "to reduce blade scrapes." It identified the graphic techniques it would use as pareto analysis, control charts, and cause-and-effect diagrams.

The team met for the first time on January 25 and considered several possible causes for the difficulty: perhaps some feature of the blade attracted the lumps. Or perhaps the presence of so much airborne flock could be the culprit. The department chief was assigned to investigate the cost of a Teflon coating for the blade; the supervisor was to seal off the Line 2 blade area from flock; and the industrial engineer would devise a form for recording the frequency of blade clearings and the location of the scrapes.

All these routes, pursued in the next month, turned out to be blind alleys. Teflon coating was impractical. Charting the scrapes by line, shift, and quadrant of material showed no discernible patterns other than a disproportionate number on Line 2. And sealing off the area didn't prevent lumps from forming.

In April, the team decided to monitor Line 2 because it was the worst. The industrial engineer would list all possible contributors to blade scrapes. In the course of his observations, he found that the blade scrapes tended to occur where the backing was lapped in a seam. Depending on which of two suppliers had provided the backing, the seams were lapped in different directions. And even a single supplier might lap in different directions.

Malden requested its suppliers to consistently lap seams in the same direction. Meanwhile, the workers were instructed to load the backing in such a fashion that all the seams would run in a direction that would not buck the blade. But to the team's surprise, these changes, however sensible, did not reduce the defect level.

The engineer also noted that the blade itself was so badly rusted and pitted that it was leaving scratch marks in the adhesive. Perhaps, he reasoned, these nicks were catching debris. The team requested a highly polished chrome-coated blade for a trial.

At last, they had the solution. In monitoring 360 pieces of fabric, figures showed that the blade operator had been forced to clear the old blade an average of once for every 2.75 pieces. After the chrome blade was installed, clearings were reduced tenfold to every 27 pieces. The seconds level showed a corresponding drop, from .638 percent to .064 percent. The team immediately obtained new or rechromed blades for all the lines, and the quality level was monitored.

In all cases, the seconds levels dropped dramatically. There were other benefits as well. The workload of the blade operator was eased, and the chrome blades required less cleaning and care. Moreover, they lasted longer. In all, the cost of regrinding and chroming the blades and fabricating two new blades cost $5,990. The annual savings were more than $125,583.

Malden learned that even unsuccessful efforts to correct a problem were worthwhile. The machine responsible for aligning fibers on finished material— a "presser"—appeared to be causing an inordinate number of defects. But nothing a team tried to correct this seemed to work. In the process, however, they were able to show with data the futility of seeking improvement with that particular machine. "We could more than justify the cost of a new one," Hudson pointed out. The new machine, which washes rather than presses the fabric, indeed did less damage—and saved enough money to pay for itself.

Multiplied throughout the division, the results of such projects added up to big savings. In using charts to control flock and adhesive weights, for example, $1 million was trimmed from costs. Today, charts on each of the flock lines indicate what adjustments should take place.

One might have expected workers to react with alarm to the introduction of charts and change. Not so. It has made the worker's job easier, said Bill Cotter, a line leader on one of the flock lines. Workers had always been required to keep records of the weights of materials once the adhesive had been added. But that was it. "All we used to do was write down the numbers. Three hours into your shift, all you saw was a bunch of numbers. Nobody paid any attention to them. . . . We'd have our weights— 8.4, 8.1, 8.5—and you'd just continue that all day long. . . .

"Now, besides writing down the weights, we also have to draw a chart, marking out the weights, so if there's something that's real uneven, we have to make an adjustment on it immediately. . . .

"It immediately made a big improvement, because everything was right in front of you. You didn't have to think about making an adjustment—it showed you what to do."

Cotter was selected with one other worker to take one of the first Deming seminars and then the statistics course. At the time, the pair wondered why. They later deduced it was because both were shop stewards in Local 311 of the International Ladies' Garment Workers Union, and Malden was anxious to enlist labor leaders in the cause.

"I enjoyed it," Cotter said of the experience. "I got a kick out of Deming. He's antimanagement. 'We don't need management. Get management out of there. Let the people do their own job. They know what they're doing. If you [the manager] knew what to do, you wouldn't be hiring these people. You'd be doing the job yourself.' "

In the post-Deming era, Cotter said, people are better trained and there are fewer of them. In the past, workers learned from other workers, who were sometimes reluctant to show them how to do a job for fear that their own job was being threatened. He explained how it used to be. "Like, if I went on the blade, I would go on for a couple of days, and whenever the person who was training me said I was trained, then I was trained. That was all there was to it. Now they set limits on training. They say, 'All right, you work with him for six weeks, that's it. It'll take six weeks to train you for this job.' They decided how long it would take the normal person to learn how to run the machines. See, there's no stress on me. I'm not afraid this person's going to take my job."

In addition, the much-resented bonus system was replaced by one in which workers shared rewards whenever productivity surpassed certain targets. Weekly bonuses usually ran fifty to sixty cents an hour, and the results were posted for all to see.

As for the union, Local President Bill Angeloni said that when the Deming method came in, grievances went out. Where there used to be three or four a week, "I haven't had a written grievance in two years." In the flock division, he said, there is now more understanding and compassion on the part of management.

In each of the divisions, a personnel coordinator was stationed on the factory floor both as a buffer between management and workers and to assist workers with both personal and work-related problems. Said Hudson, "Often the production worker feels uncomfortable going to see 'the boss' but comfortable in going to the personnel coordinators, who they know have a direct door to me. They know that their problems will be fairly and properly presented."

In flock, the second person to hold that job was Darlyne McManus, who was one of the first women to work in production at Malden. She had risen to become a line leader and then a supervisor in the fur division. When she first came to work, she said, there were rigid barriers between workers and supervisors. "If you were the supervisor, you were the boss, you were looked down upon if you went in the cafeteria and sat down with the rest of your workers.

"I think communication between upper management, lower management, and the union employees has come up 150 percent," she said. "The company is keeping the workers advised on what's going on. You're not running in the dark any longer.

"You still have a few of the supervisors that come from the old school who say that 'I'm the boss and you better do everything just the way I say it and shut your mouth.' There are still a couple of those around. They're always into trouble."

Chapter 25

---•---

Adopting the New Philosophy:

Honeywell Information Systems, Lawrence Manufacturing Operation, Lawrence, Massachusetts

Across town from the red brick buildings that house Malden Mills is another red brick mill building where Honeywell manufactures its DPS 6 family of micro- and minicomputers. Although the two companies may be generations apart in technology, there is common ground in their use of the Deming method.

A small, graceful museum on the first floor of the building recalls the history of the site. It was at this location in 1905 that a Portuguese immigrant with the anglicized name of William Madison Wood founded the American Woolen Company with a financial boost from his wife, Sasparilla Ayer, the widow of a man who made a fortune from a popular drink named for her. The American Woolen Company became the world's largest textile firm. No other textile firm before or since, says a Honeywell history, has come close to the $50 million worth of khaki cloth that the American Woolen Company produced for the U.S. government during World War I.

At one time, ten thousand men, women, and children had jobs in the building, which contains thirty acres of floor space and sixteen miles of corridors. Photographs and relics from that era in Honeywell's Heritage Room suggest the conditions under which they labored. So, too, do the memories of the "doffers," "yarn

171

boys," and "tie-over girls" preserved by oral historians and mounted on placards in the display.

Although both the jobs and the twelve-hour shifts are history, some passages suggest how little the American philosophy of supervision has changed since then. Certainly many of today's workers can relate to yarn boy Stephen LoPiano's memory of the "straw boss": "Well, the superintendent would walk by occasionally and just take a casual walk up and down and look and look. Everybody's frightened silly. 'What's he looking for? Is my job going to be depending upon what he sees or doesn't see?'

"The superintendent would wear a gray flannel jacket and straw hat. Whether that was an indication that he was superior to somebody else or that's how he had to be designated, I don't know.

"If somebody saw him two hundred yards down the road heading toward their department, immediately they would go around and make a circle over their head indicating that the man with the hat is coming. And everybody ran back and made sure they were diligently working, because they were afraid that he might report back something that was unfavorable."

Cut to the 1980s. Stanley Marsh, manager of purchased product quality assurance, whose office is four stories above the Heritage Room, was one of the key figures in turning this plant away from the "old culture" that had prevailed in this country since the Industrial Revolution and that is so graphically represented in workers' recollections. He summed up the old culture of both this plant and many others in one telling phrase: "the way we do things around here."

"Basically," Marsh said, "it was an autocratic culture. There was little training. People learned their jobs probably from somebody who'd been on the job before.

" 'How do you do this?'

" 'Well, this is the way I do things around here.'

"There were many, many informal organizations. Informal organizations tend to run things. That's the way a culture gets going. Informal groups decide what pleases management, and then they tend to do that.

"That's the way things went. 'Get it out on Friday. It's the end of the month. I don't give a damn what it looks like.' "

It was, Marsh observed, "tough to change that."

But this Honeywell plant made an all-out effort to do so through a variety of training programs that introduced teamwork and statistical thinking at all levels, from management to the hourly workers. There was a period when scarcely a week went by, it seemed, in which an employee did not find himself or herself involved in one program or another. And by 1985, there were firm indications that the effort had paid off. In the time since Marsh and nine colleagues had attended their first Deming seminar, quality levels had jumped measurably. When a system was installed, or "plugged in," at the customer's location, data were collected on the number of units, or parts, that operated without replacement. This was called "plug and play." The performance of these replaceable units rose from the low 90s in 1979 to 99.7 in 1985. Higher quality made it possible to reduce the inspection requirement by approximately 50 percent.

The Honeywell experience demonstrates that a typically American production system based on authority, quantity, and speed can be changed to a participatory, quality-oriented environment, provided, as Dr. Deming might say, there is a totally new method.

That method began with Dr. Deming himself and with his importation by GOAL.

Getting into Training

The stage had been set in 1980 by the Japanese influx. "Everywhere you looked, they were building products of higher quality," Marsh said. Although Honeywell wasn't directly threatened, the company recognized that the Japanese "were going to get into the computer market and did well in markets that they tried to penetrate."

When Dr. Deming appeared on the Lawrence scene through GOAL, a ten-member Honeywell delegation from a variety of departments attended one of the earliest seminars. On their return, they immediately wrote individual letters to the plant director, Bill Cunningham. They stressed the need to introduce statistically based quality techniques to find out what was really happening in the plant. And they encouraged him to attend a Deming breakfast.

The plant director was receptive to their ideas and okayed hiring Paul Krensky, a statistician recommended by Dr. Deming, to teach a six-week course in statistics. Krensky came once a week. His students spent mornings in the classroom learning basic statistical techniques. Afternoon sessions took place back at the plant, where teams were coached in how to apply the techniques to specific projects.

Explained Marsh, "We wanted to get the building at the management-supervisor level talking from the same base, recognizing the need for statistics, so that when somebody used statistical terminology, the staff didn't say 'What's a pareto?' or 'Who's pareto?' or 'What is a control chart?' "

At the same time, the Lawrence plant started an Employee Involvement Program dubbed "RAM," for "Reliability, Availability, Maintainability." One thing led to another. It was thought that RAM would not work unless the participants had training in teamwork, so Honeywell commissioned two of its employees to develop a program in team dynamics.

Meanwhile, a fourteen-member management steering committee was established under Cunningham to look at overall quality issues. One of the committee's first assignments was to review the team dynamics training program that had just been developed. The training was arranged in nine modules that dealt with such topics as behavior in meetings, selecting problems, the cost of quality, communication, and customer-supplier requirements. Often the sessions, Marsh said, dealt with "simple things like running meetings better, putting up your hand instead of stepping on somebody to argue, waiting for the right opportunity rather than just trying to make the point."

The steering committee decided to try out several of the modules, with unexpected results. "What we found out," Marsh said, "was that the people who needed those modules more than anybody else was us. We were not at all good working together as a team."

The management group took the course in four intense days. They decided afterward to give the team dynamics training to all salaried employees before the nine hundred hourly workers. The two original trainers trained fourteen additional instructors, including Marsh, to carry out the training more quickly. The response was heartening. "People caught on to it. They loved it."

By now, it was 1983 and Honeywell's Lawrence plant was two years into its cultural turnaround. An in-house statistics course patterned after Krensky's was developed for all salaried personnel. In addition, there was a new focus on quality at the corporate level of Honeywell Information Systems. A number of top executives were dispatched to Crosby College in Winter Park, Florida, to familiarize themselves with the philosophy of Phillip Crosby, former director of quality at I.T.T. and author of *Quality Is Free*.

The Crosby effort didn't conflict with what was already happening at Lawrence. Indeed, thanks to Dr. Deming, Lawrence had a head start.

With the workforce steeped in team dynamics and basic statistical skills, Lawrence launched a wave of temporary task-oriented project teams that cut across department lines. As soon as departments started talking to each other, some of the thorniest problems dissolved. There was, for example, a case of delays on the Honeywell loading dock. Tracking the shipments, a team discovered that there were traffic jams when outgoing orders arrived simultaneously at a single freight elevator. An elevator schedule was drafted immediately.

In a related problem, a team learned that orders often went to the wrong destination because of labels that were difficult to read, for any number of reasons ranging from sloppy handwriting to smeared printing. Sometimes the labels were slapped onto a side of the box that was hidden when the items weren't properly stacked. Eventually a computerized system was introduced for labeling, and instructions were issued for positioning the labels.

Aside from formal training, there was an ongoing effort to educate people in how their product was used—the in-house customer-supplier relationship that Dr. Deming discusses, in which the customer is the next person in the production process. To Marsh, this is of critical importance. "Quite often, work centers don't know where their output goes. They don't know where their input comes from. To me, this may be the key to getting into true, high-quality work—understanding that if I send you a round box and you're looking for a square one, then we've got a problem, but if you've never told me that you want a square one, then there's no way I'm going to know I'm doing anything incorrect or inadequate."

Much of the transformation was subtle. In the old culture, for example, performance measurements were regarded with suspicion—and for good reason. "They knew they got measured, with a carrot and a stick. If your performance was 100 percent, you didn't get hit. If your performance was 70 percent, you got called into the supervisor's office. The message became very clear that you better have a high number. So, people being people and being very bright, they find ways to provide what you want. If you ask them for a number, they'll eventually give it to you."

In the new Deming culture, people have to be shown that performance is related to the company's financial standing. "If you explain to people what the business impact is, so now there's an understanding of why that's measured, then again, the fear goes away. It's dollars lost that a lot of them don't understand."

In the old culture, when there was a downturn in business, workers were laid off. Now, the Lawrence management prefers to hire temporary people during cyclical upswings. As a result, there have been no layoffs of permanent hourly workers since 1980, even though the computer market has had dramatic ups and downs.

In the old culture, individuals were singled out for recognition of their accomplishments. The judgments were inevitably subjective, and those who were overlooked, Marsh says, would "tend to get upset." He could understand why. "It's very seldom that one person is the total reason that something occurs." In the new culture, a companywide awards program for teams has been established. "We understand recognition is a key part of any process, just recognizing people for doing a good job," Marsh said.

Each quarter, the award recipients are invited to a formal luncheon and presented with a divisional symbol of two silver dolphins encased in Lucite on a wooden base. Silver plaques note the award. On Marsh's desk is one such pair of dolphins and two plaques. One plaque is a commendation for his work in team dynamics. The other is for his role on the Heritage Room committee.

Working with Vendors

Looking back on it, it is difficult to believe that for so many years, they did it the old way. Stanley Marsh admits now that when he first heard Dr. Deming rail against the evil of "awarding business on the basis of the price tag"—his Fourth Point—he did not understand its significance.

But when the Lawrence plant decided to pare its list of sheet metal suppliers from thirty-one to five, all sorts of problems were eliminated, just as Dr. Deming had predicted.

The sheet metal suppliers made the cases that housed the DPS 6 systems. The way it worked around Honeywell in the old culture, Marsh said, "the design engineer would do a drawing, go out and work with the prototype shop—which probably wasn't the production supplier—and they would make any adjustments that were needed in the design, finalize the design, then give it to manufacturing."

Manufacturing, in turn, would estimate the quantities that were needed, then "call up purchasing and say, 'Go get me ten of these.' Purchasing would check the list of vendors and send out to several a request for price quotes. The vendors would do a quick review and price quote, and the buyer would select one and buy the things—sometimes to the surprise of the incoming inspection guys.

"We'd get a call from the docks. They'd say, 'Oh, your new sheet metal thing is here from Vendor A. Do we have an inspection docket? Who's got a drawing?'

"That's the way we do things around here."

If the order was all right, or even almost all right, Honeywell would use it. If it wasn't a new scenario came into play. Honeywell would return the shipment to the vendor—paying the freight.

Alternatively, Marsh said, a representative of the vendor might be asked to "come from their facility to see if they agreed with us, then send it back and when we sent it back, have somebody call us back and say it's all right here. We'd go down there, or they would ship it back, and we'd say, 'It still isn't okay,' and ship it back again."

Consider the absurdity of this arrangement: "One of the vendors is in Amesbury, which is a twenty-minute ride from here. Why the hell are we waiting for something to get delivered, which could take a full day in a truck, to come down here? It probably sits for another day or two before we look at it. Then we find out it isn't good; it takes another day to get it back there; then probably another two days for them to verify, and all of that is cost."

Another problem was "the late shipment that wasn't here when we needed it, which was a disaster. Having it earlier is not a disaster, but that's also a problem, because now you've got an inventory carrying charge."

It was all, Marsh said, "a lot of dumbness."

In the case of the sheet metal suppliers, that dumbness has largely been eliminated, prompting Marsh to reflect afterward that Dr. Deming "says so appropriately that you just need to think logically, and basically do simple things."

The Lawrence plant sought to make changes in its vendor program. The new approach was labeled "100-100," for 100 percent quality and 100 percent on-time delivery. The first step was to cease using supplies on an "as-is" basis. If the item was not precisely what Honeywell wanted, the company would either rework it on site or send it back to the vendor, but only once. Subsequent unsatisfactory deliveries would be refused.

This new policy was accompanied by intensified efforts to communicate with vendors. Sometimes Honeywell would find out that their own specifications or drawings were causing the problem. They therefore adopted a new-culture policy of tailoring their orders to their vendors' processes so as not to drive them out of an existing system into one that was nonstandard and rife with defects.

The old-culture policy, Marsh explained, was to develop a Honeywell specification without bothering to find out the effect on the supplier. Meanwhile, the supplier held that "it's work, and I'll do it. But I can't do it well, but they'll probably take it anyway." Usually, Marsh said, "we did. We very seldom sent anything back."

These broad changes raised the acceptance level of incoming lots from 83 percent in 1981 to 98 percent just five years later. As a result, Lawrence was able to cut down on its incoming inspection program and also reduce by two-thirds the number of suppliers.

One area in need of improvement still eluded Marsh, however. He had long been uncomfortable with the quality of incoming sheet metal. There were problems ranging from late deliveries to unsatisfactory paint jobs. What was black to a supplier, for example, might not be black to Honeywell.

Finally, in January 1985, Marsh met with the manager of purchasing and material control to try to improve the quality of sheet metal. They established a team that included representatives from quality assurance, purchasing, and material control, as well as a design engineer and an engineer from manufacturing. The team reviewed the records of its sheet metal vendors. There were thirty-one they had used in the past. The year before, they had actually made purchases from fourteen, with the orders concentrated among nine. Of those nine, the team selected the five who had done most of the work. They were not necessarily the highest in quality, but they did have the capacity to satisfy all of Honeywell's sheet metal needs. Four were in the immediate area. The largest was in Wabash, Indiana.

That same month, they invited the five suppliers for discussions. Recounted Marsh, "We opened by saying, 'We want to work with you, if you want to work in this program, and these are the requirements: defect-free product, on-time delivery. We're going to give the orders to you, and they're going to stay with you. We'll meet with you monthly, and we will tell you where we are in the business, rather than call you on the phone Thursday and tell you don't send Friday's shipment because we don't need it. We'll tell you where we're going as far out as we can see it on a monthly basis.

"Also, we recognize that we're part of your problem. And we're going to sit down with the design people, with the production people, with the quality people and with your people and define the requirements and what we might be doing to you, and we'll fix them."

Both buyer and suppliers visited each other's facilities. The sheet metal vendors saw how their product was being used. Honeywell witnessed how the suppliers filled their orders. The monthly meetings promised by Honeywell alternated between Honeywell and the vendors' plants.

The local vendors agreed that it made sense to audit the product before shipping. No longer was it necessary to return a completed order. "Now we can go right back into process as it's being made to audit and fix it if a fix is required," Marsh said.

In the start-up phase of a new piece, which is when problems usually develop, the vendor now could call for a verbal okay as it flowed through the line. Defects were detected early, before the vendor had manufactured large numbers of an unsatisfactory product. In addition, Honeywell began to consult vendors in the design stages of new products. Together, they would go through each drawing to make sure they understood and agreed on the requirements. In the old culture, Marsh said, this was done "by perception—I've got a drawing. Looks okay to me. I send it to you. I don't hear back from you. It must be all right."

After just five months, deliveries from the four local vendors met the 100-100 Rule: 100 percent on-time, 100 percent defect-free. In December, the month preceding the new program, there were thirty late deliveries. Three months later, there were none.

The largest of Honeywell's local sheet metal vendors, Cado Fabrications in Amesbury, Massachusetts, is a strong advocate of the new approach. In the past, said Cado President Rick Cayer, "the customer always viewed you as an adversary. [They thought] you were trying to get as much money as possible." All communication was with the purchasing department. "If the buyer didn't answer the phone when you happened to be having a problem in manufacturing—or, as frequently happened, wasn't much interested—you were out of luck." Now there are direct lines with quality, inspection, and engineering. "It's taken away the adversary position," Cayer said. "We're both in this in a partnership, really."

At Cado's request, he said, Honeywell allowed his management and quality staff to tour their plant and also furnished a photographer, who took pictures of final products to bring back to workers. Cado makes cabinets, panels, and chassis for internal components. Explained Cayer, "One of our biggest problems is our people asking us 'How is this product used?' 'Where does it go?' All they knew was, they were making a panel." Now the plastic-encased photographs hang where workers can see them. Although this may seem like a small thing, the photographs are not only helpful in manufacturing, Cayer said, they give workers a sense of pride.

Having assurances of long runs, Cayer said, sometimes makes it possible to offer Honeywell lower prices and also justifies purchasing new equipment for those particular orders.

Other customers, he pointed out, also benefit from Honeywell's program, since their production comes off the same lines. "We can't say we're going to give one customer that quality and Honeywell this quality." Because of that and other practices such as SQC and just-in-time inventory, Cado's in-house reject level dropped from 10 to 2 percent.

Back at Honeywell, Ron Cote, supervisor for mechanical purchasing, also welcomed the change. People in his position are "no longer off by ourselves making purchasing type decisions for the factory. When things go wrong, you're not out on a limb. In all," he said, "the communications are just unreal."

The process is time-consuming, but as issues are resolved and people get used to working with each other, Marsh predicts that the need for monthly meetings will fade. "Eventually, the goal is to get to where we don't have to meet. We'll meet because we just want to see each other and discuss our successes."

Chapter 26

·

Toward a Critical Mass:

*American Telephone & Telegraph,
Merrimack Valley Works, North
Andover, Massachusetts*

Situated an hour's drive north of Boston on a 169-acre site along
the tree-fringed Merrimack River, the long two-story yellow brick
building housing AT&T's massive Merrimack Valley Works over-
looks a lawn as large and nearly as well-tended as a football field.
The section that is visible from the road is a only quarter of the
plant. Behind are more buildings, and to the sides are parking lots
for six thousand cars. The perimeter of the main building measures a mile.

Ten thousand people work here; 6,500 of them are shop employees who turn out an array of circuit packs, bays, printed
wiring boards, quartz crystal transformers, and thin film circuits
used in the transmission of telephone messages, television programs, and data. At 3 P.M., as they stream from the plant, there
are traffic jams for fifteen minutes in both directions.

An additional five hundred are employed by Bell Labs in one
wing of the building; they design about half the products that the
plant manufactures. The remaining employees are supervisors,
managers, and engineers—known as "tech-pros," for technical-
professionals—and the clerical staff.

The plant is an enormous presence in the Merrimack Valley.
Said general manager Robert E. Cowley, Jr., a tall, balding man

with a clipped accent and a welcoming manner, "We have a profound impact on the economy of this Merrimack Valley area. . . . It would be a big bang, I'll tell you, if it were to be that we would go under."

Like Dr. Deming, Cowley believes that a company's role is to stay in business. On the wall of his spacious wood-paneled office overlooking the plant's vast expanse of lawn is a large sheet of paper containing a mandate that Deming followers would recognize as the Fourteenth Point: "Create a structure in top management that will push every day on the above Thirteen Points." Cowley had taken that command to heart. So impressed had he been with Dr. Deming, whom he first heard at a GOAL breakfast, that he had decided to spread the message by sending all the salaried employees—some two thousand of his workforce—to his seminars, and in so doing create the structure that Dr. Deming urged.

He believes that "if you're going to have an impact, you really need to get a critical mass of people educated, talking the same language, understanding the same concepts, so that these folks can really have an influence on the way we do business." He had felt a sense of urgency about the process. "After all, we can't wait as long as it took the Japanese—my stars, fifteen years. In fifteen years we'd be out of business, I'm afraid."

Not that AT&T had been in any danger of perishing. Nevertheless, the company, including the Merrimack Valley Works, was experiencing strong competitive pressure for the first time within memory, and that made it receptive to the changes advocated by Dr. Deming.

On January 1, 1984—a day known as "D-Day" in company annals—AT&T was required under court order to divest itself of its twenty-three Bell Telephone companies. Until then, the Merrimack plant had been one of several in the Western Electric Division. It remained part of AT&T after divestiture, taking the corporate name.

Even though they were not required to do so, the Bell companies in fact had bought the bulk of their equipment from Western Electric, with the exception of some specialty items. Some forward-thinking people in the company realized, however, that the widespread availability of telecommunications technology in the United States and abroad could threaten that relationship. Indeed, competing companies were poised to move into the market. Already there was some discussion of how Western Electric could best concentrate its manufacturing resources.

With the advent of D-Day, the Merrimack Valley Works discovered there were understudies waiting in the wings—companies like Nippon Electric and Fujitsu in Japan, Northern Telecom in Canada, CIT-Alcatel in France, and—closer to home—Lynch Communications, Raytheon, and Transcom, the latter founded by a group of former AT&T employees.

In sum, Cowley said, "We don't have an assured market. We really don't." Some of the former Bell companies buy the plant's products, and some don't. He continued, "That's the importance of Deming's Fourteen Points—staying in business. That's fairly critical—it is for the ten thousand people who work here, I'll tell you that."

Staying in business is Dr. Deming's First Point. As luck would have it, even before D-Day sounded a quality alarm for all of AT&T, the Merrimack Valley Works had already enlisted the man Cowley calls "The Good Doctor." In 1982, several members of the quality control department were converted to his methods at a seminar hosted by GOAL.

There was irony in this turn of events. In earlier times AT&T had been a repository of statistical methods for achieving quality. Indeed, Deming's mentor, Walter A. Shewhart, had worked for Bell Labs in the 1920s, where he developed the statistical methods that Deming teaches today. While still a university student, Deming himself had worked summers at Western Electric's Hawthorne plant in Chicago. When Cowley began his career with AT&T decades later at the same plant, he recalled, statistical techniques were still popular. The 328-page *Statistical Quality Control Handbook*, published by Western Electric in 1956, is a Bible in the field.

Gradually, however, the techniques had become less popular. Managers had begun to use them in a punitive manner, not to find flaws in the system but rather to single out workers in need of "corrective" action. There were protests from the union, and it was agreed that the control charts would come off the machines, to be filed away in binders. They thus came to serve little purpose, either good or bad.

The reprinting dates of the AT&T handbook reflected the gradual decline in quality control techniques throughout American industry. The first edition was in 1956, followed by another in

1958, and then nothing until a reprinting in 1964. The handbook was reprinted again in 1967 and 1970, followed by a seven-year hiatus until 1977. Since then, however, the dates have increased in frequency, reflecting a renewed interest in statistics among AT&T and other U.S. corporations. It was reprinted in April 1980 and again in June 1983, October 1983, March 1984, and May 1984. Much of the sales were to outside companies, including ones in Japan.

Meanwhile, in 1973, Bob Cowley's career had taken him from engineering to sales administration and from the midwest to the east. There he experienced firsthand some "rough sledding from a quality aspect." His sales division had responsibility for installation and repairs of equipment purchased by the Bell Telephone companies, and he was aware that Western Electric's vaunted reputation for high quality was not always warranted.

Cowley was concerned about quality when he took over the Merrimack Valley Works in early 1982, and his concern was reinforced by a trip to Japan that he made with several colleagues shortly after assuming his post. They visited a half-dozen or so companies, but Nippon Electric, in particular, stood out in his mind. In a presentation entitled "Inventory is Evil," his Japanese counterparts explained that Nippon had used inventory to mask problems. To illustrate their point, they used a simple line drawing of underwater rocks beneath a calm, level surface.

One day, management issued an edict ordering that inventories be sliced by 25 percent. The "water level" dropped. "Lo and behold," Cowley related, "they found a whole bunch of problems that they classified as rocks beneath the surface there. And so they were forced to solve these problems because they couldn't live with that inventory cut.

"They ran into the first problem. It stopped them dead in the water. They couldn't ship a thing. They had to solve the problem before they could ship. They finally got rid of that rock and, bang, they ran into the next one. They solved that problem. It was painful. I guess it took them close to four years. They accomplished a task. At the end, they [the employees] came in, waiting for a pat on the back. They cut it again. . . . And lo and behold, what happened? There was a whole bunch of more rocks."

The story illustrates the Japanese notion of continual improvement. But it also suggested to Cowley that his division was probably also using inventories as a crutch.

There were reasons to carry inventory. If one were to catalog the items used at Merrimack Valley, there would be more than one hundred thousand. The absence of a single one of them could stall a production line. Inventory was a hedge against running out if a vendor didn't deliver as ordered, for whatever reason.

Inventory built up when designs changed, as they often did at Merrimack Valley. So rapid were improvements in technology that the bulk of the products had a life cycle of only two to three years. Then, too, customers sometimes changed orders, leaving the plant with excess stock. And if projected needs were wrong, then still more inventory piled up. Cowley's calculations led him to believe that many millions of dollars were tied up in excess inventory. Carrying costs on that were 28 to 30 percent a year.

On Cowley's trip to Japan, Dr. Deming's name popped up more than once. Indeed, three companies who greeted the AT&T delegation had won the Deming Prize. Given this and his ongoing concern with quality, Cowley was receptive to entreaties from his engineers to hear Dr. Deming. There was a personal component to his decision: Cowley was facing up to the fact that his own new American-made car was a lemon that spent more time in the garage than on the road. He did not want Merrimack Valley to go the way of Detroit.

What would become an all-out quality effort under Dr. Deming began inauspiciously enough. Cowley was invited by Deming converts to attend a GOAL business breakfast at a nearby motel and hear both Dr. Deming and then-Senator Paul Tsongas speak. Tsongas canceled at the last minute, and Dr. Deming turned Cowley off with his irascible manner and his message, which came across insulting more than enlightening. "I didn't get too much out of the affair," Cowley said.

But his Deming disciples wouldn't give up. They urged him to attend a full four-day Deming seminar. Cowley agreed, provided that a hundred other AT&T volunteers could be recruited.

That first seminar was held at the Sea Crest Hotel on Cape Cod. (It is important, Cowley and others say, that seminar sites be located well away from the workplace, so that busy executives are not tempted to leave when crises arise. Ideally, executives should also be on hand for formal and informal discussions in the evening.)

At that four-day seminar, a format was developed that would become standard for the later AT&T sessions. The group assembled on Monday night to hear an AT&T executive talk about the purpose of the seminar. The seminar itself began Tuesday morning, and on Tuesday night there was a social hour that brought people together from throughout the plant. Explains quality engineering department chief Bryce Colburne, one of the original Deming converts, "All of a sudden, people who never even knew the plant manager before are standing there with a drink in their hands talking about quality problems. That was a very valuable outcome from these seminars."

On Wednesday night, with the seminar in full gear, the group broke into teams to address each of the Fourteen Points and several of the Deadly Diseases. The teams were organized with respect to job assignments. Someone from purchasing, for example, was almost always assigned to tackle Point Four: "End the practice of awarding business on the basis of the price tag."

The teams considered the meaning of the Points and how they applied to Merrimack Valley. On Thursday night, there was a presentation that might last as long as six hours.

The entire Deming approach, Cowley said, was "a significant conceptual notion to me." He was particularly taken with the Shewhart Cycle—the Plan, Do, Check, Act routine—which suggests that "if you're going to improve a process, you've got to understand the process—as good or as infirm as it may be."

That first seminar was the beginning of a harmonious relationship between Cowley and Dr. Deming that would be filled with mutual respect on both sides. The seminars continued at a rate of two or three a year, always at points some distance from Merrimack Valley. Although AT&T staffers also attended seminars given by GOAL and George Washington University, those that Dr. Deming arranged solely for Merrimack Valley seemed to be the most effective. When a group of coworkers attends en masse, Cowley said, "they seem to develop a spirit. It's kind of like a college class. People meet each other, and they carry on that relationship even well beyond the seminar itself."

Said Colburne, "Bob Cowley's insight was in knowing that if you only had twenty or thirty people in a factory this size . . . they could be completely swamped. There would be no way that they could even begin to have an impression. Bob Cowley recognized it was absolutely necessary that all the management people—the managers and the technical people—at least have a basic understanding of the words that Deming used, so that if they go into a meeting and somebody starts talking about 'random defects,' they understand what they're talking about." He added, "After the seminars were over, you could see a marked change in meetings around here.

"We had a meeting one day with a manager, and during that meeting the term *random defects* was brought up. We started talking about yields and defectives, and the manager wanted to be sure that we weren't talking about random defects; that we were talking about a serious, consistent problem. These were things that were never talked about before. You'd just talk about a defect, and every defect was a defect." In short, there was no distinction between defects arising from the system and those resulting from special causes.

Convincing workers that management was serious about quality was a formidable task. Each employee had been given a brochure with a letter from Cowley detailing management's commitment to the quality teachings of Dr. Deming. It contained a startling admission.

After divestiture, the Bell operating companies had formulated a set of standards called a Quality Program Evaluation (QPE) for assessing potential suppliers. Merrimack Valley had the opportunity to test itself against these standards while still in the trial stage. The plant did poorly in several of fourteen categories. "This does not necessarily mean that the quality of our products is poor," Cowley wrote. "It does show, however, that we have not focused our quality program upon the points at which the QPE team will be looking." When Merrimack Valley was tested a year or so later, it had improved in every category.

Cowley explained that he wanted Merrimack Valley employees to know the plant had quality problems. "Our people need to understand that. If you don't talk to your people, how are they going to know what we want?"

In a section entitled "The Cost of Quality," the same brochure noted that during 1982, 17 percent of manufacturing costs were devoted to finding, repairing, or disposing of defects—inspection and rework, in other words.

The brochure also included a list of the Fourteen Points, entitled with some significance, "The Fourteen Obligations of Top Management." And there was also a policy statement that "the Merrimack Valley Works commits itself to quality as its foremost business objective."

Meanwhile, the company began to demonstrate its commitment to quality. More meaningful to workers than Cowley's words was his edict that shipments must go out by Friday, when all quality controls were in place. A common practice had been to hold shipments until the weekend, when only skeleton crews were available to handle the load. (One joke was, "When push comes to shove, what are you going to shove out the door?")

Cowley says he thinks the division has made progress on all of the Fourteen Points with the exception of Point Eleven, the edict against numerical quotas. Over the years, quotas or work standards were imposed on workers through contracts with the union, the Communications Workers of America, and now they cannot be arbitrarily dropped. Only through negotiations can they be eliminated, a process that will take time.

On the recessed bookshelves of Bob Cowley's office are two framed eight-by-ten-inch color photographs. One is of a smiling, dark-haired Miss Massachusetts, and the other is of an ebullient Dr. Deming. Both were taken at an impromptu birthday party in October 1983, when Dr. Deming turned eighty-three during an AT&T seminar at the Sea Crest.

Dr. Deming later wrote delightedly about the event. "To my whole astonishment, the whole dining room was a birthday party, with a big birthday cake and fifty people. We had clams and lobster, followed by birthday cake. . . . Next day was my birthday. At lunch, all 250 people, came further celebration. Mr. Cowley brought in Miss Massachusetts, though I would say that most of the women at the seminar were equally pretty or better. Someone rolled in a huge birthday cake. Everybody was back on the job at one o'clock."[1]

Two years later, in 1985, Dr. Deming would again celebrate his birthday with AT&T at Sea Crest. It would be his eighth seminar for the company, and it would bring to close to two thousand the number of salaried employees who had taken the course.

The Big Green Wall: Breaking Down Barriers

The wall was simply a fact of life at AT&T. Built of glazed green bricks, it had been incorporated into the design when the building was constructed in 1956 to separate some operations from others. It ringed the interior on three sides, on two levels, parallel to each outside wall at a distance of about sixty feet.

With time, the wall had come to have an identity of its own. Products might come and go, but the wall remained in place, as secure and immutable as AT&T itself. Even though it wasn't load-bearing, the wall was immovable. It was an unwritten rule.

But even as the wall remained solidly in place, AT&T was undergoing a drastic transformation, losing all the "Baby Bells" that had been so much a part of the corporation. In certain shops, the wall had outlived its original justification and was becoming something of an impediment.

Such was the case in the printed wiring board shop, where the wall isolated the area in which boards were plated, etched, scrubbed, cleaned, degreased, and coated—all "wet" operations involving large-scale chemical processing.

A printed wiring board begins as a piece of laminate—two sheets of copper separated by an epoxy-glass layer. In its finished state, it is a complex circuit of copper connections, drilled with holes to receive components. It is integral to every piece of modern electronic equipment.

In the first production stage at Merrimack Valley, a film or negative of the design was made by a photographic process that took place in a small room filled with large photographic equipment. These films were hand-carried to the Yellow Room six hundred feet away, so named for the eerie amber color of the special fluorescent lights that produce no ultraviolet rays that can damage the boards. In the Yellow Room, the boards were first laminated with light-sensitive film, and then the filmed design was transferred to the boards. Next, the boards were developed in another room, eighty feet away over a zigzag course past other equipment.

When this process was complete, the board was delivered by pushcart to the first machine for tooling, then on to the next and the next, moving between and in and out of the wet chemistry areas encompassed by the green wall.

From start to finish, the board traveled a distance of 1,700 feet. To be sure, it could have—and had—been a lengthier journey. Until seven years earlier, when there was a major renovation of the shop, the trip had been 3,200 feet. The redesign had reduced it dramatically to 1,500, but with the addition of new machinery, the distance had crept back up to 1,700.

The man in charge of the printed wiring board department was Len Winn, who had started out with AT&T in 1960 as an engineer. In every organization, it seems, at least one individual emerges who embraces the Deming method as if it were a religion. If no one does, nothing happens. At AT&T, Winn was that person. Attending a Deming seminar merely confirmed many beliefs he had had all along about how a business should be run. Now it seemed as if he might have the freedom to act on them.

As an engineer, it disturbed Winn that the earlier renovation of his shop had not been as efficient as it could have been. He had known at the time of a route that could have reduced the boards' journey to much less than 1,500 feet. But because he was told that the green wall couldn't be removed, he had been forced to settle for the longer route.

Following their exposure to Dr. Deming, Winn and several engineers who worked for him set about making a number of changes over the next few years that would ultimately drive yields up 20 percent. No single dramatic change was responsible, but rather a succession of small changes. As simple an idea as layering paper between boards at critical points to prevent them from scratching each other had cut down significantly on defects. So, too, had placing control charts on ink-screening equipment, so that operators would have a clear statistical signal on when and how to adjust the ink flow, rather than having to rely on visual inspection.

One change eluded Winn, however. Analysis showed that fully 50 percent of all defects came from material handling. And in the boards' 1,700-foot journey from start to finish, they were handled a lot. Two hundred carts and dozens of people were required to transfer the boards from one point to another.

That was not the only problem. The whole layout violated Winn's notion that people need to be able to relate to each other in an easy, spontaneous manner. Dr. Deming reinforced that notion and gave it a name in Point Nine: "Break down barriers between departments."

Some of the most overlooked barriers were the most obvious: those that were physical. Even before Dr. Deming, Winn had seen to it that the offices occupied by the ten or so engineers under his supervision were connected in a way that forced people into contact. They had to thread their way past each others' desks on their way to and from their own. Although the arrangement might look awkward, and even in some cases be distracting, communication was natural and ongoing rather than formal. Winn felt that this was worth the inconvenience. He had also bought a coffeepot and placed it at a strategic point so people would gather within the office and talk to each other.

He itched to bring people together in the printed wiring board shop. It bothered him that from most of the points where a supervisor could stand, it was impossible to see who was doing what. "If you've got one operation feeding another operation some distance away, the supervisors have a very difficult time in managing," he explained. "It's sort of like having a garage with the tools down the street. You can't work that way. You've got to have your tools all together. You need to see things. Running a factory is a very visual operation."

In addition, there was a curious phenomenon that he didn't understand beyond knowing it was true. It was a kind of Murphy's Law of the factory floor. "The farther away two items are, the more likely it is that inventory will build up between them." In the printed wiring board shop, stacks of boards piled up at different work stations, representing excess inventory that was costing the company money. He knew from experience that reducing the distances would reduce the inventory.

In a sense, it was brash to propose redesigning the shop so soon after it had been done. But had not Dr. Deming ordered Winn's superiors to "drive out fear"? Coupled with the edict of "continuous improvement," as Winn saw it, this translated into not being "afraid to say I'm going to do it again, I'm going to do it better this time."

Doing something over again in a better way, Winn decided, didn't mean you had done it wrong the first time. "What it means is I've learned something new in the process. It's a great thing to have a situation where you say I can do it better tomorrow and even better the next day. Some people have that very nasty habit of saying, 'Why didn't you do it right the first time? Then you wouldn't have to do it over again.' That's a terrible detriment to progress, because you won't do anything. It's like asking why the Wright Brothers didn't design the 747 first."

Two of his engineers, Mike Sayler and Burrell Lowery, began to map out a redesigned shop that did indeed trim the manufacturing distance on a board to five hundred feet. The plan was to locate the Yellow Room next to the Camera Room, now six hundred feet away. This would cut out a big chunk of travel, and it would also eliminate having someone carry the films from one room to the other. Winn had seen films fall out of folders onto the floor, where they got dirty or scratched; left on desks during coffee breaks or, even worse, under coffee cups.

"Now," Winn explained, "the person who makes the film is talking to the person who uses it. If something went wrong with the last one, they say, 'The last one you gave me had all these scratches on it.' Or if there's a big rush on it, the person who brings over the film might say, 'Watch out for image number four—there's something wrong with it, but I had to get it out.' So you have communication that's so much better than before." Moreover, it would now be possible to eliminate one of the film files each room needed and have a single set of known quality that they could share.

Relocating the Yellow Room next to the Camera Room had another big advantage. It would mean that the humidity and temperature would be constant for both areas. In the past, no matter how hard they had tried to control them, differences had seemed unavoidable and had caused small but undesirable changes in the film and the subsequent product. Then, too, the boards became time-sensitive when they were laminated with light-sensitive film, and this rearrangement was clearly going to speed up the operation.

In the other areas of the shop, Winn and his staff wanted to station the heavy tooling in a logical, closely connected auto-mated sequence.

The cost of the project was considerable: an estimated $1.8 million. But the savings in labor, inventory, and time would be considerable. The payback period was estimated at eighteen months. And they could make use of new, nonpolluting aqueous technology. Most significant of all, the new system would cut the manufacturing interval by 75 percent. The advertised interval was now four weeks, but they knew they could do it faster, because when a customer really pressed, an order could be turned out in a day or two. The new plan would move all orders along at the same fast rate, with no delays. There would be no "hot" orders because everything would be hot.

There was only one problem with this scenario.

The green wall would have to go.

If nothing else, it was certainly going to be a test of whether management was serious about changing the old way of doing things. Winn and the two engineers, Sayler and Lowery, decided to go for it. Recalls Winn, "We said to the management, if you really want to do this job right, stop fooling around. Give us a license and let us see what we come up with."

The same boss who previously had declared the green wall off limits, but who had since attended a Deming seminar, this time adopted a wait-and-see posture. He told the engineers, "Show me what you can do."

Two and a half years later, the wall was on its way out and Winn had been promoted to quality control manager for the Merrimack Valley Works. In his place as chief of the printed wiring board shop was Mike Sayler. Together they recall that it was not all that difficult to convince the boss to do away with the wall. Said Sayler, "He went to the Dr. Deming lectures. I think he learned from that."

One of Winn's goals in his position as quality czar was to continue pressuring people to speak the same language. Like the wall, words could be a barrier. Quality engineers spoke a language that too few in the company understood, speaking of "AOQLs" (Average Outgoing Quality Limits), "three sigma limits," and "early warning" stages. In short, Winn said, "These people have created a jargon or a group of words that reduces the amount of communication between people. And I see one of my jobs here to start to create a vocabulary so that we can understand each other, so there's no mystery." People, he added, "work together when they understand each other and can see each other."

Thanks to Bob Cowley's initiative in establishing a critical mass, everyone at the management level now speaks the same Deming language. The advantage is that, as Winn put it, "if we're both trained in the same way, then there's no barrier, is there?"

The Merrimack Valley Works and the Third Deadly Disease

Perhaps none of Dr. Deming's methods gives rise to more debate than his ban on performance ratings, merit pay, annual reviews—whatever name is given to a company's practice of evaluating its employees in some fashion and doling out financial rewards accordingly.

Printed Wiring Board Shop Flow

Before   After

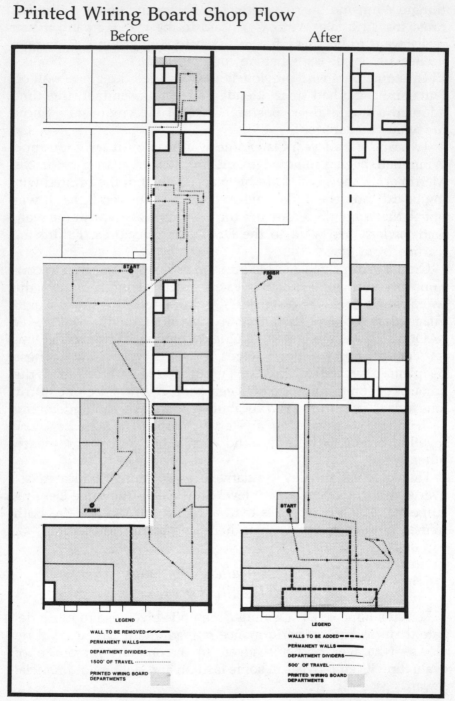

LEGEND

WALL TO BE REMOVED

PERMANENT WALLS

DEPARTMENT DIVIDERS

1500' OF TRAVEL

PRINTED WIRING BOARD
DEPARTMENTS

LEGEND

WALLS TO BE ADDED

PERMANENT WALLS

DEPARTMENT DIVIDERS

500' OF TRAVEL

PRINTED WIRING BOARD
DEPARTMENTS

—AT&T, Merrimack Valley

"The effects are devastating," Dr. Deming tells his audiences. "Such a system substitutes short-term performance for long-term planning, wrecks teamwork, and nurtures rivalry. It builds fear and leaves people bitter or despondent, unfit for work for weeks after receipt of the rating. Moreover, it encourages mobility of management."

As long as anyone could remember at AT&T, the salaries of management employees—engineers, for the most part—had been based on performance reviews. The particulars varied from time to time, but the basic theme had remained the same: supervisors were to rank their subordinates on the basis of performance, which would determine salaries.

The Merrimack Valley management knew that dissatisfaction with performance reviews was widespread among the engineers, or tech-pros. It was a factor in an organizing drive by the Communications Workers of America, who represented the hourly workers in the plant. Indeed, General Manager Bob Cowley thought it might be the principal factor. (The drive was derailed in part when AT&T mounted a successful legal challenge to the composition of the group the union sought to represent. Another damper was the failure of a similar drive at AT&T's plant in Reading, Pennsylvania.)

Whenever the subject of performance reviews came up at a Deming seminar, there was a long and spirited discussion. "Deming hated it," said Robert Pettirossi, department chief of technical-professional relations. "He thought it was one of the worst things we did, but he really didn't offer any concrete solution to the problem or an alternative, other than just pay everybody at the same level the same salary. I think people still have a real problem with that."

Finally, Merrimack Valley decided to bite the bullet and change its system. A committee of twelve engineers and five department chiefs, all selected by their peers, was formed. The committee was charged with studying the current system and recommending changes.

At Merrimack Valley, engineers are divided by training and experience into three categories: engineering associates, occupational engineers, and senior engineers. For the purpose of rating, each category was divided into eight "bands" based on performance. It was the supervisor's job each year to decide how well an employee had performed and then to assign that employee to the appropriate band. Salaries were set according to band number, the eighth band receiving the lowest amount and the first band the highest.

Because of the way the money was divided, the system required that there be a set number of people in each band. Thus, if band six was short a person, then someone had to be bumped up from band seven or bumped down from band five. Not the least of the problems with the system was that an employee's rating was always relative. No matter how well an employee did a job, others thought to be doing better were ranked higher. A supervisor could not tell an employee what to do to rise in the hierarchy since it always depended on what others were doing.

Another problem was the subjectivity involved in the decisions. An employee who was having problems with a supervisor could be in big trouble. No matter how hard supervisors might try to be objective, Pettirossi said, "some subjectivity gets into it. There's just no two ways about it."

Also, those on top tended to stay there—a phenomenon that the committee believed derived from human nature. Supervisors just didn't like to tell people they were being demoted. An employee in question might well challenge the ruling, and then there could be a confrontation. Unless a supervisor had kept careful notes of the employee's mistakes or shortcomings, the ruling could be difficult to defend. The whole process was so unpleasant that it was easier to leave people where they were. This tended to limit mobility for people at the bottom, regardless of their talents.

When workers complained about not getting ahead, no one took responsibility for it. "Don't blame me, blame the system" was an easy way out for supervisors. In fact, there was a good deal of justification for that response.

Although the names and band levels were a closely guarded secret, the number of employees at each pay level was public knowledge, and employees could see where they ranked, which didn't do a lot for morale.

Such was the system as the committee began the meetings, which would take place weekly for longer than a year. Not everyone, they discovered, disapproved of the system. There was support for it among people who were at the top and among those, Pettirossi said, "who thought they had a shot of getting there." And no one, it turned out, was in favor of throwing out the merit system altogether.

What they fashioned, however, was a radically different procedure. Instead of eight categories, there would be only three: "exceeded expectations," "met expectations," and "didn't meet expectations." The "expectations" would be goals set at the beginning of the year between the employee and the supervisor.

Unlike the old system, categories would not carry fixed salaries. A change from one to another would determine only the amount of the raise or its absence. Moreover, each time an employee exceeded expectations, expectations would rise for the next year. Thus, the theory went, it would be progressively more difficult to exceed these rising expectations. In time, there would be slippage into the "met expectations" category. This would mean that the best employees would not always be in the number-one category, which meant, in turn, that there would no longer be a rank order in effect.

Nor would there be quotas. If everyone was in the "exceeded expectations" category, then the available funds would be divided among whatever people were there.

An appeal procedure was also built into the new system. An unhappy employee could ask for a review of the decision by a supervisor higher than his immediate boss. If still dissatisfied, then the employee could request a review by an ad hoc committee of four volunteers, drawn from a list kept by Pettirossi's office. The committee would have to include two supervisors. The others could be either supervisors or peers, as the employee wished. The appeal committee would vote by secret ballot. No member would ever know the outcome.

Their proposals for reforming the system completed, the committee received management approval to take them to the engineers for a show of support. After much discussion and some minor modifications, the committee's recommendation to adopt the new proposals received a hearty 88 percent endorsement. Cowley and his staff okayed the plan, and it was used for the first time to determine 1984 salaries.

Pettirossi conceded that, in time, failings may become apparent in the new system. For the moment, however, it has one distinct advantage. Under the old system, "you could sit down and ask your boss, 'What do I have to do to get into the top band?' He could not tell you what, because in a system of forced distribution not everybody can be in the top band. Under our system today, he can tell you what you must do to meet or exceed expectations."

Perhaps the best thing going for it, he said, is the way it was developed. "The people who were going to be affected by it really generated the plan. That's the big plus."

Chapter 27

•

The Philadelphia Model:

Philadelphia Area Council for Excellence, Philadelphia, Pennsylvania

At the stroke of 11 A.M. on July 3, 1985, in Philadelphia, a gathering of men and women in business dress filed into a small, brick colonial building known as Carpenters' Hall, where the first Continental Congress had met more than two hundred years earlier. Composed of bankers, lawyers, congresspeople, CEOs, and labor leaders, the group was present on this sunny summer morning to sign a "Second Declaration of Independence"—a document whose contents sounded extraordinarily like Dr. Deming's Fourteen Points.

"We shall adopt a new philosophy for a new economic age," this second Declaration began. It continued, "We shall create a constancy of purpose for improvement of product and service." And so it went, through nine such statements, concluding with "It is essential to eliminate fear in order to foster a creative environment."

After introductory remarks by Mayor Wilson Goode, the signers stepped up to attach their names with yellow-plumed ballpoint pens to the parchment document on which the Declaration was scripted. Edward Toohey, the small, wiry president of the AFL-CIO Philadelphia Council, delivered a spontaneous endorsement. "We subscribe fully and completely to the principles involved in all the foregoing statements," he said.

The event was largely the work of the twentieth person to sign the Declaration, a dark-haired dynamo named Mary Ann Gould, the chair of an organization called the Philadelphia Area Council for Excellence (PACE), an arm of the Greater Philadelphia Chamber of Commerce. The similarity of this Declaration to the Fourteen Points was no accident. Gould was a fervent Deming disciple who was successfully using Deming's methods in her own company, Janbridge, Inc., a young, growing electronics manufacturer.

Under her prodding, the Chamber of Commerce had mounted a major drive for quality, sponsoring several Deming seminars and establishing a coalition of nine companies known as the Quality Round Table, which was working with a Deming-endorsed consultant. The nine included several of the largest companies in the area—Campbell Soup Company, Rohm & Haas Company, and Philadelphia Electric—as well as an assortment of smaller firms like Janbridge.

Housed in Chamber offices, PACE is now that organization's single largest program for improving the area's business climate. PACE has its own budget and staff, plus access to the Chamber's resources and the endorsement of Philadelphia's business leaders. In short, it represents a major commitment to change the way business functions in the Delaware Valley and to establish the region as a pioneer in quality products and services.

Several weeks after the July 3 gathering, the framed Declaration came temporarily to rest on an easel in Mary Ann Gould's Janbridge office, near a fishbowl filled with the red and white beads that any Deming follower would recognize instantly as props for the bead experiment. Gould, a founder of PACE, was the only woman on the Chamber's executive board; she is a spokesperson for small and medium-size companies in the area.

The effort had begun in 1983, a year the Chamber was in the midst of change. A new generation of business leaders was looking for ways to overhaul the Chamber as part of a larger campaign to stimulate the Philadelphia business environment. Like much of the Snow Belt, Philadelphia was having severe economic problems, reflected in high unemployment and shuttered industries. A coalition of business and civic leaders agreed to mount a drive to attract new business. But Gould argued that the first step had to be a campaign to help existing industries prosper. She reasoned that unless the area had a healthy economic base, it was unlikely that any company would relocate. "If we can show we're doing something extraordinary here, everybody will be beating at your door."

Not everyone saw it that way. But there was enough support for her position that the Chamber forged ahead. It organized a "business improvement council" whose governing board drafted a mission statement: "to help the existing companies of the Delaware Valley grow and prosper and secondly to position the Delaware Valley as a leader."

In considering how to accomplish these lofty goals, the group bandied about a number of ideas. One option was to offer management seminars and programs on a wide variety of useful subjects. But they decided instead to concentrate on a single path so as not to fragment the effort. Given Gould's passion and firsthand knowledge of Deming, it was not surprising that "quality" became that path.

Explained Gould, "We had the environment in which Deming could be more readily accepted than in many other sections of the country—for the same reason as Japan. Japan probably never would have listened to Deming if they hadn't lost the war and recognized that their old ways couldn't make it. Here in Philadelphia, we weren't nearly that badly off, but we were losing jobs and our managers were willing to listen and act." Within the Chamber, she advocated the idea of "excellence," which she explained means "all-encompassing quality" in manufacturing, service, education, and government organizations. The business council became PACE.

As much as she was "scared to death" at the idea of involving Deming, whose ideas and personality might cause controversy, she was convinced that no one else could offer such "totality." The Deming method was not just another program or project. At Janbridge, where she had implemented his principles, she was seeing barriers fall and teamwork flourish, costs drop and productivity go up—all as Dr. Deming had predicted. Most of all, quality was improving dramatically.

She booked Dr. Deming for a half-day "overview" on January 19, 1984, along with two enthusiastic practitioners, John E. Driscoll, manufacturing director at AT&T's Merrimack Valley Works, and James K. Bakken, Ford Motor Company vice president.

Dr. Deming was in good form. "You say you can't do it?" he thundered at the half-awake executives who had gathered at 8

A.M. in the ballroom of the stately Bellevue Stratford Hotel. "Can't hold up against the Japanese? Such nonsense. You mean Americans can't do it? I don't believe that."

Gould need not have worried about the reaction. When Dr. Deming returned for full four-day seminars, first in March and again in July, the executives came back in force. Several hundred people representing more than a hundred companies attended each time.

Under the auspices of PACE, the Chamber scheduled a number of seminars on statistics and quality and brought in more speakers from companies with experience in Dr. Deming's methods.

But Gould was troubled. She realized that people were struggling with how to put the new methods to work in their companies. She wondered how to create a broad-based approach that would snowball among the Chamber of Commerce's constituency. She had a vision of companies working together in some fashion, sharing their experiences, learning from each other. Dr. Deming was intrigued by the idea. "He thought it was unique," she said. And when she suggested such a joint effort to the people attending the second seminar, several companies indicated strong interest.

On Dr. Deming's recommendation, she approached a statistical consultant, Brian Joiner of Madison, Wisconsin. Joiner had had a tangential relationship with Dr. Deming for nearly twenty years. Originally an industrial engineer, Joiner had taken a minor in statistics while in a master's degree program at the University of Tennessee, where he first learned of the work done by Shewhart and Deming. Later, working at the National Bureau of Standards, he had met Lola Deming and then Dr. Deming himself. Joiner had had little contact with Dr. Deming in later years as he pursued his career in academia first at Penn State, then at the University of Wisconsin. Joiner went on to Rutgers where he obtained a Ph.D. in statistics. But Dr. Deming reappeared in his life via the NBC White Paper. Joiner renewed his acquaintance in person. He began to study his books and other materials seriously. Seeking hands-on manufacturing experience, he worked as a statistical consultant at Hewlett-Packard for a summer and became familiar with what that company's Japanese affiliate had done to win the Deming Prize. In the fall of 1983, he and his wife Lauren founded Joiner Associates, marketing a statistical software package to help in the quality area.

When the call came from Mary Ann Gould on behalf of PACE,

Joiner reacted with apprehension more than appreciation. "They want me to transform the Delaware Valley," he told his wife that evening. She said she thought the project was too big. But Gould repeated her plea, and Dr. Deming personally urged him to take part. Finally, Joiner agreed. He hired an associate, Peter Scholtes, to share the responsibility. Scholtes was a management consultant with the city of Madison who had experience in team dynamics, leadership training, and organizational development. He was no Deming expert—he would later joke that his first week of on-the-job training was attending a Deming seminar—but Scholtes was impressed with Deming's belief that "people are inherently good."

Gould realized that Joiner would be feeling his way like the rest of them. "He was really just learning, too," she said. "Nobody really is an expert in this. . . . We knew we'd have to build the program. Nothing existed." Gould agreed to give a substantial amount of her own time in the first year.

So began a pattern in which Joiner and Scholtes typically spent three to four days out of each month in Philadelphia. Part of the time, representatives of the companies would gather for joint sessions, which almost always included a CEO session. The remaining time was spent in site visits. Gould, Joiner, and Scholtes met monthly to plan the structure of the Quality Round Table as well as the course content. They were assisted by the manager PACE had hired, Richard Ross, as well as PACE board members.

As a game plan, the group agreed that the companies had to come away from each monthly session having learned something new in statistics and human relations. As they put together a model for the companies to follow, they made several basic decisions. The first was to rely heavily on interdisciplinary project teams. This was based on the belief that, as Dr. Deming indicates in Point Nine, "some of the biggest problems are caused by barriers between departments." In addition, project teams were a way to "drive out fear," as mandated in Point Eight. When people work together as peers, without regard to status, fear is reduced. People in managerial positions, of course, would have to learn to give advice, not orders.

Project teams were not a new idea. But more emphasis was placed on using them in a way that would require commitment from top management, as Dr. Deming insists. So a second basic decision was to make top management—preferably the CEO or someone at the next level—responsible for the teams. This, Joiner reasoned, would emphasize "that management really wants to do this." It would make management available to give direction. "Otherwise, the team could go the wrong way or spin its wheels." And finally, the management team would learn from the experience "what barriers are out there—ignorance, lack of supervision. It also would learn what it takes to support a project team."

Gould, Joiner, and Scholtes believed in the top-down rather than the bottom-up approach to change. His experience with companies had taught Joiner that "things don't move up very much in organizations at all. They move down much more easily." Although it was easier to try to change things at the bottom, because workers were generally more enthusiastic than managers, there was low impact that way. Working at the top was difficult, but it had a high impact. Thus, the first project team would be at the top, among managers.

Finally, after deciding to use project teams and make top management responsible for them, the planning team made a third basic decision: to minimize up-front training. Not only was such training expensive, but the retention rate was low and "real-world problems are never like those in the classroom," Joiner says. Training is popular because it provides "the illusion that you've done something. You hear managers say, 'We've sent so many people to training. How many have you sent?' " Instead, Joiner and Scholtes would train people in the statistical and organizational skills on an as-needed basis. It was called "just-in-time training."

From the outset, Joiner and Scholtes realized that they were dealing with typical American companies, whose structure they characterized as "management by control." Top management sets goals based on projected profit levels and return on investment. The next level of management translates these profit-centered goals into production, sales, cost reduction, and time-saving objectives. Jobs throughout the organization are tuned to department objectives, performance standards, and production quotas, reinforced by rewards like bonuses and merit increases. Typically, bosses use pep talks, exhortations, and slogans to reinforce the effort. At the same time, there are penalties to discourage people from straying off the course. The system is logical and ingrained but is also authoritarian, inflexible, and stifling.

The PACE Quality Round Table companies, in one respect,

were more enlightened than the rest of corporate America: they recognized the need for change. At the outset, they outlined the following nine-phase approach.

Phase One: *Education and/or reeducation of top management in the Deming method*. Companies are instructed to form a management team, consisting of the manager or CEO and those reporting directly to the CEO, which meets on a regular basis. The job of this team is to develop strategies, set goals, identify priorities, and plan changes consistent with Dr. Deming's teachings. In time, the structure will prevail throughout the company. Each manager will be a member of a team led by his or her immediate supervisor and the leader of another team composed of direct reports.

Phase Two: *Systematic review of targets of opportunity*. The management team targets areas for improvement and decides how to expand such efforts throughout the company.

Phase Three: *Planning for the first projects*. The first project is selected and planned in detail. This requires the support of certain individuals. The services of a statistical consultant are required, or someone can be trained in-house. By whatever name— "organization development specialist" or "facilitator"—someone with skills in team-building and leadership training is needed. To support these individuals, a network of internal "Deming consultants" must be trained in basic statistical tools, group development, scientific approaches, and planning.

Phase Four: *First project is carried out*. A project team is established and educated in the Deming method. The team studies and defines its project, and work begins. It reports to the management team on a regular basis.

Phase Five: *Other preliminary implementation projects are planned and carried out*. The steps in Phases Three and Four are repeated. This is done until the management team feels it is ready for a comprehensive plan.

Phase Six: *Top management develops a comprehensive plan, a major escalation, especially in terms of the number of people who will be affected*. In this stage, Joiner and Scholtes envision waves of projects throughout the organization.

Phase Seven: *The first large-scale wave of projects is begun*. Previously only one or two projects have been done at a time. Now the first of an ongoing series of annual project waves is begun.

Phase Eight: *Succeeding waves of projects are done*. Each year another wave of projects is begun. The processes of annual corporate planning and annual implementation planning are merged.

Phase Nine: *Institutionalization.* This occurs when all of Deming's Fourteen Points are the natural way to carry out operations. Pervasive, never-ending improvement, with a constancy of purpose is a way of life.

At the end of the first year, it was possible to draw certain conclusions about how the Phases worked. First, Phase One—the education of top managers—is never-ending. Second, while Phases Two through Five are sequential, companies would do well to repeat Phase Five until they feel confident with project teams. Only then should they take them companywide in Phases Six through Nine, which represent a major commitment of planning and resources.

In later materials, Joiner and Scholtes elaborated on processes that have to be established to propose and respond to changes. Proselytizing, education, and training would have to continue until there was a critical mass of managers and employees at every level committed to and involved in change.

Gould, working with the two consultants, developed guidelines for managers undertaking the effort. Scholtes put them in writing as a working paper for Round Table members.

1. The top manager and his or her immediate subordinate manager should consider themselves the premier project team whose assigned improvement goal is to implement Deming's teachings. . . . The top manager is the prime mover and team leader of this project team. This team should hold for themselves the same high expectations they will have for other project teams. . . .

2. A manager should demonstrate to the rest of the organization that a never-ending process of improvement has begun. . . .

3. The manager should be a role model. . . . His or her behavior must demonstrate what the new way will look like and sound like. . . .

4. The top manager and each of his or her subordinate managers should convey to others in the organization that this decision to change is an irrevocable commitment and among the highest of the organization's priorities.

5. Managers should pay attention not only to the current implementation activities . . . but also to the next phase or two of the implementation process.

6. The top manager in particular must suppress the appetite for "instant pudding" [Dr. Deming's term for instant results]. . . . His or her rule of thumb should be "It's better to do it right than do it fast."

Scholtes cautioned that "a premature proliferation of projects and teams will not have an adequate system of managerial oversight, support and followup."

In the first year, companies progressed at different rates. There was friendly competition at the monthly PACE meetings, which proved helpful. Said Mary Ann Gould, "The very fact we had scheduled meetings provided discipline. We probably did more because we were committed to participating in those meetings. There were a million reasons why we could put off doing certain things. This forced us to follow through."

As the year drew to a close, she concluded that the project teams were indeed "the best way to get started and to show some results," especially to a CEO. In that sense, they catered to short-term American vision, while planting the seeds for long-term change in the way a company tackles problems. She compared them "to sticking your toe in the water, teaching people to swim a little bit before they're ready to go."

She proselytized for Short-Term Projects (STP) to "get some gas into the system." Brandishing a bottle of STP, she would read from the label: "specially formulated to fight the accumulation of dirt, gum and varnish in the carburetor and water in the fuel system that can harm performance, waste gas and cause corrosion."

As Joiner had foreseen, she said the project teams have had "tremendous value in breaking down barriers between different departments."

Finally, the candid Round Table discussions revealed that no matter what their size, companies have many of the same problems. "That was one of the major benefits our company got out of the Round Table," she said. Until that point, Gould said, her people "felt the problems we had in our company were unique to us. . . . When you see that Campbell Soup has many of the same complaints as Rohm & Haas or Philadelphia Electric, it enables you to put things out in the open. A lot of times you're afraid in companies to bring things up because you're going to step on somebody's toes. Once you realize it's a universal problem, it's different.''

Chapter 28

•

The Evolution of a "Demingized" Company:

Janbridge, Inc., Philadelphia, Pennsylvania

It was 8 A.M. on a Friday in midsummer, and the first shift was under way at Janbridge, Inc. This printed circuit board manufacturer is housed in a 60,000-square-foot, two-story building in a quiet, leafy northeast Philadelphia neighborhood. Production manager Dennis Sweeney, who had joined the company five months earlier, was just beginning his morning rounds to observe production start ups in each department. That morning, as usual, he had driven in from Allentown, sixty miles to the north, where his previous job for RCA had been terminated—making him yet another casualty in the all-but-decimated U.S. semiconductor industry, which in a few short years had plummeted from riches to rags. Sweeney was acutely sensitive to competitive pressures from Japan.

A few days earlier, Janbridge President Mary Ann Gould had remarked that scarcely a day went by without incident in this highly integrated type of manufacturing, which combined mechanical fabrication, photography, and numerous chemical and computerized processes. Sure enough, a problem had cropped up in the drilling department, where a newly acquired machine called a "deburrer" wasn't meeting expectations. The deburrer mechanically removed rough spots after drilling from the laminated

209

copper-clad panels and cleaned excess copper and other residues. It was a critical step in production. Failure to remove these residues could cause adhesion problems in subsequent chemical processes. But a decision to shut down the deburrer would temporarily affect production flow in the next departments.

Yet there was no way around it: the deburrer simply wasn't working right. Employees suspected that vibration in the gearbox was the culprit. Sweeney decided he had no choice but to shut the equipment down for repairs rather than risk excessive rework or, worse, rejects.

As he stopped in the adjoining departments, Sweeney discussed with supervisors and line leaders how production schedules could be adjusted while the deburrer was being repaired. "They [the people] do the job," Sweeney observed. "It's very important they have a strong say in solving the problems which relate to their work."

It was apparent from his decision to throttle the deburrer and from his ear for listening that Sweeney was not an order-barking, get-out-the-numbers kind of boss. As the day progressed, it was also clear that Sweeney fit into a larger corporate culture in which communication, respect, and teamwork were values (Gould used the acronym CRT) and quality, not only of the end product but also of the overall process, was the benchmark.

As Gould was the first to admit, Janbridge had not always been so quality-conscious nor so humanistic. Alvin Harrison, the supervisor in plating, spoke for several when he said that in that not-so-distant past a visit from the person in charge of production often meant trouble. It gave him the feeling that "they were after me." He felt personally at fault for problems, and that made him defensive. "We felt we were the accused: 'What or who is causing this problem or that problem?' I became tense, paranoid. My health was affected. I told my wife, 'Something's got to change.' "

Something did change.

"Luckily, Mary Ann Gould got Dr. Deming." Harrison said this as if he were talking about someone who had got religion, and he was not far off.

As much as, if not more than, any company in the country, Janbridge has sought to practice the Deming method. Thanks to that commitment, Janbridge today is a bright spot in an industry picture that is otherwise grim. In 1985, a year when the printed circuit board industry as a whole suffered a 30 percent downturn along with massive layoffs, Janbridge sales and productivity increased nearly 20 percent, creating new jobs in the process. And the company was looking forward to yet another growth year.

Meanwhile, the company established itself as the number-one printed circuit board vendor with most of its customers. Employees proudly framed and hung quality awards and citations from companies like Honeywell and Northern Telecom on the lobby walls.

Equally important, Janbridge has built an enthusiastic and supportive workforce through participation in decision making and the stability that comes from working for a growing company with a bold new no-layoff policy.

Partly because the company's size (roughly two hundred employees) allowed it to move quickly, but mostly because of Gould's imagination and unbending determination to adopt and adapt the Deming method, Janbridge is proof of the Deming chain reaction: Improving quality reduces costs and improves both productivity and market share. Janbridge is a success story whose lessons can be learned by others.

The conversion to the Deming method was not easy. Gould and her colleagues engaged in months of painful self-examination that focused on the company and their roles within it. Employees openly mistrusted their intentions. There were mistakes along the way.

What she learned from the experience, said Mary Ann Gould, is that "you can't put Deming's ideas into most corporations the way they stand today. You can't superimpose Deming's views of the roles of workers and management on the present organizational structures. It just won't work."

What it takes, she said, is a "thought revolution. You have to think in new ways about quality, systems, priorities, and your own job. New relationships must be forged between people. Quality must be all-pervasive—the driving force of change.

"I sometimes call quality 'holistic innovation.' It's not a great term, but it's the best I've found to convey the way you have to treat the *total* system, not just the individual part.

"Too often in America, we value people as bodies, a pair of hands. We've never tried to win their minds and hearts.

"There is no pat formula, no perfect set of techniques. At Janbridge, we've moved through stages, learning and changing as we did so. It's hard work, sometimes frustrating, especially for management. But it can be exhilarating when you see people working to their fullest potential. It *can* be fun."

In the spring of 1981, Mary Ann Gould was attending an industry convention in Washington where W. Edwards Deming was scheduled to speak on quality. Founded in 1976, Janbridge now occupied a niche in the high-reliability end of the printed circuit board business, with customers who manufactured customized equipment for the computer, telecommunication, medical diagnostic, and energy conservation fields. Gould had never heard of Dr. Deming, she would later say, but "quality was very important to our company. I decided I would attend."

The meeting was in a large amphitheater, with listeners looking down upon Dr. Deming. He was not at his best that day, as he seldom is in a short session. His delivery seemed rambling, and he reacted with his customary irritation to questions he considered irrelevant. On top of that, most of what he said sounded pretty radical. When he introduced Point Eleven, attacking the practice of relying on quotas and numbers, Gould was shocked.

"I thought, 'What the heck am I going to do? Just throw out the numbers and say quality first?'" But she also listened carefully to his statements about problems in the system, the fears and barriers that existed, and what top management had to do.

When she got back to Philadelphia, she thought more about what Dr. Deming had said. Some of it hit home. Gould sincerely believed that Janbridge needed to change. The company organization was a triangle, with what seemed like everything coming up to the top for a decision while everybody else waited for something to happen. Meanwhile, "people at the top were so busy trying to handle problems, they weren't doing the job of figuring out where the company was going."

She believed there were too many rules and no overriding principles. If you had a framework of corporate values and long-term objectives to guide decisions, then you wouldn't have to make rules for everything. She readily understood that change, as Dr. Deming said, had to start with top management—in other words, with her. She was by training a financial analyst and planner with what she knew to be a "take charge" personality, and she realized that it was easy for people in the organization to let her run things. She had to divorce herself from giving instant answers and consider where the corporation was going in an ever-more-competitive marketplace.

Gould took a four-day Deming seminar and traveled to AT&T's Merrimack Valley Works to visit firsthand with people who were working on the Fourteen Points and Seven Deadly Diseases as well as Statistical Quality Control. She became convinced that the Deming method was more than just a new program that would wear itself out in time. It was, rather, a corporate way of life that would ensure longevity for Janbridge.

For the first year, she and her top managers—particularly Vice Presidents Robert Petherbridge and Marty Jansen, who had founded the company and had combined their names into "Janbridge"—met and talked about the Fourteen Points and how they related to their firm. In one of the more important transformations, they began to think of themselves as the management team.

In addition to in-house meetings, there were four off-site weekend conferences where they wrestled with what Janbridge stood for—its future, its strengths, and its weaknesses. They made lists of what they were unhappy with and what they were happy with. They brought in other managers for consultations. "To be honest," Gould recalled, "we were struggling with 'What do we have to do to get these people [the employees] to do what they should do?' " They thought perhaps that procedures weren't clear enough. Later, they would realize that that was a simplistic solution. They debated why supervisors didn't seem to take the initiative. Gradually, they reached the painful conclusion that they were the ones who needed to change first.

From these conferences, a vision evolved. It incorporated new technology, a set of corporate values, an operating philosophy, and a firm commitment to Dr. Deming's methods. "We wanted to be in a position to choose customers—preferably those who believed in Deming—instead of customers choosing us," Gould explained. In a major mind-shift, they came to accept that short-term profits should be second to the long-term interests of the business and its employees.

Toward the end of that first year, several top managers attended a four-day Deming seminar that deepened their commitment to his philosophy. They began to hold meetings of all employees to outline where they wanted Janbridge to go. Their understanding of Deming had been limited. It would grow with time, but then, Gould recalled, "we were still talking about quality of the product rather than a process. We were still doing too much fire-fighting."

As a practical matter, they decided to make no changes in the manufacturing processes until they were running in the same way day-in and day-out, so that they could be analyzed in systematic fashion. As in all companies, well-meaning employees introduced variation into the processes by trying to fix things as they went wrong. "We decided to keep the processes running consistently—exactly the same way every day—before improving them," Gould said. "That took a good year." This decision was made even before Janbridge became well-versed in SQC. "It didn't involve a lot of control charts," she said. "If something's been running a certain way for a certain time, you could say it's predictable. In the beginning, you don't need statistics all over the place. You can think in terms of input and output. If the output has changed, then some input has changed. Statistics become valuable as you progress."

When something did go wrong, Janbridge repeatedly closed down the line. That, more than anything else, convinced doubting workers that management was serious about quality. "Management had to show they would sacrifice that day's production to find out what had really happened and what had to change," Gould explained. "Once wasn't enough, twice wasn't enough, three times wasn't enough."

In the second year, Janbridge sent ten additional top and middle managers to four-day Deming sessions and began to train supervisors within the company to see themselves less as bosses and more as leaders who were there to help workers do their jobs, as Dr. Deming suggested. Janbridge hired consultant Phyllis Sobo to coach people in the basic skills of supervision: how to handle conflicts, for example, and how to train people in their jobs. There was role-playing, with supervisors alternating roles as both workers and supervisors. Several sessions were videotaped for subsequent viewing and discussion.

Every supervisor went through two ten-week sessions, meeting three hours one day a week. Top management did not attend. But after each session Sobo would conduct an hour-long review of what she had presented and what supervisors thought were barriers to team-building and improvement. "The first sessions were bitch sessions," Gould said. "Problems were aired and put on the table." Once past that hurdle, people began to discuss what to do about them. Leaders emerged. In all, she said, the group forged "new relationships at the middle-management level. They came out a much stronger team."

In the second set of sessions, Sobo introduced some of the simpler statistical tools, and Gould put in occasional appearances to explain the Deming method and how it related to the future of Janbridge. She and other top managers began to take the message companywide. After the supervisors were trained, they in turn trained workers. Workers were shown such films as *Staying in the Race*, which showed how Malden Mills had averted bankruptcy after joining the Deming camp, and *Road Map to Change*, which detailed work at the General Motors Fiero Division under Dr. Deming's tutelage. Gould developed a shortened version of the bead experiment and kept a bowl of red and white beads at the ready.

In 1983, Janbridge introduced a no-layoff policy. Again, people did not believe the company would stick by it—until there was a slow period and excess workers were kept on the payroll. The company diverted them to cleaning, maintenance, and repairs, as well as to additional training. When new contracts came through, employees responded with high-quality work and productivity in record time. "It was unbelievable the way people responded," Gould observed. "They felt they had a stake."

In the next stage, Janbridge joined the Quality Round Table sponsored by PACE, which had been founded by Gould and others in 1984. Although Janbridge previously had experimented with project teams, now there was a formal structure and a plan to follow. As a strategy, Janbridge at first promoted Short-Term Projects (STP) that could be carried out in sixty to ninety days, thus creating a series of successes that proved the merit of the Deming method and gave team members confidence. These were not necessarily minor projects, but rather major projects broken into smaller ones. Thus, Gould explained, "every project developed from the company vision." Each project also had a learning goal—the use of a certain statistical tool or teamwork technique, for example. The idea was to build a force of mini-experts to deploy throughout the company.

"We began with the decision that quality came first," Gould reflected as 1985 drew to a close. "We were always known as a quality company, but quality improved dramatically."

As Dennis Sweeney made his rounds on this summer day, he told stories of this or that worker being promoted, of problems detected and solved by project teams. "I look for natural leaders," he said. It was, he said, his responsibility to bring them along. "If they fail, then I'm not doing my job."

As he walked through the shearing department, where the three-by-four-foot copper-clad panels are cut to smaller sizes, he recalled a worker who insisted he would be more productive on the night shift. Although it was a departure from procedure, the worker's request was granted. His productivity rose almost 20 percent.

In that same department, a project team was initiated to cut down on scrap. A manager involved with the project team developed a computer program to maximize the yield of each panel. Leftover material dropped from 8 to 1.5 percent. In an area that used to be so stacked with odd-size panels as to be nearly impassable, only a few remnants leaned against the walls.

At 9 A.M., Sweeney joined the daily staff meeting. One by one, individuals reviewed the work that they planned to move through their respective departments. They discussed how they would readjust their plans while the deburrer equipment was being repaired.

Janbridge had always held these morning meetings, but they were smaller and emphasized production ("the numbers"). Recently, more supervisors and line leaders were invited as part of the ongoing process to delegate responsibility for production planning. And now quality was just as important. Each morning, a member of the quality assurance department reported on some aspect of their operations: an overall analysis of defects, perhaps, or customer complaints, or a particular issue on which they were gathering data. Lynne Wolkiewicz, a young woman promoted from inspector, was giving more and more of these presentations, but today she was on vacation, and Barbara Hysek, the manager of quality assurance, presented a quality report for the week, with the sources of rejects displayed on a pareto chart. As anticipated, a preventive maintenance program in plating during vacation the week before had improved consistency, but the results had exceeded expectations. "We should . . . plan a schedule for continuing this type maintenance in the future," she suggested in a written report.

After the meeting, at 9:30 A.M., two men from the Honeywell, Inc., process control division in Fort Washington, Pennsylvania—buyer Dave Homiller and production engineer Bob Altimari—arrived for the official closing of a Janbridge project. At the outset,

Janbridge had set as its goal "to provide Honeywell with consistent quality to meet their expectations of better than 95 percent acceptability." In fact, the company had done even better. The month before, Homiller had written Marty Jansen, who was in charge of marketing, a letter of congratulations "for achieving a 100 percent quality rating with Honeywell for two consecutive months, May and June.

"We at Honeywell," Homiller continued in his letter, "know that these results were attained only with great effort and adherence to the Deming Statistical Process Control methods. Please extend my congratulations to all members of Janbridge on a job well done. Your achievements have been noticed most favorably throughout the Honeywell PCD division."

Now that Homiller and Altimari were here in person, implementation coordinator Carol Tunstall outlined for their benefit precisely how Janbridge had accomplished its quality goal. A soft-spoken blond woman with an MBA, Tunstall had started her career in personnel at a large pharmaceutical company. Attracted by "the excitement of manufacturing," she became a production supervisor, then a plant manager for a composite can manufacturer. In June 1984, she answered an ad for a project manager with "empathy for people." The advertiser was Janbridge. It was Tunstall's job to promote the Fourteen Points, squelch the Seven Deadly Diseases and Obstacles, and arrange resources for project teams. Janbridge now had an in-house statistical assistant as well, and retained consultants on an as-needed basis.

The firm had devoted considerable resources to the Honeywell project. It had taken longer than four months and involved detailed statistical studies in several departments, working with vendors of both equipment and raw materials, daily test runs of panels under varying conditions, new testing methods, and new equipment.

One cause of returns was copper plating in certain holes designed to be nonplated. There were three ways to keep the plating out. One was to plug them; another was to cover them with "tents" of dry film; and the third—and most expensive—was to drill after plating, which involved rerouting the boards back to the drilling department.

In their search for defects, inspectors developed a simple but effective plastic overlay, which made it possible as well to gather data on the size and location of defective holes. It was evident that there was a pattern to both. People were sure that broken tents were the major cause of most rejects. To their surprise, the data showed that tents worked well, depending on the size and location of the hole, and the dry film thickness of which the tents were made. Time, temperature, and speed of processing were also factors. Data also showed that an additional problem was the cone-shaped plugs used on larger holes, which had an unfortunate tendency to fall out. Knowing this, Janbridge began to use straight plugs that fit more tightly. With solid data on all these variables, and knowing the capabilities of the process, the project team developed a decision-making grid for the engineering department that showed them when to specify the use of plugs, when to use tents of whatever thickness, and when to drill after plating. Each decision was based on which was most cost-effective while still meeting customer requirements.

The project team, by using an analytical, systematic approach, had been able to identify the problems and their causes and bring about permanent solutions. That had improved the system, not "Band-Aided" the problem. The accomplishment drew a compliment from Honeywell's buyer. "It's well appreciated and very well noticed there [at Honeywell]," Homiller said.

After the Honeywell team disbanded, another project team claimed the conference room. Promising that theirs would be the most "boring" meeting of the day, the Military Specifications Project began their labors during the lunch hour, ordering sandwiches from a local deli. Its task was to translate a two-inch-thick manual of military specifications for printed circuit boards into language that operators and inspectors could quickly understand. The team consisted of Tunstall, Quality Manager Hysek, Inside Sales Representative Craig Johnson, Engineer Ricci Lubinski, and Image Department Supervisor Don Poirer, whose department transferred designs to the boards.

The project was initiated when Janbridge decided to go after more military business. In reviewing the situation, Janbridge discovered that in the past, inspectors had ignored complicated and confusing military specifications, substituting the simpler, more familiar ones used for commercial customers. It was not as if the inspectors didn't try to find out the proper procedure. But when they would ask supervisors a question, the typical response would be "What do the specs say?" The inspectors would answer, "I don't understand them."

Finally, several inspectors confronted Sweeney with their concerns. He initiated the MIL-P Projects. Until the team examined the specifications, Barbara Hysek said, "we didn't know what they were running into."

What they were running into were military instructions like the one for solderability standards, which said to refer to "paragraph 3.5.6." Looking up "paragraph 3.5.6" on "Solderability," the inspector was told to "See 4.8.2.6." But "4.8.2.6" on "Solderability" directed the inspector to "See 3.5.6." In other words, it was one big circle.

Once a week for three months, the MIL-P team had given up its lunch hour to ponder such matters as the allowable limits for printed circuit boards on bowing and twisting, solderability, conductor spacing, solder mask thickness, and plating and coating thickness. This was their final session. As a result of their labors, the complex requirements for final visual inspection had been reduced to a mere two pages of simply written instructions.

At 3 P.M., the White Glove Project filed into the conference room. This was the front office team and they, too, were involved in the transformation. Their objective was to "define and evaluate data needs and reorganize what is to be kept and where. Set up program to maintain and monitor cleanliness and orderliness of each work area as well as total office." For the next hour, they reviewed floor plans and equipment purchases that would make the office more efficient and attractive.

The day was drawing to a close. Back in plating, the second shift had arrived, and Alvin Harrison was putting his papers in order. As Harrison prepared to leave, he was joined by Process Engineer Ed Patton, a retired engineer from Ford Aerospace Division. The two explained with some pride how a team had completed a highly successful project to eliminate a costly procedure called "destructive testing." It had been exactly what the name implied. Standardized, industrywide test coupons—small test patterns etched along panel edges—weren't reliable for some of the complex boards Janbridge produced, and only by destroying an entire board was it possible to measure accurately the thickness of the plating. After much analysis and repeated testing, Janbridge had developed its own sophisticated coupon, reflecting the circuitry and other characteristics of the more demanding boards and putting an end to destructive testing. That and other changes in plating that developed from the project had resulted in a $70,000 annual savings and a 30 percent gain in productivity.

During the day, workers in all departments—now called "operators" because, Gould noted, "that's what they're doing"—had spoken freely of how much their jobs had improved.

In the image inspection department, where Blanche Slovinsky spent each day at a desk station touching up minor defects with a brush, the boards now came in almost "100 percent clean," she said, adding with a laugh, "I don't feel like I'm being Rembrandt anymore, but there's satisfaction in being able to complete a job faster."

In the past, she said, "we would show them [supervisors] things, and they didn't act like it was a problem. When you see things wrong and you can't define them, and you can't make anybody understand, it's very frustrating. Now they want to know all about it. We can go to anybody and tell them and they do look into it. They don't act like it's nothing."

Engineers reviewing customers' designs now have the confidence to call customers immediately as potential difficulties surface that in the past were caught downstream in production. Observed Mark Rosenbaum, "You open up doors and talk, instead of just putting things through." He added, "We do really try to make every board a Cadillac."

In the film department, Jim Wright, a supervisor, said that intradepartmental contacts mean "you get to hear more of the problems from department to department. There might be things we could do to really help them, but we wouldn't really be aware of the problems before."

In "electroless," a long, narrow room with a series of tanks through which boards passed for the purpose of applying .00001 inch of copper to the boards and holes, Ken McAndrew, as line leader, has been given the authority to halt production in response to any problem, as have others in their departments. "I feel a lot safer by stopping the line," he said. "Believe it or not, it saves a lot of time. We used to have a lot of rework time. Now panels don't leave this room until they're right and I make sure of it. Before, they used to say 'Ship them.' "

In the old days, he said, "It was hell. You'd have people breathing down your neck, checking the boards. 'Why are they so bad?' " As far as he was concerned, he said, there had been no real interest in improving the process. Indeed, he had been on the verge of quitting. Some thought of him as a difficult employee.

Now he has only praise for the way Janbridge responded. "Since they started talking to this Dr. Deming, they're starting to pay attention," he continued. "Now I can voice my opinions. . . . You used to come up with an idea and they'd say, we'll check into it, and we'd never hear anything about it." Today, he said, "Nobody comes running down saying 'You do this. You do that.' They *ask* you to do it. 'Can you do this?' It's a lot better that way."

Having learned how to use control charts, McAndrew recently led a team that evaluated the chemical solution baths in the electroless copper plating line and found ways to extend their life at significant cost savings while also improving product consistency.

Although he has subsequently been made supervisor of both electroless and drilling, the greatest reward was not his promotion. Rather, he said, it was being able "to let management know what we're doing down here and that we're not kids. We do give a damn. We do care. Just trying to do it right, that's all. I don't like rework, and I don't like returns from customers."

Not all the raves come from operators. Managers have positive things to say as well. Said cofounder and General Manager Robert Petherbridge, "For my part, I think it has helped me tremendously. People respond without having to go back over things several times. They've picked up the responsibilities. That's the relief I personally get out of it. That, and the fact that we're able to service the customers with a quality product with on-time delivery to meet their needs."

From John Miller, head of engineering, came this endorsement: "I was of the old school: a boss is a boss is a boss. . . . 'Do it my way, or this is it.' I've found it's a much easier life for me to share responsibility. People know more than we give them credit for. You can listen to them. It's strange at first. . . . But then you can concentrate more on the planning stages. Before, you were tied up with all the little things going on."

From Milton Reid, director of technical services: "Now that the day-to-day processes are under control, we can plan where we want to be twelve or eighteen months from now."

From Mary Ann Gould: "I think there's a trust now between everyone. . . . I think they believe in us and we [management] believe in them. It's not 'us' and 'them' anymore, it's a 'we.' "

Perhaps the most remarkable endorsement came from Alvin Harrison, the plating supervisor, who once regarded the quality department as his enemy. "It used to be a defensive thing when quality came down. We used to be at each others' throats. Now nobody gets offended when you find a mistake. They look to find what has changed in the system, not 'who did it wrong.' "

"No one wanted to hear what I had to say," Quality Manager Barbara Hysek agreed in a separate discussion. "I was the policeman. Mary Ann Gould was the only one who listened to me."

On this day at Janbridge, Hysek had a memo from Harrison posted on her door. "In the six years I have been here," he had written, "I've never seen an organization running more tightly than these past four months. I am proud and much more confident of our area. They understand and have participated and created what I call 100% togetherness of teamwork.

"Barbara . . . I thought I owed this memo to quality control to show that I and the other members of this area have appreciated your help. Thank you."

Chapter 29

---•---

The Transformation of
an American Manager:

Microcircuit Engineering
Corporation,
Mt. Holly, New Jersey

"It takes courage to admit that you have been doing something wrong, to admit that you have something to learn, that there is a better way."

DR. DEMING

"Top management must feel pain and dissatisfaction with past performance, and must have the courage to change."

PHYLLIS SOBO, MANAGEMENT CONSULTANT

The word that Stewart G. Stalnecker, Jr., uses to describe his former posture toward employees is *autocratic*. "I ran a tight ship. Tell them what to do, and they'll do it. If they don't, blow them out."

He was the kind of CEO who retreats to his office with the door closed, venturing onto the factory floor only when there is a crisis having to do with production. "People problems" were the responsibility of his personnel manager, who seemed to know what she was doing. He didn't get involved.

For Stalnecker, the company picnic and the Christmas party were obligatory functions where he had to mix one-on-one with employees of Microcircuit Engineering Corporation (MEC), the company that he had started in the basement of his Medford, New Jersey, home in 1967. No liquor was served at the Christmas party. He had heard stories of employees downing a few stiff ones and telling managers and supervisors just what they thought of them. God forbid that that should happen at MEC. So employees drank soft drinks and probably were just as happy as Stalnecker when the affair was over. It was merely a formality, really.

Stalnecker, forty-eight, had attributes that were not in and of themselves negative ones, like a passion for detail and structure. But he also believed in discipline and was not, by his own admission, "a very open person." He was, in short, like many, if not most, American managers.

If he was as rigid as he says he was, of course, he would not have changed. But he did change. In 1984, his wife Joan read an article in the *Philadelphia Inquirer* magazine about W. Edwards Deming, announcing one of his seminars in Philadelphia. That Mary Ann Gould, president of Janbridge, was prominently mentioned in the article as a Deming disciple gave Deming credibility in the eyes of the Stalneckers. Janbridge was a respected MEC customer.

Given that there were problems at MEC with both productivity and the workforce—two topics Dr. Deming seemed to know a lot about—Stalnecker was more than a little interested in finding out just what he had to say. But he was not, it must be noted, interested enough to attend the seminar himself. Instead, he asked his wife if she could go and take the new personnel manager with her. Joan Stalnecker obligingly called the Chamber for information. "I found out it was a four-day seminar and said, 'Oh, well, which day can you go?' " When she learned that attendance was required on all four days and that it cost nine hundred dollars, she informed her husband that it was out of the question.

"He said," she recalled, " 'Would you go?'

"I said, 'Oh, I can't do that. Who's going to teach nursery school and do all the carpooling?'

"He said, 'If you can get a substitute teacher, I'll do the carpooling and help out at home.' "

Stalnecker unwittingly had embarked on a course that would be, in a word, painful, but that would deliver unanticipated rewards.

Stalnecker had never given management much thought. By training an engineer, he had been employed for a number of years at Corning Glass Works, where his last job was senior process engineer in charge of a prototype production group that produced precision stencil screens for printing electronic circuits on ceramic foundations. Automobile makers, telephone companies, and defense contractors were just a few of the firms that purchased this customized tooling.

But because there were so few manufacturers, many companies were compelled to make their own screens. When Corning decided not to pursue ceramic circuits, Stalnecker thought he could fill the need for precision stencil screens by starting his own company. For the first year after MEC was founded, he taught school to make ends meet.

After two years, Stalnecker was having a problem with outside suppliers for his artwork and photographic needs. He established a photo division that supplied the needs of the screen division and provided reprographic services for architectural and engineering firms, aerial mapping, cable television systems, and printed circuit board manufacturers.

By the mid-1980s, MEC had more than six hundred accounts. The company occupied a 22,000-square-foot former shoe factory in Mt. Holly, New Jersey, twenty miles northeast of Philadelphia, and employed 120 workers with varying skills. Managers were selected primarily for their technical expertise.

From the beginning, price was not the major emphasis. "The most important thing," Stalnecker said, "was quality and delivery and the know-how of how to use the product. If it didn't work, we knew what to recommend that would work."

In the early 1980s, sales were escalating as much as 40 percent a year. But the volume was creating problems from a quality standpoint. Explained Stalnecker, "We had so much work, and there was so much pressure to get the product out, there were a lot of internal problems with rework and rejects. Basically, once it went out, it was very good; but it was taking longer and longer to get it out."

Meanwhile, his personnel manager of five years left the company and a new one was hired. The new manager began to hold meetings with workers, who complained bitterly about working conditions. Stalnecker found it impossible to ignore long-standing undercurrents of dissatisfaction.

The former personnel manager, he said, "had set up a very tight system—personnel handbook, a lot of policies, regulations, rules. She was pretty much an enforcer." After she resigned, "a kind of wave of relief went through the organization. I found out that even management people were afraid to talk to me about her because she was so powerful."

Occupied with the technical end of the business, Stalnecker had chosen to trust her, in part, because "it seemed very convenient to have her take over all the dirty work, so to speak, of personnel management."

Meanwhile, Joan Stalnecker, a former school psychologist who was teaching nursery school, was hearing secondhand about these problems at her husband's business. An attentive woman who speaks in the slow cadences of one who has spent years talking to children, she concluded that under the old regime employees "weren't made to feel like adults; they were made to feel like children who were incapable of making decisions."

At the Deming seminar, which she attended in the elegant gilded ballroom of the turn-of-the-century Bellevue Stratford Hotel, Joan Stalnecker heard what was to her a radical message. "The thing that impressed me the most: 'American management's greatest resource is their people.' " Although she instinctively agreed, "I just couldn't believe that anybody that old, after all the years he'd been around, would say that people were very important, and that they were going to make the difference, how you handle them. And how he actually, right in the meeting . . . didn't tolerate any type of question from a person that in any way was disparaging toward the workforce."

Joan returned from the Deming seminar with a message for her husband. "I came back and I said we really should focus on the people because they are all we've got."

Stalnecker, who had just posted a sign in the cafeteria announcing that MEC had shipped a record 3,085 screens in a single week, hadn't anticipated this reaction. Personally he thought the company had a lot more going for it than its workforce, with its absenteeism and rising defect levels. "We've got this terrific product and these neat processes and all this great equipment," he told his wife. "Why can't we run it? Why can't people just go out and do their jobs?"

He was more enthusiastic about Joan Stalnecker's report on statistical techniques. "It made so much sense to me," she said, "that you could actually keep track of certain things and give people the answer on a concrete foundation." That also made some sense to Stalnecker, who had already used control charts for some operations.

At the invitation of the new personnel manager, Joan attended one of the meetings with workers. Even the presence of the president's wife did not stifle the pent-up unhappiness. The workers believed the company was far more interested in making money than in the quality of the work. And they believed their welfare was at the bottom of the priority list.

In the months following the Deming seminar, Joan began to take an active interest in the business. But she found it frustrating. "I believed in Deming, and I wanted to do something, but I didn't know how. . . . As people would present me with problems, I was beginning to feel overwhelmed."

But her husband was gradually beginning to believe in the need for reform. As evidence of his goodwill, he initiated a "prosperity-sharing" arrangement of up to seven hundred dollars, based on seniority. He thought MEC workers would be grateful. Such was their alienation, however, that "they thought the main reason we gave money was to avoid paying taxes."

In late summer of 1984, when PACE was announced, Joiner Associates of Madison, Wisconsin, was hired as a consultant and Joan Stalnecker felt a surge of relief. MEC became a charter member of the Philadelphia Quality Round Table. At last, someone was going to help MEC carry out the methods. "For better or for worse," Joan Stalnecker said, "we just did what they told us to do. We got a project team together, and we gave them their project." As Joiner had instructed, the first team was to be no larger than eight, with representation from management and the people who worked in the area. The team was to cut across all organizational lines and include a facilitator and a statistician.

Following the Joiner model, what had been known as the "staff" renamed themselves the "management team." It consisted of Stewart Stalnecker as CEO and Joan as "implementation coordinator," plus the managers of the screen and photo operations and the directors of sales, personnel, and accounting.

The launch of the first project team was not without glitches. When the employees selected for the team were asked to come to a meeting, Joan got an indignant note from one supervisor that said, in effect, "Very typical MEC policy. You call a meeting and you don't tell the supervisors what it's about, and you don't even tell them why you need the person. When are you going to start communicating with us?"

Joan was startled. She apologized to the supervisor and invited him to the first meeting.

She had learned a lesson. "If you think about it," she said, "he made a valid statement. He didn't know what we were going to set up, but anything you set up—which is our project team—and they're going to meet for two hours every week, and you're not going to tell their supervisors what you're doing, that's kind of crazy."

At that meeting, she told the prospective members that they were not being forced to serve on the project team but that their involvement would have priority over their other work. Everyone accepted. Taking the name of START, for Statistical Techniques and Responsive Teamwork, the team included the division production superintendent, a statistical coordinator, an order entry clerk, a supervisor from the screen division, the artwork department supervisor from the photographic division (the outsider that Joiner recommended), a technician, and an hourly worker representing the second shift. Joan was the facilitator.

It was a new experience for everyone. John Criqui, the statistical coordinator, who had taken the Paul Krensky training in Philadelphia, was barely one step ahead of what he was supposed to teach team members. (Brian Joiner called it "just-in-time training.")

The project team took as its mission the task of pinpointing delays in the progress of screens through the eight-step production process. It turned out to be a mammoth project, perhaps too large in retrospect, for it really meant no less than analyzing the entire manufacturing process for problems that caused delays.

Because there were five kinds of screens, each had to be traced separately. The team ended up attaching a "trip ticket" to fifty orders, on which each department would record time-in and time-out. That was a threat of sorts. Said Joan, "We realized people were going to be afraid to fill out the trip ticket, to admit how long the order stayed with them. So the team decided to invite everyone to a meeting who actually handled orders—seventeen people." The presentation was made by the project team leader, who was the production superintendent. He assured the people that the team was interested only in an honest picture of the process, not in information that could be used against them. Recalled Joan, "He had to say it three, four times. The project team told him he would have to say it a lot, because 'they're not going to believe you.' "

It took the project team six months to gather data. The resulting pareto chart showed that the screens spent the bulk of their time in the department where they were coated with emulsions. Two "focus" teams were set up to study the issue, staffed by the hourly workers in that department, who were called "coaters," but they were chaired by a member of the project team. They immediately set up a time study on the screens and a "life study" on the tools, which the coaters said were their greatest aggravation. Rather than feeling under attack, the coaters, Joan said, were flattered that "somebody really thinks we know something about what we do."

The sixteen coaters had traditionally felt isolated from the rest of MEC—and for good reason. Because of a requirement for a dirt-free environment, the coating area was sealed off from the other production areas. With rare exceptions, no one but the coaters ever entered it. All women, they changed into special clothing each time they entered and did not leave on casual missions. The coaters seldom socialized with other employees, not even in the cafeteria, and very few ever came to the company picnic or Christmas party.

As the screen division team met week in and week out, there was growing pressure from the photo division for its own project team. The photo division, which was a quarter of the size of the screen division with only thirty people, suffered from a stepchild complex anyway, and now they felt totally ignored. Although preoccupied with the screen division, the management team felt it was important for morale to establish another team.

Suddenly, there were teams all over. Joan called it an "adopt-a-team" philosophy. In addition to the management team, two START teams, and two focus teams, there were now two STP [Short-Term Project] teams, an idea that the Stalneckers had brought back from one of the PACE meetings. The safety committee became a safety team; the "sunshine committee," which handled proceeds from the vending machines, became the sunshine team, and when it came time to plan a company picnic, there was a team for that as well. The event was dubbed a "MECnic" and was, everyone said, the most successful event of its kind. Twice the usual number of people volunteered to help, and those who went remarked that it was like "a family picnic." By this time, team participation had risen to the point where 50 of the 130 employees at MEC were involved on one team or another. It was perhaps not surprising that there appeared to be a new mood of togetherness. Indeed, eight coaters attended the MECnic—more than anyone could remember seeing at any company event.

On his own, though with management approval, the production supervisor set up an ad hoc team to design an orientation tour for both new and long-term employees to learn how screens were made. Each employee would make a sample screen, spending the amount of time in each department necessary to complete that particular step. In all, the cycle took a week.

On unsigned surveys afterward, the first group to complete the tour was extraordinarily enthusiastic. "I feel that the information accumulated on the tour is very helpful in my 'home' department," wrote one. "I think *everyone* should get to take this tour. I thought it was awesome!" Concluded another employee, "This whole program really helped to break barriers between departments and helped them work together." Another ended with a note: "I feel if everyone does a tour they and there [sic] supervisors will be more informed on the other areas and appreciate there [sic] own jobs more. . . . Keep up the good work. . . . Gang! There's no stopping us now!"

Several months before the first project team was formed, another development took place that would claim the attention of Stalnecker. MEC gave birth to an underground paper called *The Merri-MEC*, a clever, photocopied publication that made its appearance in the men's room on a more-or-less monthly basis and provided a running, barbed commentary on the company's programs. Articles were written by "Emmy Cee" (MEC) and "Mike Rowe" (Micro), among others.

Issue number four told of a quality foe called the "MECness Monster" but reported that "all hope is not lost. A call has gone out for the renowned dragon slayer, Sir Deming of the round table. Sir Deming has agreed to organize teams to subdue the MEC-ness Monster and make Microcircuit Engineering a safe place for quality once again."

Stalnecker was known as "Sigis" and Joan was "Jips" in *The Merri-MEC*. The paper had a cartoonist—"Wunuv Armen" (One of Our Men)—whose character, a big, ambulatory foot with sunglasses, was named "Blind Baby." Wunuv Armen liked to depict Sigis in plaid pants. He owned seven pairs.

The Merri-MEC took a skeptical view of the changes. In one issue, the broadside announced its own team: "S.T.O.P.P.E.D.," for Secretive Techniques of Paper Pushing and Efficient Distribution. It also promulgated an inspired parody of the Fourteen Points that suggested, if nothing else, that a savvy workforce was not easily persuaded of management's new philosophy. *The Merri-MEC*'s version was "Fifteen Points," and it presented an employee's view of what motivates bosses.

Point One read: "Create inconsistency of purpose toward improvement of product and service, with the aim that if they can't figure out [what] we're doing or when we're doing it, they can't stop us."

The parody continued in the same vein. Point Nine read: "Create barriers. People work best when they're motivated by revenge." And Point Twelve read: "Keep those barriers up. If someone does a good job, wait until they're not looking and mess it up. Reserve pride of workmanship for yourself."

If possible, *The Merri-MEC* outdid itself in a later issue with a parody of statistical techniques. The underlying theme of the pseudocharts was that training was taking such a chunk out of profits that employees could expect a smaller-than-usual distribution when prosperity-sharing gifts were handed out at the close of the fiscal year. The paper was on top of things, that much could be said. In fact, the small company spent upward of $100,000 on training the first year—easily 25 percent of its profits before taxes and depreciation.

The Merri-MEC was willing to give credit where credit was due. When liquor was served for the first time at the Christmas party, the paper gave thanks in its version of *A Christmas Carol*. At the end, the enlightened Scrooge shouts, "I'll give them off on Christmas Eve. They'll like that. I'll give them off on New Year's Eve. They'll certainly enjoy that. . . . I'll even give them a company-paid Christmas party with music, dancing, food and drinks! (and by the way, they did like that)."

These jibes notwithstanding, Stewart Stalnecker was discovering that workers were not necessarily the cause of whatever difficulties MEC might be having at the moment.

After the Fourteen Points were handed down, a respected employee wrote a devastating commentary on the way they were constantly being violated at MEC. On constancy of purpose, Point One, the employee wrote, "We have yet to walk into a meeting and discuss what we are actually going to do aside from 'increase sales,' which is meaningless without improving profitability. On Point Two, "Adopt the new philosophy," the employee observed that "you [Stalnecker] tell us to continue to make defective products until we can work out the bugs. . . . It is demoralizing and counterproductive to deliberately make bad parts. We should not make them—PERIOD."

The critique continued. On "Institute leadership," Point Seven, the employee informed Stalnecker, "Your solution to any problems we have brought to meetings has been to [tell us to] figure the problems out ourselves or put us off." On removing barriers affecting hourly workers, Point Twelve: "Ask THEM. They DO have brains." And finally, on Point Fourteen, to create a structure to push on the other Thirteen Points, the employee wrote "DITTO—you FIRST! Let's hear YOUR plan."

In early 1985, Stalnecker received a request from the first project team that he talk to all MEC employees. The project team had grown weary of trying to explain to others what they were doing during their meetings and the mysterious trips to Philadelphia to attend the PACE Round Table. They felt, said Joan, "as if no one believed that anything was really going to happen as a result of their activities." They wanted Stalnecker to make it clear that he supported the program. "So the team asked Stewart to give a talk on the Fourteen Points."

Stalnecker gave the talk, as requested, to each of the three shifts, and he prefaced it with assurances that the company was genuinely serious about the Deming philosophy; that it was not "just a gimmick, and if that doesn't work we'll try something else, and if that doesn't work, we'll try something else again." He explained that MEC was in a leadership position but that it was threatened by competition, particularly from overseas, and that the company needed to keep up with the latest techniques and programs to survive.

"When you say you want to survive, that's pretty emphatic," Stalnecker later reflected. "You think you're doing fairly well. The employees may think we're doing extremely well around here. But then they're finding out maybe things aren't as good as they're led to believe or they see or they think. So I wanted to explain how it's related to the overall goals of our company." Everyone in the company was given a copy of the Fourteen Points.

Stalnecker had done what the project team asked him to do, but he wished there had been time for questions and answers. He volunteered to hold additional, smaller meetings with time for discussion. Project team members suggested he go into the workplace, department by department, lab by lab.

Even though it had been his idea, Stalnecker didn't know what to expect. Would anyone say anything? Would there be only silence? Or would they be hostile? He wasn't sure which would be worse.

With care, he chose the site for the first of thirteen meetings. The supervisor was on the project team and was certain to give him support. Joan was there as well.

Stalnecker need not have worried about people speaking up. Scheduled for thirty minutes, the sessions were extended to sixty and even ninety minutes to accommodate the lively discussion. Stalnecker described the experience. "You go into a meeting and you're nervous. I'm nervous, and they're nervous. And then you wait, and we look at each other. And we try to relax and we try to open up some discussion. The first ten or fifteen minutes are awkward. By the end of an hour, we're talking so much and we've got so many things going that we don't want to stop.

"I'd take a point and I'd say, 'Here's a point—driving out fear. What in your department are you afraid of? Are you afraid of making mistakes? That you'll be embarrassed by your supervisor, or you will not get an increase? If your manager comes in and says I want you to do one hundred pieces today, and you work hard and you do one hundred and fifty of them are bad, how do you feel? Would you feel better doing sixty or seventy and getting them all right, and how can we eliminate this pressure so you can do a better job and be proud of what you do every day?' "

Gradually, people would speak up. The trickle of comments turned into a torrent. There were common themes. "I come in and they give me this job, and then ten minutes later say, 'Forget about that job, push this one ahead of it, I've got to have this one out by noon.' And then you rush and you make mistakes and you feel bad, and then they come in and they say, 'Why didn't you get it done?' And then you have to try to explain what happened. And there's a lot of pressure, frustration, and confusion. 'Well, we can't get it done because the department before us didn't get their job done.' "

Some departments labored under adverse environmental conditions. "One department said, 'It's too cold in here. Then it goes up and it's too warm. We can't control the thickness [of the emulsion] when it's too warm or too cold.' ''

To Joan, listening in, ''the thing that impressed me the most, the people didn't have any problem with the Fourteen Points. It may have made you feel bad, but it was impressive that they could actually say to you, 'Well, how are you going to take down the barriers? We see real barriers here.' Focus on teamwork? They would say, 'Well, we don't work as a team.' ''

At the end of one of the meetings, an employee asked Joan, ''Are you sure you can trust this Dr. Deming?''

With each meeting, Stewart Stalnecker was revising his opinion of the people who worked for his company. ''I think there are a lot of good people here. People that I thought weren't doing a good job are not doing a good job because they don't know how. They don't know the importance of their job. They're not trained properly.''

He even concluded, ''It's amazing they do as well as they do. We have to convince them that this is serious, and this is what we want to do in the long term; it's not just a quick-fix program. . . .

''I'm learning recently, you can't motivate people. You've got to provide the work environment that's going to make them want to do a better job. You just can't make them do a better job by paying them more money.''

In the spring, members of the management team decided that they themselves needed help. MEC hired a consultant, the Deming disciple Phyllis Sobo, recommended by Janbridge. For three months, she held weekly training sessions.

Sobo thought the management structure at MEC was vague. Her first task was to identify precisely what their jobs were. She went through a similar process with supervisors. In addition, she taught the supervisory skills of motivation, counseling, time management, orienting and training new employees, and appraising the performance of people who worked for them.

Fifteen months after Joan Stalnecker had sat through the Deming seminar, she and her husband reflected on the experience. Certainly they had had their ups and downs. Although they did not question that Deming's philosophy was indispensable, they had not been prepared for the way in which people would react. Who could have foreseen, for example, that workers would be irritated because supervisors left their shift to go to weekly two-hour training sessions? Or that supervisors would feel threatened by Stalnecker's meetings with workers, wondering, as one put it, "Are you going to let them take over the business?" Or that six months into the project teams, one member would resign because the slow pace was demoralizing?

Joan Stalnecker was able to woo that person back. She well understood his frustration. The former teacher had been forced to learn to keep silent, stifling an impulse to tell people what to do, as if they were students. She lectured herself before each meeting: "These people are all adults just like I am. If I make them feel like I have all the answers, then they'll never learn to think for themselves. They'll always be coming to me."

In short, she said, "It isn't easy. It takes a long time and a lot of patience."

On June 20, 1985, MEC held its first Employee Recognition Day. Three sessions, one on each shift, took place in the cafeteria, a small room with painted wooden floors and a row of vending machines. On one wall were displayed the screens people had made on their orientation tour. Employees sat on metal folding chairs. Stewart Stalnecker had good news and bad news as he addressed each of the shifts.

The good news was that sales were up 13 percent. The bad news was that profits were down 49 percent. He gently explained why.

"Profitability, or profits before taxes and depreciation, is a measure of the performance of our company so far as the money earned by the corporation," he said to the workers, who were nothing if not attentive. Many were wondering whether the bottom line would permit a cash distribution, as it had the year before.

Stalnecker was careful not to blame the workers for the decreased profitability. He confirmed that training had cost a good deal. "We have to pay fees to organizations and individuals to be trained. . . . Now, there's also costs of training we can't measure, and that's the cost of having a meeting, having people come for an hour, two hours a day, to talk and solve problems, be away from production. We had a big cost incurred in the last twelve, fifteen months on training because we weren't available to do production. We understand this, and we said this is what we want to do and that's why we're doing it, but we knew it was going to affect profitability in the long run."

He also mentioned problems in production. "We had more work than we could really handle, so we ran into difficulty. We worked a lot of overtime, plus there was a lot of pressure, haste, waste, confusion. . . . Our system had problems. Not the people. People tried very hard to do their jobs, worked their butts off trying to get the work out, but we were overloaded."

Stalnecker went on to mention other problems in production, materials, and management. "All in all," he concluded, "1984 was a hectic year, a frustrating year, a difficult year. I'm kind of glad we got through 1984. I'm sure a lot of you feel the same way. All that overtime, all that pressure, all that hassle, agony, and frustration. There were a lot of difficult situations that we were faced with. So it wasn't one of our best years. It was a very difficult year."

As for profits, he continued, "I'm not going to say, 'Next quarter we want a 30 percent profit or a 15 percent profit, and that's what we're going to work for.' . . . Let's say next quarter we're going to do the best job we can . . . We want to assure our survival long-term."

Stalnecker also announced that the company was considering continuous employment, or a no-layoff policy. "We want to be able to keep you people working at Microcircuit Engineering. You're good people, we have trained you to be good people, and you can do the work, and you are productive, and we need you."

The ceremony concluded with the employee recognition for which the day had been titled. Certificates were handed out to the supervisors who had completed their training and to the employees who had completed the orientation tour.

Finally, Stalnecker announced that the company was giving employees a gift day—the Friday following the July 4 holiday. And he ended speculation about whether there would be prosperity-sharing by announcing the distribution of checks based on seniority, as before. Even though 1984 profits were down, he said, the prevailing sentiment was that employees had "worked hard" and therefore deserved something. "We know in the future with quality improvement, we will see increased productivity and increased profitability."

By the time the third shift rolled around, there had been several unforeseen developments. When Stalnecker concluded handing out the certificates, the production superintendent handed him a certificate. It was addressed to "the outstanding president of the year." He was also presented with a hastily drafted sheet signed by sixty employees thanking him for the gift day. But what gave him perhaps the greatest twinge of satisfaction was a sketch, on a transparency suitable for display, that arrived on the speaker's stand between the first and second of the three scheduled meetings, courtesy of the anonymous *Merri-MEC* cartoonist. It showed Blind Baby extending a hand to a man seen only from the knee down and saying, "Ya done pretty good yourself." Stalnecker recognized himself by the pants legs. They were plaid.

Chapter 30

———•———

Lew Springer—
The Role of a Zealot:

Campbell Soup Company,
Camden, New Jersey

In the sunny brick courtyard behind historic Carpenter's Hall, Lewis W. Springer mingled with others of the fifty business, industry, and labor leaders who had just signed the "Second Declaration of Independence" promulgated by the Philadelphia Area Council on Excellence. The short, vigorous senior vice-president from Campbell Soup Company showed little interest in the rose-colored punch or the fastidiously sculpted tea sandwiches at the postceremony reception as he enthusiastically recapitulated what Campbell was doing to implement the Deming method: 210 upper-level managers had been sent to the four-day Deming seminar; fifty-five people had been dispatched to statistical training at the University of Tennessee; and two thousand hourly workers had been exposed to a four-hour Deming overview that included the rudiments of statistical methods, with plans to include an additional eight thousand.

It wasn't so much that the workers would begin instantly to employ the methods. After forty years in manufacturing, Springer well knew how suspicious workers might be of a sudden switch in management styles. "We want them to understand what we're doing," he said. "We don't want them to think we've developed a new way to fire them."

In addition, at each plant Campbell had established a team that included a statistical coordinator, an engineer, and a systems manager to introduce the Deming method. Springer had also enrolled Campbell in the PACE Quality Round Table sessions, often bringing in people from distant plants for the sessions. He himself was on the road 75 percent of his time, "spreading the gospel," as he put it. Campbell President and Chief Executive Officer R. Gordon McGovern, in extending his blessing to his chief of manufacturing, joked that Springer had been "born again."

To help carry out the effort, Springer had recruited a longtime associate, George Hettich from Campbell's Vlasic Foods Division. As vice-president for manufacturing technology, one of Hettich's first assignments was to attend a Deming seminar. He became a believer almost immediately. "It doesn't make any sense at all for the first two days," Hettich reported. "Then all of a sudden the light goes on and you say, 'This guy's got something.' "

For his part, Springer had discovered Dr. Deming when he appeared in Philadelphia in January 1984. Campbell at that time was pushing Quality Control Circles among its hourly workers. The company also wanted to get into the Japanese art of just-in-time inventory management. But these plans were akin to making soup with meat and vegetables but no stock. When he heard Dr. Deming, Springer would later say, "then I knew what else we had to do." The Deming method tied together employee involvement and long-term planning. It offered the statistical methods that would get the glitches out of manufacturing processes, so that just-in-time could work.

The news that a Japanese company was building a canned soup company in Fresno, California, provided a further incentive. Springer, for one, did not believe the Japanese had gotten where they were merely by singing songs, wearing uniforms, and doing exercises. He had no qualms about borrowing their successful techniques. "I hope we can learn their system of managing," he said, "before they learn our system for making soup."

Springer was in a position to make things happen. He was, in effect, the CEO for U.S. operations, for each of the U.S. division's twenty-two manufacturing sites. He had come up through the ranks and knew Campbell inside out. So did Hettich, who had been with Campbell for twenty-four years. He had previously reported to Springer in various roles, including plant engineer and manager of maintenance.

In discussing the critical need for leaders to get things moving, Brian Joiner and Peter Scholtes, the PACE consultants from Madison, could have been describing Springer. Such leaders, they said, would have to be people "with zeal, knowledge, and sufficient influence to spark and sustain interest in others." They would have to be persistent, clever and able to circumlocute obstacles, of which there would be many. The consultants suggested various names: "prime movers," "champions," even "zealots." That was Springer to a T.

In George Hettich's view, what Springer was doing to change things was, in a word, paramount. He had become a living example of the Deming philosophy. Given Springer as a role model, Hettich said, it followed that at a meeting of plant managers, "all of a sudden, everybody wanted a piece of the action."

Campbell was not, let it be said, in any immediate danger of going under. But revenues were far below the 15 percent mark that McGovern had projected upon his promotion to CEO in 1980. And the rapid introduction of new products had met with mixed success.

"Intrapreneurism"—harnessing independent entrepreneurial attitudes within large corporations in the spirit of innovation—was a popular idea at the time, and McGovern was a believer. He split the company into fifty autonomous business units, each with its own general manager and a charter to operate like a minibusiness. Some of the new products were wildly successful: the Prego line of spaghetti sauces and the Le Menu frozen dinners headed the list. And some, like Pepperidge Farm Star Wars cookies, were duds. The jury was still out on others.

McGovern decided to slow but not halt the pace. It was clear that Campbell could no longer survive with long runs of old-time favorites. "When I got here, we were driven by the consumer about five percent," he told a magazine interviewer. "We made the tomato soup, and you bought it."[1] In all its product lines, Campbell would have to adapt to shorter runs, fast changeovers, smaller orders and more of them, with speedier deliveries. But the company also needed to act with reason as well as dispatch. That was where Dr. Deming came in.

The Wall Street Journal took note of Campbell's change in emphasis on August 14, 1985, in a story headlined "Revised Recipe: Burned by Mistakes, Campbell Soup Co. is in Throes of Change." Asserted the story, by staff reporter Francine Schwadel, "R. Gordon McGovern, the president and chief executive of Campbell

Soup Co., was so obsessed with cooking up new products a few years ago that he sent key executives copies of 'In Search of Excellence,' a primer on corporate innovation. Partly as a result, the company had introduced 334 new products in the past five years—more than any other company in the hotly competitive food industry.

"But now Mr. McGovern has decided that Campbell may have done too much innovating too fast. His new reading assignment has a different emphasis: This year, he sent his executives a book about how to improve product quality and production efficiency to hold down costs. 'Read it carefully,' Mr. McGovern wrote in an accompanying memo. Failure to control costs, he said, could leave Campbell without enough money to support its new-product strategy."[2]

The giant food corporation, with 44,000 employees and close to $4 billion in 1984 sales, quietly outlined an internal four-year game plan that sounded not unlike the Total Quality Control agendas followed by Japanese companies. The first year, which Springer described that morning of July 3, 1985, was dedicated to education, training, and setting up the mechanics of carrying out the plan based on the Deming management method. In the second year, with a nucleus of people that understood the philosophy, Campbell planned to get its systems into a state of statistical control, form partnerships with vendors while narrowing their numbers, and perhaps see initial results. In the third year, the company anticipated moving into just-in-time inventory management, in which supplies arrived on an as-needed basis, meanwhile slicing in half the time it took to fill orders. By the fourth year, the company hoped to have all its systems running smoothly and efficiently, with improved quality and increased productivity.

That timetable represented the company's best guess as to how long it would take to convert to Deming-style management. But Springer's right-hand man, George Hettich, emphasized that the period could be less than four years, or more. "No one's done this before," he said. "At least, not in the United States."

A week after the "Second Declaration," Springer bounced to the front of a long, narrow meeting room at the Hilton Hotel in Mt. Laurel, New Jersey, that was filled with Campbell employees, most from the general office in Camden. Bathed in a pallid yellow glow from cone-shaped chandeliers, they sat at long tables covered with sky-blue cloths.

One of many such sessions, this was a day-long crash course in the Deming method. That method, Springer told the Campbell employees enthusiastically, was not a nebulous, human resources "type of thing. . . . It's a very, very disciplined way of solving problems." He assured them it had the blessing of the board of directors, and McGovern's as well. Its introduction signaled a new era, he said, in which workers would no longer be blamed for problems but would be given responsibility for dealing with them.

Already, he said, there had been changes. Campbell had not undertaken the usual seasonal layoffs, because "you don't have people involved with you and then go lay them off." He took note of the fear in middle management that "hourly people are going to run the plants and top management is going to make decisions," and he reassured them that it was not so.

Springer introduced Dr. Deming's 85-15 Rule, which holds that 85 percent of the problems in any operation are within the system and are the responsibility of management, while only 15 percent lie with the worker. And he aired Dr. Deming's dislike for MBO, or Management by Objective, in which goals are set and rewards distributed according to whether they have been met. Declared Springer, "Nobody knows how to set an MBO that's going to make the system better."

He discussed the Deming chain reaction, in which improved quality leads to lower costs and improved productivity, allowing companies to capture the market, stay in business, and provide "jobs and more jobs." And he outlined the following points from Dr. Deming's teachings:

- The failure of management to understand variation.
- Management's responsibility to know if the problem is in the system or with a person.
- The importance of teamwork based on knowledge of the need to design and redesign for constant improvement.
- The need to distinguish between design quality and conformance quality.
- The importance of training people until their work is in statistical control.

Moving on, Springer briefly discussed how Campbell planned to use the Deming method in its new "task force" approach to problems. Unlike the existing Quality Control Circles, which chose their own assignments, the task forces would be selected and targeted by management. In choosing priorities, however, management would also depend on its people to help. In the future, Springer told his audience, "the people who are going to get ahead are problem solvers who can work with people."

And finally, he reminded them of an old Campbell slogan: "Every can of soup contains our reputation." Campbell now had a new goal, he said. "We want to be a world-class manufacturer."

Springer's energetic presentation was followed by others on quality and statistical methods. The employees also broke into discussion groups on Dr. Deming's Fourteen Points. Late that afternoon, they left the meeting wearing buttons that read, "I've been Demingized at Campbell Soup Co."

The Campbell Soup Company was founded in Camden, New Jersey, in 1869 by Joseph Campbell, a fruit merchant, and Abram Anderson, an icebox manufacturer, as a company that canned vegetables and other products. In 1876, Anderson left and Campbell formed another partnership with Arthur Dorrance. Campbell died in 1900, but the company continued to bear his name, while rapidly expanding nationwide. Campbell never abandoned its Camden base. When the city fell prey to deep-seated urban blight in the 1960s and 1970s, Campbell remained one of the few bright spots in an otherwise bleak economic picture.

In the mid-1980s, there were signs that Camden had bottomed out and might be on the rebound. And the Camden plant, where Campbell turned out its familiar red and white line of soups, plus its new Prego sauces and Franco-American spaghetti and pork and beans, was also poised for change.

"It's kind of like we're building a house," said Plant Manager David Winkler. "We've engaged the services of an architect. We're getting to the point where we'll start putting the side walls up."

If Deming was the architect, then the contractor was Lew Springer, whose job it was to convince people like Winkler that Campbell was serious. But even though Springer said so over and over, money spoke louder than words.

Campbell was not known as a big spender. In contrast to General Foods's space-age headquarters in Rye Brook, New York, a five-story rotunda flanked by large, aluminum-clad wings that was reached by bridging a shimmering seven-acre pond, the Campbell headquarters in Camden is an unassuming two-story brick building overlooking a parking lot. The company paid what it had to for good people. But offices are utilitarian and expense accounts modest.

So it was that Winkler was at first surprised and then convinced of the company's serious intent by "the amount of money and commitment being spent on training." The purse strings were loosened as well for necessary travel, and Winkler was given the discretion to decide what was necessary. If he felt he needed to visit the plant of a supplier, for example, he was told to do so. Also symptomatic of the new way of managing was that "the boss doesn't call every day." The boss, of course, was Lew Springer.

Just six months into its first year of Deming, the Camden plant, to Winkler's way of thinking, was poised for a breakthrough. A three-person statistically trained team had been installed in an air-conditioned, computer-equipped module on the plant floor next to where the fast-moving line of Franco-American cans received their allotted dollop of sauce and meatballs. The man in charge was Edward H. Krystek, an industrial engineer who had worked first in research and development and then in production in his eleven years with Campbell. Most recently, he had been product manager for cream soups and noodles.

Already there had been training in statistical methods under two Drexel University professors. In six four-hour sessions, task forces were assigned problems on which to practice their education. The small but not insignificant accomplishments of the task forces had done a public relations job for the new methods. In one instance, exploring a yield problem, the team discovered a worker who couldn't read a scale. For years, he had managed to add the proper ingredients by watching the needle and relating it to what a coworker did. That method no longer worked when that scale was replaced with a digital model. Just four months from retirement, the worker took himself off the job at no loss in pay when the problem was discovered.

In another minor victory, a team had discovered that a mixup in labels was taking place because the manufacturer's code was almost identical for two products' labels. The manufacturer agreed to change one. It was just that sort of mistake that previously would have been blamed on the worker, Krystek noted.

Next, Winkler assigned Krystek to set up eight task forces on "Cream," the production unit that made the cream soups. They would work on such issues as narrowing the range of fill, limiting the amount of salt, and lessening warehouse damage. In the past, it had been necessary to grossly overfill the cans to make sure they were full. Salt was a problem in consumer complaints. One of the experimental task forces had established that Campbell was adding the customary amount of salt. That conclusion suggested that consumers must be demanding less salt than in the past. This task force would have to work with marketing to determine the truth of the matter.

It was not that Cream had more problems than other lines, but that its operation was simple enough to increase the odds that problems would be solved with dispatch. Cream used fewer ingredients and simpler machinery than the other lines and required no changeovers. In addition, the plant had begun to work with its label, tin plate, and case suppliers.

Krystek looked forward to a future in which the quality control department "will become auditors, working with vendors" and supervisors "won't have to worry about day-to-day problems. The system will be under control." Supervisors then would be free to consider long-range issues.

Each plant in the Campbell complex was proceeding in much the same fashion as Camden. Meanwhile, the education continued apace. When Dr. Deming gave a Philadelphia seminar in September 1985, a quarter of the four hundred attendees were either from Campbell or from its vendors.

Springer saw no reason to proceed at a cautious pace. "We just decided we don't have to start slow," he said. "We know it's right."

Epilogue

In November 1985, W. Edwards Deming returned to Japan for the thirty-fifth annual award named in his honor. The Deming Prize ceremony took place November 11 in Tokyo's Imperial Hotel. The large meeting room was filled with close to seven hundred Japanese businessmen in dark suits drawn from the ranks of upper management. Also present was a delegation of Americans attending under the auspices of the Philadelphia Area Council for Excellence as well as others who have appeared in these pages: Mary Ann Gould, Bob King, Lew Springer. It was for them both an affirmation of the course they were following and an opportunity for advanced study.

As TV lights blazed, Dr. Deming took his place at the podium, which was draped with a white banner emblazoned with a large red "Q" for Quality.

Although titled "Foundation for Success of Japanese Industry," his discourse had more to do with the mistakes of U.S. industry than the accomplishments of Japan. Just as he had once helped rescue that nation from postwar devastation, he now thought it important to warn the Japanese against adopting any of America's desperate efforts to badger its workforce into solving the problems that rightfully should be handled by managers themselves.

Dr. Deming had said on earlier occasions that he was not impressed with the way things were going in his own country. To be sure, in 1985 some 3,800 people had attended his seminars sponsored by George Washington University, more than twice the 1,500 who attended in 1984. As recently as 1979, there had been just one seminar, with fifteen registrants. Such major companies as Procter & Gamble, Campbell Soup, AT&T, Rohm & Haas, Exxon, and Control Data were sending large numbers of people. Still Dr. Deming wasn't satisfied with the way U.S. industry was responding to his message. Among those companies that had sought him out, Dr. Deming said he saw "great advancement in spots." But for every company that advanced, he said, "others remain in the dark ages."

Each day the business press brought bad news. Corporate profits were down. American industry was gypping the Pentagon. A blue-ribbon presidential commission reported that the ability of American business to compete with other countries had been in a downward slide for twenty years. The United States became a debtor nation for the first time in seventy-one years.

In response, a wave of protectionism had swept over America. Acquisitions and takeovers proceeded at a feverish pace. And the corporate search for the deadly sin of "instant pudding" continued. *The New York Times* reported that "Now 'Intrapreneurship' Is Hot."

At Harvard, economics was the most popular major. A new generation of financial whiz-kids was being readied.

No one was talking about quality and productivity. No one was making the pie bigger.

Now, he had a chance to address an audience in a country whose history he had influenced in a very significant and positive way. To them, he was a hero, the American who had taught them about quality and given them the key to unlock world markets.

The Japanese listened intently as Dr. Deming recalled his visit to their country in the summer of 1950. No doubt, for many in his audience this was a new and intimate glimpse of history.

"It was in July 1950—my third trip to Japan—when Mr. Ichiro Ishikawa assembled at the Industry Club the top twenty-one men of Japan, and I had the privilege to talk to them and try to explain what they could do," Dr. Deming began. "I did not just talk about quality. I explained to top management their responsibilities. I taught hundreds of engineers that hot summer. There was no air conditioning, remember that. Management of Japan went into action, knowing something about their responsibilities and learning more about their responsibilities."

But Dr. Deming was not here thirty-five years later to dwell on history, nor to praise Japan for its accomplishments. He viewed with alarm joint business ventures that would expose the Japanese to the diseases that infected American business.

In contrast to Japan, he said, "management for the most part in the western world has abandoned their responsibilities, delegating their responsibilities to other people, focusing their efforts on outcome."

He had, he told them, invented a new description for western management. "It is 'retroactive management.' Western management operates on management by numbers, MBO or management by objective, QC Circles, quality of work life, employee involvement, daily reports on people, and/or rating on performance of people."

The Japanese, of course, had invented Quality Control Circles and put them to good use. But Dr. Deming worried that they would become acquainted with some of America's homegrown fads.

"It is important," he warned, "that Japanese management remain strong, not weakened and diluted by adoption of some of the practices that are largely responsible for the decline of western industry. It is possible for a strong body to become infected, to become weak. Japanese management has responsibilities to continue to be strong and not to pick up infections from western management."

In particular, he cautioned his listeners against the use of performance ratings to determine salaries or bonuses, reminding them that differences between people for the most part are caused by the system, as the use of control charts—which he introduced thirty-five years earlier—so clearly indicate.

"Thousands of people understand that investigation of ups and downs within the control limits creates trouble, increases variation, causes severe loss. These same people forget the basic principles that they have learned on the factory floor; those same scientific principles apply to people. People are the most important asset of any company.

"Western management, having abandoned the responsibility of leadership, as I said, depends on reports. Too late! Retroactive management reports on people. They don't know anything else. How could they know?"

His voice became grim. "Failure to understand people is the devastation of western management. It's obvious. America has people. America has natural resources. Japan has people and no natural resources. The difference is management. Is Japanese management to become infected with the diseases of western management? Rating people? Is Japanese management going to become infected? Japanese management has an obligation to Japan and to the rest of the world to remain strong."

As he himself had once taught practices of good management, Dr. Deming now charged the committee that bore his name with protecting Japan against this new threat from America. "It is important," he said, "for the Deming Prize Committee to understand their obligations to Japan and to the world. It is important that the Deming Prize Committee beware of the poison that can come from unstudied practices from the western world."

One might ask what lasting effect Dr. Deming has had upon Japan. Consider only that the modest Deming Prize award of 1950 has evolved into a feverish month-long celebration of quality. In 1985 more than 550 presidents and vice presidents attended the annual conference for top management at which Dr. Deming spoke. More than 2,000 middle managers and staff attended a three-day conference at which 108 case studies were presented. [It took a translator an entire evening merely to translate the titles for an American visitor.] More than 2,000 foremen attended a three-day conference where there were 150 case studies. An annual national QC-Circle competition drew 2,000 finalists. And in 1985, for the first time there was a conference for service industries.

What had Deming done? Exactly what he said in the five words with which he always concluded his seminars.

"I have done my best."

Chapter Notes

PART ONE:
W. EDWARDS DEMING—THE MAN AND HIS MISSION

Chapter 1 W. Edwards Deming: A Biographical Note

Information on Dr. Deming's life came primarily from interviews with him; his brother Robert E. Deming; his sister Elizabeth Hood; and his daughters Diana Deming Cahill and Linda Deming Haupt. His secretary, Cecelia Kilian, also contributed to this chapter. Clare Crawford-Mason and William Conway provided the account of the "discovery" of Dr. Deming.

1. Dr. Deming's diary, "Travel Logs, Around the World by Air," 1946–47, p. 88.
2. Ibid., p. 91–92.
3. Ibid., p. 92.
4. Ibid., p. 100.
5. This formation of JUSE is described in "Notes on the history of JUSE and the advent of the control of quality in Japan before 1950—Conference with Dr. E. E. Nishibori on Sunday the 14th December 1982 in my room at the Hotel Century, Japan," given to the author by Dr. Deming.
6. Dr. Deming's correspondence with Kenichi Koyanagi, as well as a reminiscence of Dr. Deming's visits in 1950 and afterward, and his 1960 speech at the Deming Prize awards appear in a pamphlet, "The Deming Prize," by Kenichi Koyanagi, published by the Union of Japanese Scientists and Engineers, Tokyo, 1960. Hereinafter cited as "Prize."
7. Dr. Deming's diary, "Japan, 1950," p. 14.
8. Ibid., pp. 30–31.
9. Dr. Deming's diary, "My Third Trip to Japan (1951)," p. 18.
10. Dr. Deming's Diary, "My Sixth Trip to Japan—June 1960," p. 3.
11. "Prize."
12. William Horwitz, W. Edwards Deming, and Robert F. Winter, "A Further Account of the Idiot Savants, Experts With the Calendar," American Journal of Psychiatry, 126: Sept. 3, 1969, pp. 160–63.

Chapter 2 The Deming "Four-Day": A Seminar Begins

Except where noted, quoted material for this chapter comes from Dr. Deming's seminar, "Management Methods for Quality and Productivity," February 5–8, 1985, West Springfield, Massachusetts, sponsored by the Growth Opportunity Alliance of Greater Lawrence, hereinafter cited as Seminar, February 5–8, 1985. The author attended at Dr. Deming's invitation.

1. W. Edwards Deming, *Out of the Crisis* (Massachusetts Institute of Technology Center for Advanced Engineering Study, Cambridge, Mass. Scheduled for publication June, 1986) p. 3. Hereinafter cited as *Crisis*.
2. *Crisis*, p. 5.

Chapter 3 An Introduction to the Fourteen Points, the Seven Deadly Diseases, and Some Obstacles
1. Dr. Deming discussed the history of the Fourteen Points and Seven Deadly Diseases in an interview with the author in April 1985, in Valley Forge, Pa.

Chapter 4 The Parable of the Red Beads
1. This rendition of the red bead experiment took place on February 6, 1985, at the seminar in West Springfield, Mass.

PART TWO:
THE DEMING MANAGEMENT METHOD

Chapter 5 Point One: Create Constancy of Purpose for the Improvement of Product and Service
1. Deming, *Crisis*, pp. 24–25.
2. Ibid., p. 25.
3. Ibid., pp. 25–26.
4. Seminar, Feb. 5–8, 1985.
5. Seminar, Feb. 5–8, 1985.

Chapter 6 Point Two: Adopt the New Philosophy
1. W. Edwards Deming, *Quality, Productivity, and Competitive Position* (Massachusetts Institute of Technology Center for Advanced Engineering Study, Cambridge, Mass.), 1982, p. 21. Hereinafter cited as *Quality*.
2. Interview, Dec. 21, 1985.

Chapter 7 Point Three: Cease Dependence on Mass Inspection
1. Author's interview with Dr. Deming, June 9, 1985, Washington, D.C.
2. June 9 interview.
3. June 9 interview.
4. June 9 interview.
5. Author's interview with Dr. Deming, Dec. 21, 1985.
6. Seminar, Feb. 5–8.

Chapter 8 Point Four: End the Practice of Awarding Business on Price Tag Alone
1. Interview, Dec. 21, 1985.
2. Interview, Dec. 21, 1985.
3. *Quality*, p. 23.

4. Interview, Dec. 21, 1985.
5. Seminar, Feb. 5–8, 1985.
6. *Crisis*, 1985 draft, p. 34.
7. Seminar, Feb. 5–8, 1985.
8 Interview, Dec. 21, 1985.

Chapter 9 Point Five: Improve Constantly and Forever the System of Production and Service

1. *Crisis*, p. 46.
2. Seminar, Feb. 5–8, 1985.
3. Seminar, Feb. 5–8, 1985.

Chapter 10 Point Six: Institute Training and Retraining

1. Seminar, Feb. 5–8, 1985.
2. Interview, Dec. 21, 1985.

Chapter 11 Point Seven: Institute Leadership

1. Seminar, Feb. 5–8, 1985.
2. Seminar, Feb. 5–8, 1985.

Chapter 12 Point Eight: Drive Out Fear

1. *Quality*, p. 33.
2. *Crisis*, p. 59.
3. Seminar, Feb. 5–8, 1985.

Chapter 13 Point Nine: Break Down Barriers Between Staff Areas

1. Interview, Dec. 21, 1985.
2. Interview, Dec. 21, 1985.
3. Seminar, Feb. 5–8, 1985.

Chapter 14 Point Ten: Eliminate Slogans, Exhortations, and Targets for the Workforce

1. *Crisis*, p. 67.
2. Ibid., p. 66.
3. Interview, Dec. 21, 1985.
4. Seminar, Feb. 5–8, 1985.

Chapter 15 Point Eleven: Eliminate Numerical Quotas

1. *Quality*, p. 40.
2. *Crisis*, p. 71.
3. Interview, Dec. 21, 1985.
4. Seminar, Feb. 5–8, 1985.

Chapter 16 Point Twelve: Remove Barriers to Pride of Workmanship

1. Seminar, Feb. 5–8, 1985.

Chapter 17 Point Thirteen: Institute a Vigorous Program of Education and Retraining

1. *Crisis*, 1985 draft, p. 75.
2. Seminar, Feb. 5–8, 1985.

Chapter 18 Point Fourteen: Take Action to Accomplish the Transformation

1. Seminar, Feb. 5–8, 1985.
2. *Crisis*, p. 88.
3. Seminar, Feb. 5–8, 1985.
4. Seminar, Feb. 5–8, 1985.

Chapter 19 The Seven Deadly Diseases and Some Obstacles

1. Deming seminar sponsored by George Washington School of Engineering and Applied Science, San Diego, California, Jan. 24–27, 1984.
2. Seminar, Feb. 5–8, 1985.
3. Seminar, Feb. 5–8, 1985.
4. *Crisis*, p. 102.
5. Seminar, Feb. 5–8, 1985.
6. "Foundation for Success of Japanese Industry," speech to 23rd Annual Conference for Top Management, Nov. 11, 1985, Tokyo.
7. *Crisis*, p. 121.
8. Ibid.
9. Ibid., 1985 draft, p. 111.
10. *Crisis*, pp. 136–37.
11. Ibid.
12. Ibid., p. 143.

Chapter 20 Doing It with Data

1. "Prize," pp. 43–44.
2. *Quality*, pp. 47–48.
3. Kaoru Ishikawa, *Guide to Quality Control* (Asian Productivity Organization, 1976), pp. 24–26.
4. *The Memory Jogger* (Growth Opportunity Alliance of Greater Lawrence, Lawrence, Mass., 1985), p. 24.
5. Ibid., p. 7.
6. Ibid., p. 19.
7. Ibid., p. 30.
8. Ibid., p. 39.
9. Ibid., p. 44.
10. *Quality*, pp. 126–27.
11. *Memory Jogger*, p. 48.
12. Ibid., pp. 56–57.

PART THREE:
MAKING DEMING WORK

Chapter 21 The Deming Prize

Information for this chapter is based on interviews with William Conway and Tsotumu Nakayama, and on interviews and research materials from the Growth Opportunity Alliance of Greater Lawrence (GOAL).

1. Kaoru Ishikawa, trans. David J. Lu., *What is Total Quality Control?—The Japanese Way* (Prentice-Hall Inc., 1985), p. 45.
2. Ibid., p. 103.
3. *Kayaba Industry Co. Ltd.*, Report 101 (GOAL, 1984).

Chapter 22 Shifting Gears: Ford Motor Company, Dearborn, Michigan

Numerous Ford executives and employees were interviewed for this chapter, including William Scollard, James K. Bakken, William Scherkenbach, John Manoogian, Lewis C. Veraldi, Lionel Rivait, Wayne Richard, Harry Artinian, Edward Baker, Robert Linklater, George Brooks, Michael Moulder, and Joe Abela; from the United Autoworkers Union, Len Campbell; from A. O. Smith, Paul Smaglick.

1. William W. Scherkenbach, "Performance Appraisal and Quality: Ford's New Philosophy," *Quality Progress* (April 1985), pp. 40–46.
2. Ibid.
3. Edward M. Baker and Harry L. Artinian, "The Case of Windsor Export Supply," *Quality Progress* (June 1985), pp. 61–69.

Chapter 23 Spreading the Deming Word: Growth Opportunity Alliance of Greater Lawrence, Lawrence, Massachusetts

This chapter is based on interviews with Bob King, Michael Brassard, and Diane Ritter.

Chapter 24 Deming to the Rescue: Malden Mills, Lawrence, Massachusetts

This chapter is based on interviews with Bob King, Marshall Hudson, Bill Cotter, Bill Angeloni, and Darlyne McManus.

Chapter 25 Adopting the New Philosophy: Honeywell Information Systems, Lawrence Manufacturing Operation, Lawrence, Massachusetts

This chapter is based on interviews with Stanley Marsh, Rick Cayer, and Ron Cote.

Chapter 26 Toward a Critical Mass: American Telephone & Telegraph, Merrimack Valley Works, North Andover, Massachusetts
This chapter is based on interviews with Robert Cowley, Bryce Colburne, Len Winn, Michael Sayler, Jack Driscoll, and Robert Pettirossi.

1. W. Edwards Deming, memorandum, undated.

Chapter 27 The Philadelphia Model: Philadelphia Area Council for Excellence, Philadelphia, Pennsylvania
This chapter is based on interviews with Mary Ann Gould, Brian Joiner, and Peter Scholtes.

Chapter 28 The Evolution of a "Demingized" Company: Janbridge, Inc., Philadelphia, Pennsylvania
Numerous Janbridge executives and employees were interviewed for this chapter, including Mary Ann Gould, Dennis Sweeney, Alvin Harrison, Marty Jansen, Barbara Hysek, Carol Tunstall, Blanche Slovinsky, Jim Wright, Ken McAndrew, Robert Petherbridge, John Miller, and Milton Reid; from Honeywell: Dave Homiller and Bob Altimari.

Chapter 29 The Transformation of an American Manager: Microcircuit Engineering Corporation, Mt. Holly, New Jersey
This chapter is based on interviews with Stewart and Joan Stalnecker.

Chapter 30 Lew Springer—The Role of a Zealot: Campbell Soup Company, Camden, New Jersey
This chapter is based on interviews with Lewis Springer, George Hettich, David Winkler, and Edward Krystek.

1. Joel Kotkin, "The Revenge of the Fortune 500" *Inc.* (August 1985), pp. 39–44.
2. Francine Schwadel, "Revised Recipe," *The Wall Street Journal* (August 14, 1985), p. 1.

Index